THE
DEATH
SHIP

THE
DEATH
SHIP

RECOVERING THE BODIES OF TITANIC'S DEAD

VICTORIA BROWN
FOREWORD BY STEVE HALL

Please be aware that some parts of this book may prove upsetting. Chapters Two and Three go into detail on certain aspects of death, as those on the ship may have experienced it, and body decomposition.

First published 2025

The History Press
97 St George's Place, Cheltenham,
Gloucestershire, GL50 3QB
www.thehistorypress.co.uk

British Library Cataloguing in Publication Data.
A catalogue record for this book is available from the British Library.

ISBN 978 1 80399 803 9

Typesetting and origination by The History Press
Printed and bound in Great Britain by TJ Books Limited, Padstow, Cornwall

MIX
Paper | Supporting
responsible forestry
FSC
www.fsc.org   FSC® C013056

Trees for LYfe

Contents

PART THREE: THE AFTERMATH: *TITANIC'S* LEGACY

Foreword

With most tragedies throughout history, it's the loss of human life that we remember most. The loss of the *Titanic* in 1912 remains one of the worst maritime disasters outside times of armed conflict. In this book, Victoria Brown looks into how and why so many of those aboard *Titanic* lost their lives.

The principal reason so many were lost that night was the insufficient provision of lifeboats carried, but as the reader will find, there are other factors that need to be considered. Not all boats were lowered away full, and there was no other ship in close proximity to render timely assistance. The bitterly cold conditions that prevailed at the time were also critical.

Titanic carried sixteen lifeboats under davits, with the additional provision of four 'collapsible' Engelhardt lifeboats. The total indicated capacity for all boats was 1,178 persons. When *Titanic* left Queenstown, there were 2,208 on board. Making up the number of souls the ship carried were 1,317 passengers and 891 crew members. This meant, in a worst-case situation, whereupon every person on board needed to be evacuated, 1,030 would have to be left behind.

On the night of 14 April, *Titanic*, as we know, collided with an iceberg. An assessment of the damage sustained was made by Harland & Wolff's Thomas Andrews. His inspection revealed that the ship had been mortally wounded. For Captain Smith and his officers, their ship's insufficient lifeboat capacity was soon to be realised. Although the *Titanic* carried 3,560 lifebelts, they would prove to be of limited value for those who hadn't found a seat in a lifeboat. With a sea temperature of little more than 28°F, their immersion in water that cold would result in death from cardiac arrest, a phenomenon known as hydrocution. In the aftermath of the sinking, all these lifebelts ultimately achieved was to keep their deceased bodies afloat.

For those fortunate enough to have found room in a lifeboat, their salvation would be met by the arrival of the Cunard ship *Carpathia*. CS (Cable Ship) *Mackay-Bennett* was contracted by the White Star Line to search the wreck vicinity for bodies, departing from Halifax on 17 April. The crew recovered 306 bodies. Of that number, 116 were buried at sea and 190 returned to port.

Days later, CS *Minia* was likewise engaged to further search the area. Unfortunately, due to the stress of weather, her crew only recovered seventeen more bodies from the icy sea. In the following weeks, the ships CGS *Montmagny* and SS *Algerine* would further search the area, recovering an additional five bodies between them.

In all, 209 bodies were brought back to Halifax and 128 were buried at sea. Sadly, all those other souls lost would remain unaccounted for, lost to the North Atlantic. When looking at the complete number lost in connection with *Titanic*, a further eight need to be added: those of the Harland and Wolff workers killed during the ship's construction. The total now amounts to 1,504.

In *The Death Ship*, Victoria Brown examines in detail the fates of the 1,496 people who perished on that cold and moonless night, examining how those lost died, how their bodies were recovered and where their remains were interred. Did the initial lack of urgency contribute to earlier lifeboats being lowered not fully loaded? And could the provision of additional lifeboats have saved more? Was there anyone to blame? These questions and hundreds more were subsequently asked at post-disaster inquiries, and have fascinated the public ever since.

As for the *Titanic*, that marvel of the Edwardian era, today she rests over 12,000ft below those icy waters of the North Atlantic – nothing more than a rapidly collapsing and disintegrating hulk on the seafloor, and to many maritime historians, a victim herself.

Steve Hall
Titanic historian and author
January 2025

Introduction

When I was a little girl, my mum and dad took me and my sisters to the Ulster Folk and Transport Museum in Cultra, Northern Ireland. Certain exhibitions always stand out in my mind whenever I think of the museum – the enormous steam trains; the recreation of a rural Victorian primary school, complete with chalkboards and wooden hula hoops for playtime; the preserved heritage buildings that line the streets, including an old-fashioned sweetshop with Lime Fruit, Twisted Barley Sugar, Strawberry Drops and Lemon Drops, all weighed and placed into delicate brown paper bags – but the one I remember in the most vivid detail is its *Titanic* exhibition.

Before Titanic Belfast opened in 2012, the Ulster Folk and Transport Museum was the place to go in Northern Ireland for information about RMS *Titanic*. While the *Titanic* museum does a wonderful job of putting the *Titanic* into context, looking especially at Belfast's history and legacy as a centre for ship works in the nineteenth and twentieth centuries, it features few artefacts salvaged from the ship itself. The Ulster Folk and Transport Museum, however, is home to several items, including a porthole, part of the ship's hull, and part of the engine telegraph. They also have garments worn by survivors on the night of the sinking on display.

The most emotional part of the exhibition, for me as a child, lies in the centre of the room. A huge glass case houses a replica of the *Titanic* mid-sinking, its hull disappearing beneath the black seawater. Around the outskirts of the water, labelled and arranged by class at three of the four corners of the case, are the survivors. These mini figurines are clad in Edwardian garb, coloured in reds, yellows, greens, blues. Beneath them are those who were lost. They are not colourful – they are a ghostly grey. There were many first- and second-class survivors, as to be expected, but the discrepancy between them and the loss of third-class passengers and the ship's crew was astounding and heartbreaking to me, even as a young child. I remember looking up at my mum, with big sad eyes, and asking her, 'Why didn't they save them?'

I couldn't get over how many little grey figures stood there, lost.

Even at a young age, I was familiar with the *Titanic*. It's difficult not to be when you're from Northern Ireland. My mum adored, and still adores, James Cameron's 1997 adaptation of the story, so she watched it a lot when we were growing up. Mum never hid the tragedy of the sinking from us, or the horrors that were part of it: she didn't see the point in trying to shield us from it. Her efforts would have been in vain anyway, for I was a very curious and conscientious child, so I would've found out for myself one way or another. My mum always knew how best to answer questions we posed to her, depending on how old we were at the time, and she always did her best to give us as succinct an answer as she could to satisfy our curiosity. She did not forbid us from watching the film, but she would warn us if a potentially scary or upsetting scene was coming up so we could brace ourselves. For me, this was always the scene when the glass dome over the famous Grand Staircase explodes from the sheer force of the water, sending ice-cold waves rushing into the ship and pinning passengers to the stairs, as sparks from the electric lights fly in every direction. Even as an adult, it is a scene that pulls at my heartstrings.

To this day, I remember how scared and sad I used to be while watching *Titanic*. I love the horror genre but I find it easy to separate myself from it, even from some of the most brutal true crime, but watching *Titanic* as a kid felt like I was trespassing on something I wasn't old enough to see yet. I felt mature watching it, but *Titanic* scared me – not because it was especially scary in the way horror films are, but because I couldn't help but feel how utterly terrified those people must have been. The opening shot of the film is filled with such hope, and it makes me so sad, even now, because all those smiling, waving people standing aboard the ship's decks are sailing towards their deaths. Some would die alone, freezing, terrified and confused. Some would die with family, watching their loved ones fight for breath while they were unable to help, as they themselves strug-gled to stay afloat. Crew members helped passengers before themselves, many going down with their friends inside and alongside the ship. *Titanic* made me sad, more than anything I had ever come across, more than any other tragedy in history I had known about up to that point. I remember vividly watching television late one night from behind the sofa – my dad had no idea I was there – and he was watching a documentary about the firefighters' experiences during 9/11. That footage spooked me and upset me a little, but it felt somehow removed from my experience: I had never flown on a plane or been in a high-rise building.

I had, however, been on a boat and set foot in the ocean. I had never felt blistering smoke fill my lungs or flames scorch my skin, but I had felt the roll of a boat deck and ice-cold waves pull the legs out from under me, leaving me powerless and terrified. I could put myself in the position of those who died on the *Titanic*, and because I could understand (as best as an 8-year-old could, anyway) how they must have felt, that terrified me and upset me to my very core. I used to imagine what it would be like to be on the ship, and the idea of having to leave my dad behind made me cry. Even Jack and Rose, who we know were James Cameron's fictional creations, broke my heart because they represented so many real people. Rose, trapped in a wealthy but monotonous, depressing life of meaningless and superficial pageantry, betrothed to someone she hated and given no agency just because she was a woman, and Jack, a man whose optimism and genuine love for life brought him as far as the ship's decks, on his way home, though he never got there. Rose's lament of 'he saved me in every way a person can be saved' is one of the most beautiful and heart-wrenching lines in cinema because it is true, and it is one of the best examples of just how much a single person can alter your entire sense of humanity and experience of life. One person can save another in more ways than one, and Jack did that for Rose. The romantic in me treasures their story. I know some people roll their eyes at the love story at the centre of James Cameron's version, but for me it makes it. Jack and Rose are two of my favourite fictional characters on screen, not just because of who they are as individuals, but because of what they come to represent for me: real people with real hopes and dreams shattered by that fateful, arguably easily avoided, collision with one block of ice in the middle of the ocean.

I can imagine myself on board the *Titanic*: I can feel the iron and steel of the steps through my shoes, feel the sharp wind on my cheeks, the rough texture of the ropes against the palm of my hand, the roll of the waves beneath the ship, the polite yet awkward clinking and clattering of cutlery. I can feel the pain in my back from having to sit straight in first class while wearing beautiful but uncomfortable clothing. I can taste Guinness and cigarettes, smell sweat, and hear the boisterous and uninhibited laughter in third class. The moon and stars the passengers and crew watched and died beneath are the same ones above us now. For me, *Titanic* represents just one of a million ways in which human beings are connected. And it breaks my heart.

There have been many worse tragedies, but the *Titanic* always sticks with me. The people on the ship thought they were sailing towards New York, the place where anyone could make it no matter how poor they were, where they came from or how educated they were. America represented hope to hundreds of people aboard the *Titanic*: people who walked the same paths as me through Belfast Harbour, past Harland & Wolff, along the River Lagan. Some may have even sat in the same spot at City Hall, where I go to drink my coffee, or maybe they sat on the very spot where the *Titanic* memorial to those who were lost now stands. Their determination to make their dreams come true in the Land of Opportunity was rewarded with an ice-cold watery grave.

I loved history as a child. I wanted to be the Indiana Jones of Egyptology (I know my family are laughing reading this). I was fascinated by the Egyptians' art, their culture and their gods, but mostly I was obsessed with mummies and the preservation process. I used to go around telling everyone about how the ancient Egyptians pulled the deceased's brain out by their nose with a long hook and separated their organs into jars. I also loved graveyards, especially a small, overgrown one in Carnmoney, Belfast, where I have family buried. My dad used to play a game with my sisters and me, where we had to find the oldest grave we could. No one ever got an actual prize – it was more a matter of pride – but it was the best part of visiting the graveyard for me. I was a bit of a macabre child, obsessed with the more tragic and sad parts of history – captivated by death as a philosophical concept and an aesthetic, as well as a concrete reality – so, in hindsight, it's not surprising that a story such as the *Titanic*'s would stick with me well into adulthood.

I think a big part of my fascination with the *Titanic* also comes from it being connected to the country where I was born. Northern Ireland has a troubled and turbulent history, and to be honest it's not one I'm particularly drawn to, but the *Titanic* always pulled me towards it. Perhaps part of it was growing up by the sea, in a small village called Groomsport, where the vast ocean was literally on my doorstep. Having the ocean at my fingertips was a great inspiration for imagination for me as a child. In primary school, one of my favourite craft activities was making a replica of the *Titanic* using an empty cereal box and old toilet rolls for the funnels (young Victoria usually only gave her little ship three funnels, but I think we can forgive her). Groomsport's play park is right on the seafront and its biggest climbing frame looks straight out on to the ocean. My sisters and I, along with my childhood best friend Nicola, used to pretend that we were sailors adventuring on the high seas (though, if memory serves me, we more often pretended to be pirates because I think we considered that more exciting).

Perhaps it's the knowledge that anyone with family from Belfast likely knew and/or is directly related to someone who worked on the ship in Harland & Wolff's world-famous shipyard. In my case, I know for certain that my great-great-grandfather Thompson worked on it and my great-great granny McVeigh watched it travel down Belfast Lough when it left Belfast for the last time. She also watched the sea trials from the top of Belfast's Cavehill. Whenever my great-granny Bash spoke about *Titanic*, she always prefaced it with 'she was doomed from the start', based on what her father, my great-great-grandfather Thompson, told her. He also spoke of a woman in black, who was supposedly seen in the ship's interior during the fit-out. He said that the ship never had any rats inside or outside when it was being fitted out – a bad omen, for rats are known to flee sinking ships. Maybe it's just some good ol' Belfast superstition, but it's compelling, isn't it?

The story of the *Titanic* stayed with me as I grew up. The first short story I ever had published in my university newspaper, *The Piano*, was a *Titanic*-inspired ghost story about a young girl who helps reunite the lost spirit of a third-class passenger with his fiancée, who survived the sinking. Looking back, it was not very good – and was maybe a little more sentimental that I'd like to admit – but I like knowing that my first ever published piece of fiction is directly connected to Northern Ireland and to something I loved as a child. The *Titanic* has a wealth of possibilities for storytellers for numerous reasons, but Sam Willis, author of *Shipwreck: A History of Disaster at Sea*, puts it best: 'tales of shipwreck are attractive as straightforward descriptions of human tragedy, in which heroism, sacrifice, and villainy all bubble to the surface in conditions of extreme physical and emotional suffering.'[1] He also reflected on the attractiveness of the *Titanic*'s story. It has endured so long in our popular imagination, he said, because it has 'such socially and politically charged undercurrents'. Few stories within history so 'magically captured the essence of their age as did the *Titanic*'.[2] My story was certainly tragic, but it also had a cathartic element: my ghostly passenger got to reunite with his lost love. But the families of many of those who died never got that chance. I think my story was a way for me to explore the part of me that was always heartbroken by that fact.

About halfway through university, when I got into the death positivity movement, spearheaded by US mortician Caitlin Doughty, I started thinking about it in the context of the *Titanic*. What happened to the *Titanic*'s dead — those little grey ghostly figures I saw represented at the Ulster Folk and Transport Museum? Were their bodies recovered and buried? Where were they buried — Belfast? Maybe New York, the *Titanic*'s intended destination? Were they buried at sea? How many? Did people want to help retrieve the bodies? How many were recovered from the water? How did the victims actually die — drowning, injuries from falling into the water, hypothermia? What happened to the bodies that sank with the ship? Are they still down there?

Most research into and documentaries about the ship tend to focus on Harland & Wolff and the building of the ship, the actual sinking (the timeline between hitting the iceberg and the final submersion in particular), the rescue effort, the subsequent inquiries into the sinking, and the discovery of the wreck. But what happened to the dead is usually either glossed over or missing altogether. Then Caitlin Doughty answered my (atheist) prayers and released a video conveniently titled 'What Happened to Titanic's Dead?'[3] She had the same concern I did. In her video, she says, 'Dead bodies don't just disappear. Where did they go?' Thank you, Caitlin — that is *exactly* what I want to know.

The video is just under six minutes long, but it gives curious researchers such as myself a great starting point for exploring the topic in more depth. Through Caitlin's video, I learned that over 300 bodies were recovered by several smaller ships, including the *Mackay-Bennett* – which was nicknamed 'The Death Ship' by the local papers, hence the title of this book – and taken to Halifax in Nova Scotia, a place I had never heard of, where they were stored at a makeshift morgue pending identification and burial. I learned how the bodies that stayed in the ocean would have decomposed and how the Atlantic's underwater climate means there are likely no recognisable bodies on the sea floor, or even trapped within the ship (unlike other sinkings, which will be discussed later in this book). Caitlin also briefly touches on the now infamous photograph of the leather shoes taken at the wreck, and the tension between treasure hunters and marine archaeologists regarding the wreck as a gravesite.

Caitlin's video is fantastic, but it wasn't enough for me: I wanted to know more. I wanted every tiny detail I could find. With this idea firmly in mind, I contacted the Titanic Society in Belfast to see if they would be interested in me presenting a talk on the subject. I liaised with the wonderfully enthusiastic Aidan McMichael, who was keen for me to get involved with the society because he shared my interest in a part of the *Titanic*'s story that is seldom told. I figured that if I'm fascinated by this element of the story, there are bound to be other people who are interested too, but who don't want to say so because it's seen as morbid or creepy. Even now, I find myself censoring myself so as not to offend or trigger someone who isn't as interested in this kind of thing as I am.

But we must remember that part of the *Titanic*'s enduring legacy is its tragic loss of life. The *Titanic*'s sinking wouldn't be nearly as famous had the loss of life been significantly lower; and, on a personal note, I think it's disrespectful to avoid talking about the victims altogether and what happened to them after they died. The dead body is not a thing to be feared or to shy away from; after all, if the wonderful people of Halifax had turned their backs on the *Titanic*'s dead, very few of them would have been recovered.

The only things every single human being on this planet have in common are that we are born and we die. We're happy to discuss birth, but talking about death and dying is avoided at all costs, much to our detriment. Not only are death and dying genuinely interesting things to learn about, but they are something each one of us will have to face, whether we want to or not. That makes it one of the most important things we can talk about while we're here on earth.

This book is split into three parts:

Part One is about death: the infamous and contentious lifeboat issue that surrounds almost every piece of *Titanic* scholarship, how those on board the *Titanic* likely perished, and how their bodies would have decayed.

Part Two is about the body recovery effort. It explores the ways in which the various recovery ships found, identified, and took care of the bodies before bringing them to Halifax. It looks at how the people of Halifax bonded together to care for the dead, including by organising their memorial services and burials. It concludes with an overview of some key *Titanic* memorials around the world. At the end of this book, I have compiled a list of the souls lost. Even if you don't read every single name, please take a second to really think about them as individuals. They were people with hopes and dreams for a better life, and the least we can do for them is to think of them, even for a moment. They deserve that.

Part Three explores the proposed legislative changes that came about as a result of the inquiries into the sinking, the cultural interest in the wreck and the numerous proposals to salvage it, and, finally, the contemporary controversy of *Titanic* as a shipwreck versus a graveyard. It considers the ethics specific to maritime archaeology, the efforts to protect *Titanic* and its dead, and the concept of dark tourism in light of the recent *Titan* submarine tragedy. It concludes, for what it's worth, with my own opinion on what to do with the wreck.

It is important to acknowledge, before diving into this book, that the statements and testimonies of the passengers and crew who survived are not the most reliable. Any seasoned historian knows this, but for those of us who are starting out on our journeys, it's crucial to address this from the outset. It's also important to know that this book does not intend to give definitive answers to the questions it explores. There are much more intelligent people out there who have done, and will do, a much better job than I at tackling the enormity of them. And there are many more *Titanic* historians and scholars who have explored the stories I have included in *The Death Ship* in much more depth. Many of them are listed within the bibliography and I highly recommend seeking them out. I, like many readers of this book, am at the beginning of my *Titanic* scholarship journey and a big part of writing this book has been deciding what to include, where to hold back and when to redirect you to the true experts.

Consider this book more of a prompt – an easy way into this extremely detailed and complicated historical topic. I do also hope that this book teaches you a little about the kind and heroic people of Halifax and that it prompts you to learn more about the *Titanic*. I hope you will even come away with the knowledge and reassurance that talking about death doesn't have to be quite so scary.

PART ONE

Death and Decomposition

1

Titanic's Lifeboats

One of the biggest issues people have with *Titanic* is its lifeboats: were there enough? If not, why? If they had been filled to capacity, how many people would have been saved? Were the crew adequately trained to evacuate the ship? Did the crew dispatch them quickly enough? It is often the first issue people turn to when discussing the sheer number of fatalities during the sinking.

Many of the questions surrounding the lifeboats come from the idea that the ship was unsinkable. A publicity brochure from White Star Line in 1910 for *Titanic* and *Olympic* stated that they were designed to be practically unsinkable, though White Star Line stuck to its assertion that the ship had been *designed* to be unsinkable, not that it was *actually* unsinkable. There isn't much of a difference between those two, if you ask me, but White Star Line was always quick to cover its own back. Other publications supported this notion of the ship being unsinkable: the *Irish News* and *Belfast Morning News* reported in June 1911 that the hull's watertight compartments and tried-and-tested watertight doors – which would fall by gravity via hydraulic cataracts when the electric magnet that held them open was deactivated on the bridge – meant that the ship was practically incapable of sinking. *The Shipbuilder* magazine's article on *Titanic* and *Olympic* agreed.[1]

Supposedly, a deckhand stated that 'God himself could not sink this ship' when asked about it,[2] inspiring the famous line in the 1997 film. This notion of the ship's unsinkability also reached the ears of passengers: Thomson Beattie wrote in a letter to his mother in Fergus,

Ontario, that he was 'coming home in a new, unsinkable boat';[3] and Margaret Devaney said that she boarded the *Titanic* because she 'thought it would be a safe steamship' and 'had heard it could not sink'.[4] It was not that passengers had an almost religious belief that the ship was unsinkable, but that they believed it had been built so well that it could only sink in the most unlikely, nigh-on impossible, of circumstances.

In 1912, the Board of Trade was trying to make ships watertight and become lifeboats in themselves. The Board of Trade rewarded shipbuilders with having to carry fewer lifeboats if their ship was properly sub-divided, which the *Titanic* was. The ship's eventual lifeboats numbered twenty – fourteen traditional, two emergency and four collapsible – but the boats could not accommodate everyone; in fact, they could only fit 1,178 of the 2,208 passengers and crew on board. But the ship was unsinkable, a lifeboat in itself, so surely it did not need to fit all those people? This view was supported by Archibald Campbell Holms, a shipbuilding expert (and spiritualist) from Scotland whose 1904 work *Practical Shipbuilding: A Treatise on the Structural Design and Building of Modern Steel Vessels* became a go-to for industry professionals. In a second edition of the book published in 1918, Holms stated:

> The fact that *Titanic* carried boats for little more than half the people on board was not a deliberate oversight, but was in accordance with a deliberate policy that, when the subdivision of a vessel into watertight compartments exceeds what is considered necessary to ensure that she shall remain afloat after the worst conceivable accident, the need for lifeboats practically ceased to exist, and consequently a large number may be dispensed with.[5]

This was not an unfair assessment to make and was, in fact, backed up by evidence. In 1909, White Star Line's ship RMS *Republic* was sailing from New York to the Mediterranean when it encountered dense fog off the coast of Massachusetts. Despite precautions, it collided with SS *Florida* of the Lloyd Italiano Line. SS *Florida*'s bow was crushed, killing three crewmen, while RMS *Republic* was sliced open on its portside. Two passengers who were asleep in their cabins – William J. Mooney and Mary Lynch – were killed instantly, while a third, Mary's husband Eugene, would later succumb to his injuries at Long Island College Hospital in Brooklyn, New York. The ship began to list as its boiler and engine rooms flooded with water, thanks to a rip in its side not dissimilar to the damage *Titanic* later fell victim to. Like *Titanic*, it did not have enough lifeboats to accommodate all its passengers, but it stayed afloat long enough to transfer everyone via the lifeboats it did have to SS *Florida* and the *Greshem*, a cruising cutter and auxiliary gunboat that answered RMS *Republic's* distress call. RMS *Republic* did sink, despite efforts to tow it to New York for repairs as SS *Florida* was, but the evidence, in White Star Line's eyes, was clear: in the event of a major accident and/ or disaster, its ships could stay afloat long enough to avoid loss of life, and it provided the number of lifeboats accordingly.

It is worth noting, however, that it took almost half a day for RMS *Republic's* passengers to be transferred to a rescue ship, and the ship sank at a much slower rate than the *Titanic*. White Star Line could not accurately predict how fast or slow *Titanic* would sink (two hours, forty minutes in the end) in the event of a collision, be it an iceberg, rocks or another ship. Even if *Titanic* had had additional lifeboats, it's unlikely that they would have saved more lives, unless *Titanic* had stayed afloat longer, allowing *Carpathia* to reach more survivors. This was addressed in a speech by Lord Charles Beresford, Chief of the British Channel Fleet, a few weeks after the disaster, in which he lamented that 'it might be fairly supposed that had the *Titanic* floated for twelve hours, all might have been saved'.[6]

The *Titanic* carried the number of lifeboats – twenty – it was legally required to. At the time of its launch, *Titanic* was subject to the requirements of section 427 of the Merchant Shipping Act 1894 and the Merchant Shipping Act 1906. These outlined the rules and regulations ships were required to follow to keep their passengers safe. At the time, the number of lifeboats required was based on the tonnage of a ship, not on the number of passengers and crew it could carry. The highest requirement, applied to ships over 10,000 tonnes – *Titanic* was 46,328 – was to have at least sixteen lifeboats able to accommodate a total of 990 people. The ship's design would have enabled it to carry over sixty lifeboats, but as these weren't required within the current regulations, they weren't incorporated into its construction.

These regulations were wildly outdated. When the regulations were outlined in the 1880s, the largest liners at the time – *Etruria* and *Umbira*, sister ships of the Cunard Line, one of White Star Line and Harland & Wolff's biggest competitors – had a tonnage of 8,000grt (gross registered tonnes). By the time the legislation came into effect, White Star Line's own *Oceanic* surpassed the 10,000-tonnage mark at 17,272 gross tonnes, so the legislation was practically outdated as soon as it was passed. Shipbuilding had advanced unexpectedly quickly in less than twenty years and ships had become much larger than anyone could have predicted. RMS *Carmania*, another Cunard Line ship, had berths for 2,650 passengers but only enough lifeboats for 29 per cent. In fact, only six of the thirty-nine British liners at the time had enough lifeboats to accommodate all their passengers, and these were the ones that were registered as over 10,000 tonnes.

Ships from companies across the water did not fare much better. SS *Amerika* (recommissioned USS *America* during the First World War), launched in 1905 by Harland & Wolff for the Hamburg America Line of Germany, for example, was a 22,225-tonne passenger liner with only enough lifeboats for about 55 per cent of its crew. (Interestingly, SS *Amerika* also reported icebergs on 14 April 1912, not far from where *Titanic* struck hers). The legislation had not been updated to reflect any of this, so while White Star Line's decision not to include more lifeboats did result in a loss of life that could have been avoided, it was covered legally. When asked during the British inquiry why the regulations had not been updated since they had been drawn up, Sir Alfred Chalmers of the Board of Trade stated:

> Due to advancements that had been made in shipbuilding it was not necessary for boats to carry more lifeboats. The latest boats were stronger than ever and had watertight compartments making them unlikely to require lifeboats at all. Sea routes used were well-travelled meaning that the likelihood of a collision was minimal. The latest boats were fitted with wireless technology.[7]

The ship's lifeboats had the capacity for 1,178 people – far more than what was required in line with the Table and Rules within the Merchant Shipping Acts of 1894 and 1906. So White Star Line, technically, acted within the requirements of the legislation placed upon it and actually provided *more* lifeboats than legally required. It was only in hindsight, following investigations and inquiries into the sinking, that the British Commissioner recommended that the appropriate number of lifeboats and rafts on board ships such as *Titanic* should be based on the number of people the ship could carry, not on its tonnage. Many of these recommendations were incorporated into the International Convention for the Safety of Life at Sea, just two years later.

The confidence in *Titanic*'s unsinkability is arguably evident in the ship's owners and builders rebuffing plans early on that called for additional lifeboats in the early stages of the ship's design. At the British inquiry after the sinking, Harold Sanderson of Harland & Wolff argued that more lifeboats than legally required wasn't feasible. He stated that the proposal was ridiculous and that there were positions on board 'where only ignorant persons would put boats'.[8] Alexander Carlisle, the brother-in-law of Harland & Wolff's managing director William James Pirrie, had expected the Board of Trade's regulations regarding the number of lifeboats legally required to be increased by the time *Titanic* was launched, but they weren't, so it is unsurprising that a proposal for more lifeboats was rejected. Following a meeting with Harold Sanderson and the chairman and managing director of White Star Line, Bruce Ismay, Pirrie suggested bringing this number down to forty-eight with the innovative use of a new type of davit, the small crane used for suspending or lowering a lifeboat. It would have provided enough seats for everyone on board, should an emergency occur. It would 'be a good thing to make reparations for supplying the larger number of boats',[9] Pirrie had said, and Ismay agreed. This was rejected. It was implied at the British inquiry that the real reason for this rejection was that White Star Line objected to 'depriving the boat deck of space for promenading',[10] but this was staunchly denied by Sanderson.

It is worth noting, too, that it was found at the American inquiry that a new type of davit was fitted 'throughout in view of coming changes in official regulations. It was considered wise by the owners that these changes should be thus anticipated, and so make it possible to double, or even treble, the number of boats without any structural alterations, should such increase ultimately prove to be necessary.'[11] When questioned about this at the British inquiry, Sanderson claimed that his firm had not authorised the production of these davits, that he was unaware that the ships he was working on should have a larger capacity of lifeboats, and that the davits were not installed, as far as they were concerned, with the anticipation of expected changes to the legislation.

A final proposal for thirty-two lifeboats was put forward later, but it was also rejected, as it was not required by the Board of Trade. At the British inquiry, Sanderson was asked, 'With your experience, which is a very extensive shipping experience, and also in the light of this recent calamity, do you not think now that some of this space which is devoted to millionaires' suites and extra deck promenades could not possibly be better utilised for the purpose of ensuring the safety of all the passengers?' He responded simply, 'If there was anything we could do to ensure the safety of the passengers the question of millionaires' suites would disappear in a moment.'[12]

The final agreed number of lifeboats was twenty. Sanderson stated during the British inquiry that the 'additional boats were put on, to be on the safe side'.[13] Carlisle was not happy with the decision, firmly believing that *Titanic* did not have enough lifeboats, but he signed off on the lifeboats anyway. When questioned about signing off the report after the sinking, he said, 'I do not know why I did. I am not generally soft … but I must say, I was very soft the day I signed that.'[14]

Walter Lord, author of one of the most famous books about *Titanic*, *A Night to Remember*, argued in his later work, *The Night Lives On: Thoughts, Theories and Revelations about the Sinking of the 'Unsinkable' Ship – Titanic*, that money was a factor in White Star Line's decision to cut the number of lifeboats originally proposed. He believed that equipping *Titanic* with enough lifeboats to accommodate all passengers and crew would have drawn attention from the press, who would put two and two together and realise that many, if not all, modern ships did not have enough lifeboats for everyone on board. This would have led to a review of the regulations, which would, in turn, cost White Star Line and shipbuilders money they were not willing to part with. This is supported by the testimony of Alexander Carlisle, who noted that changing the number of lifeboats would have meant that White Star Line would have had to 'consider their other fleet and their own steamers'.[15] Reverting to the previous proposal of thirty-six lifeboats would have cost under £1,300, a fraction of the £1.5 million (the equivalent of £170 million today) it spent on *Titanic*. This is likely speculation on Lord's part, but given what we know about White Star

Line's attitude, it would not be surprising to find out that this concern influenced its decision.

Contrary to the argument that more lifeboats would have saved more lives, Sir Alfred Chalmers of the British Board of Trade believed if there had been *fewer* lifeboats, there would have been more of a rush to fill the boats and more people would have been saved. We'll never know if this would have been the case, but it is an interesting point to note. In fact, in a documentary for National Geographic, *Titanic: 20 Years Later with James Cameron*,[16] it was argued that more lifeboats may have been a hindrance to the people on board, as the lifeboats that were there were coming down on top of each other and they would have got in the way of people trying to make it to higher ground. In the end, around 1,496 people perished, so even if the lifeboats had been filled to capacity, many passengers and crew still wouldn't have survived.

In the end, while *Titanic* carried lifeboats that could fit 1,178 passengers (a measly 53 per cent – still not enough to accommodate everyone on board), it only managed to successfully launch eighteen on the night of the sinking and saved slightly over 710 people. There were fourteen traditional lifeboats, 30ft (9.1m) long by 9ft1in (2.77m) wide, which held sixteen people (this applies to the guidelines at the time – in *Report into the Loss of the SS Titanic: A Centennial Reappraisal*, Dave Gittins notes that under current SOLAS guidelines, the lifeboats would carry twenty-four, or at a push thirty-four).[17] These were the lifeboats you would ideally want to be placed in. Built by Harland & Wolff, these lifeboats were designed with strength in mind. They were made from wood in a lapstrake or clinker style, a building technique originating from the Vikings that was favoured for its lightness atop the waves and easy buildability. They were designed to withstand potential flooding from waves breaking over the boat by having two bows rather than a bow and a stern, and their sides were filled with airtight copper tanks for extra buoyancy. These boats were inspected by Board of Trade ship surveyor William Henry Chantler, who found that they were 'well-made and of good material'.[18]

Many of the officers didn't believe the boats were strong enough to hold sixty-five, but they were unaware of tests conducted in Belfast before the ship's maiden voyage that proved they could hold up to seventy. In May 1911, Harland & Wolff conducted tests on *Titanic's* sister

ship, *Olympic*. At the British inquiry, Harland & Wolff naval architect
Edward Wilding explained:

> We put into one of the lifeboats of the *Olympic* half-hundredweight
> weights distributed so as to represent a load equal to about sixty-five
> people, and then we raised and lowered the boat six times. It was
> done with the object of testing the electric boat winches, not with
> the object of testing the boat. I happened to see it coming up one
> time myself after the weights had been removed [the boat was lowered
> without weights into the water], and there was nothing the matter
> with her; she was watertight. I do not think there was any doubt the
> boats were strong enough to be lowered containing the full number of
> passengers, and I think that it was in the evidence of [Joseph] Wheat
> [assistant second steward] that he lowered a boat with about seventy
> in her. I think that confirms our Belfast test.[19]

Perhaps if the crew had been aware of these tests, they would have been
willing to fill more of the boats to capacity (some passengers would have
had to stand, but that's a small price to pay), thus saving more lives. Saying
that, however, could be wishful thinking. At the British inquiry, Second
Officer Charles Lightoller explained that this capacity would only be
possible if conditions were favourable, ideally water that was absolutely
smooth. Lightoller referred to this as a 'flat calm',[20] which the sea was
when they hit the iceberg. Lightoller assured investigators at the British
inquiry that he filled the lifeboats with as many people as he considered
to be safe, i.e., not overcrowded enough to risk tipping or capsizing while
out at sea but, even more importantly, not at risk of the mechanisms that
held and lowered them collapsing, which would have inadvertently led
to more deaths. This is a major area of contention in the history of the
Titanic, for the crew manning the lifeboats were also scared the boats
would sink should more people climb aboard, so they sailed away from
the wreckage and the passengers who were stuck in the freezing water.
Perhaps more people would have been saved if the crew had known this.

Four of the lifeboats were Engelhardt boats, 27ft5in (8.36m) long by
8ft (2.4m) wide, which held forty-nine (some sources claim they held
forty-seven). Built by McAlister & Son of Dumbarton, Scotland, these
were not so much boats as they were boat-shaped rafts. They were made

from cork and kapok (coconut fibre) and had heavy canvas sides that were designed to be raised to form a makeshift boat. They took up little space on deck, as two were able to be stored on the roof of the officers' quarters at the foot of the first funnel and two were stowed alongside the emergency lifeboat cutters.

Finally, there were two emergency lifeboats, 25ft (7.6m), which held between thirty-five and forty passengers. These were essentially miniature versions of the traditional lifeboats. They were kept ready to be launched at all times in case of an emergency that required the crew to act quickly, such as someone falling overboard, and had all their equipment stowed inside. One of these boats, the fourth to be launched on the night of the sinking, contained only twelve people, many of whom were first-class men, including the infamous Cosmo Duff-Gordon. Witnesses claimed that Duff Gordon and his wife, Lady Lucy Duff Gordon, bribed the crewman in charge with £5 to not return to rescue people struggling in the water. When he was questioned about the incident during the British inquiry, they accepted his explanation that it was not a bribe but a generous donation to the crew who had lost their livelihood. I personally find this hard to believe, but his testimony stands.

The British inquiry found that the arrangements for manning and launching the boats on board the ship in case of an emergency were insufficient. Drills were conducted in Southampton, which consisted of loading and lowering two lifeboats on the *Titanic*'s starboard side (it was docked to its port side so the lifeboats on that side could not be used). This drill was attended by White Star Line's Marine Superintendent Captain Benjamin Steele, the British Board of Trade's Captain Maurice Clarke, and *Titanic* crew members Second Officer Charles Lightoller, Third Officer Herbert Pitman, Fifth Officer Harold Lowe and Sixth Officer James Moody. The drill involved almost all seamen on board the ship, but not everyone. Quartermaster Robert Hichens, for example, did not take part because the quartermasters had been posted at gangways to prevent unauthorised visitors from boarding. It was also found that the crew, according to Sanderson, refused to participate in said drills, despite being offered half a day's pay (though he did specify that he was talking strictly about the firemen and the Commissioner shot him down, arguing that it was wasn't unreasonable for that part of the crew to reject the lifeboat drills).

Despite it being part of White Star Line's rules, no thorough lifeboat drill had been carried out since the *Titanic* had docked at Southampton, meaning that the crew had limited knowledge of what to do in that specific situation and were unaware of their lifeboat assignments until the voyage started. However, it should be noted that the crew were experienced, so they would have been able to use their best judgement during the disaster, as far as reasonably possible. As standard, a list had been drawn up to dictate which crew members were responsible for which lifeboat in a case of emergency. According to Second Officer Lightoller, it was the first officer's responsibility to draw up the boat list – that first officer was William Murdoch. But either the crew did not read it, didn't read it thoroughly enough, or were unaware it was there at all. In fact, a lifeboat drill had been scheduled for the morning of 14 April, the day of the sinking, but was cancelled. The real reason for the cancellation remains unclear, but the British and American inquiries revealed three possible reasons: Lookout Archie Jewell testified that it was cancelled due to strong wind that day; First-Class Saloon Steward Edward Wheelton claimed that a drill would have disrupted the meal prep for the third-class passengers that day; and Steward George Crowe stated that a church service was held at 10.30 a.m. that day instead of the drill, which was unusual, as drills always took place on a Sunday. This was supported by other surviving crew members at the inquiries, including Saloon Steward James Johnson, Third Officer Pitman, and two able-bodied seamen by the names of Lucas and Jones.

Others claimed that drills had been conducted, but insufficiently. One first-class survivor, Emma Bucknell, criticised this strongly in an interview with the *Philadelphia Inquirer* on 20 April 1912. She stated that the 'greatest crime was the "unpreparedness" of the lifeboat equipment', and argued that the crew on board her lifeboat did not know how to row. Regarding the drills themselves, she claimed that she 'had not seen a lifeboat drill while she was aboard the *Titanic*'.[21]

The crew's limited knowledge of what to do in that specific situation probably cost lives (please note that I am not blaming the crew here; they did their best given the horror they were a part of). Getting over 1,000 people off a ship that was safely docked would have been stressful enough to coordinate effectively, never mind getting them into a limited number of lifeboats the crew were inexperienced at manning. In *Titanic:*

20 Years Later with James Cameron, Cameron and his team re-enacted the lifeboat procedure using a lifeboat prop from the film and discovered that, done correctly, it probably took around thirty minutes to lower the boats fully. Once people understood the magnitude of the sinking and panic began to ensue, this procedure was bypassed altogether, and passengers and crew alike cut the ropes connected to the lifeboat davits. In his re-enactment, it took Cameron one minute, forty seconds to cut one piece of rope, and that was without disruptions or distractions. Now imagine trying to do that with ice-cold sea water rushing at you, and as people scream and clutch at your arms, legs and torso for dear life. Those men had a momentous responsibility thrust upon them and it is astounding that they managed to save as many as they did.

Newspapers were quick to jump on *Titanic's* lack of lifeboats, with one reporting on 20 April: 'U.S. Probe Shows *Titanic* Raced to Doom with Insufficient Lifeboats.' After reading what you just have, you now know that *Titanic* had more lifeboats than legally required, but that still wasn't enough to save everyone who could have been saved. Knowing that the ship was within the confines of the law does little to soothe those who lost loved ones, however. As Alan Ruffman notes, 'If you didn't get a place in a lifeboat, you were lost.'[22]

2

Death

Given that *Titanic* sank, one would assume the most likely cause of death would be drowning. Newspapers at the time unwittingly encouraged this misconception, with one local Washington paper, the *Tonopah Daily Bonanza*, running the headline 'Hundreds Drowned at Sea'[1] and the *Hawaiian Gazette* reporting that 'twelve hundred and upward certainly drowned in wreck of *Titanic*, drowned like rats in a hole'.[2] The notion that most people drowned was also encouraged by the coroners' reports, which simply stated 'drowned' on many death certificates because they did not have the time or resources for autopsies. In cases such as this, the cause of the actual sinking usually took priority over the overall cause of death.

But there are many ways to die in a shipwreck. The main ones I will discuss are drowning, injuries/crushing, suicide and – the leading cause of death – cold water shock and hypothermia.

Drowning

We'll start with drowning. The World Health Organization strips drowning down to its most basic form: 'the process of experiencing respiratory impairment from submersion/immersion in liquid.'[3] Drowning is, therefore, death brought on by suffocation. It can take several minutes – in some cases, up to twelve – and occurs in stages:

1. Stage one occurs within the first few seconds after the water is inhaled. Your body immediately goes into its fight-or-flight mode as you try to breathe.

2. Stage two is the narrowing or closing of your airways. Once your body senses hypoxia, or oxygen deprivation, it will close your airways to prevent more water from getting into your lungs. Your body will hold its breath without conscious thought and can hold it for up to two minutes. The pressure of water submersion can also cause your chest cavity to fill with fluid, both external and internal, which will put pressure on your heart and disable it from pumping blood efficiently. In some cases, this can lead to cardiac arrest and death.

3. Stage three is when you fall unconscious. Your breathing stops completely and, while your heart slows, it continues to pump blood as best as it can.

4. Stage four is when the body can start hypoxic convulsions, which can look like seizures. The lack of oxygen will turn your body blue. If you can be removed from the water at this stage, you have a good chance of being revived by resuscitation.

5. Stage five, the final stage, occurs when your body – specifically your lungs, heart and brain – reach a point where they cannot be revived. Your body will go into a cerebral hypoxia state, meaning that all oxygen sources have been cut off, and your body will eventually shut down completely, leading to clinical death.

It is unclear how many passengers and crew were trapped on *Titanic* as it sank, but many of those who were deep within the belly of the ship likely drowned. It is often theorised that the first to drown would have been the boiler- and engine-room operators (Lightoller specifically stated seeing them on deck during the British inquiry). People are quick to argue that they would have been trapped in the different compartments as the watertight doors in the bulkheads lowered, giving them absolutely zero chance of survival, and those who did manage to escape the closing of the bulkheads still perished once the bulkheads were breached, due to the sheer pressure of the water. This is highly unlikely. The crew knew the ship like the back of their hands, and many ships of that era, which they would have worked on previously, had similar designs. The crew would have had ample time to escape via catwalks and ladders, as we know that while the water did rush in, it wasn't quick enough to make escape impossible.

The only crew members who would have drowned there would be those who chose to stay behind – this is possible but we'll likely never know – or those who were injured and couldn't leave. 32-year-old Junior Assistant Second Engineer Jonathan Shepherd is one man who likely suffered this fate. He is considered by some historians to be the first person to die as a result of the disaster, but there is some conflicting evidence that he was taken to the aft boiler room or the upper deck. Since the evidence leans towards Shepherd being in Boiler Room 5, that is the most likely scenario we are exploring here. Shepherd had broken his leg after slipping into an access hole, which had been uncovered (the stokehold floor had access plates that could be removed to get to pump valves, etc.) in Boiler Room 5 while he was helping his fellow engineers rig pumps. He was taken to a pump room, assisted by Lead Stoker Frederick Barrett and fellow Junior Assistant Second Engineer Herbert Gifford Harvey, to recover but he likely drowned in that very room when the structural integrity of the non-watertight coal bunker was ruptured. Barrett reported that when the call to evacuate the boiler room sounded, Harvey ran to rescue Shepherd, but the last he saw of the two men was their bodies disappearing under the torrent of water, swept away by a wave of sea foam. Neither man, if their bodies were recovered, was identified.

Also still aboard the ship as it sank were postal clerks, kitchen crew (Paul Mauge, secretary to the chef of the restaurant Ala Carte, claimed at the British inquiry that many of his colleagues were kept down by stewards blocking the entry to the second-class deck, but it is unclear as to whether this was intentional or not),[4] stewards and officers, as well as passengers (mostly third class) making their way up to the decks but not making it in time. In some cases, passengers remained in their cabins out of fear, confusion, denial or acceptance. In fact, some testimonies stated that many third-class families – women and children among them – *chose* to remain in their cabins, perhaps waiting for officers to direct them to the upper decks or, the more heart-breaking consideration, resigning themselves to their fates because they knew they were the last priority. A brave and dignified choice, if true.

Those who entered the water without life jackets also likely drowned.

Injuries/Crushing

One of the more gruesome ways people on the *Titanic* died was from injuries sustained during the sinking and the breaking apart of the ship. If you feel triggered by this kind of content, please skip to the 'Cold Shock Response/Hypothermia' section. We'll start with some of the more unusual and rarer cases of injuries first. Some are detailed in witness accounts in sources I found during my research and others are educated guesses that we can make based on what we know about the sinking.

One type of injury that is highly contentious within *Titanic* scholarship is the injuries that may have been sustained by the stokers in the ship's engine rooms. While eyewitnesses claimed that they heard the boilers explode, Robert Ballard and Jean-Louis Michel, who co-discovered the *Titanic* wreck in 1985, found that the ship's boilers were intact and had not exploded, despite eyewitnesses claiming they heard them explode. The seawater would have been very unlikely to crack or damage the boilers: they were Scotch boilers, which do not explode when hit with cold water. The boilers themselves would not have exploded, but connected pressurised piping could have been compromised. Excess steam pressure in the foremost boiler rooms was reduced by the stokers, who blew off the safety valves. According to Frederick Scott, one of the ship's greasers, the safety valves were lifted early on into the sinking, letting off huge amounts of steam as the lifeboats were loaded. Scott, ironically, would die just three years later from being too close to an exploding boiler – the deaths of he and other crew members caused by the rupturing of steam pipes, resulting in extreme steam scalding – on SS *La Marguerite* in 1915.

Arguments have been made that the noise the eyewitnesses attributed to exploding boilers was more likely to be machinery crashing through the ship or the shattering and breaking of steel as *Titanic*'s bow tipped and stern lifted,[5] causing the hull to separate. Lawrence Beesley, *Titanic* survivor and author of *The Loss of the Titanic*, wrote:

there came a noise which many people, wrongly I think, have described as an explosion … It was partly a groan, partly a rattle, and partly a smash, and it was not a sudden roar as an explosion would be; it went on successively for some seconds, possibly fifteen to twenty …

It was as if all the heavy things one could think of had been thrown downstairs from the top of a house, smashing each other and the stairs and everything in the way.[6]

What he heard was the steel of the ship itself ripping and tearing.

The loud explosions eyewitnesses attributed to 'exploding boilers' was near the end of the sinking, as the ship was breaking in two. According to Bruce Beveridge, if injuries did occur, it would have been scaldings from the stream mains in Boiler Room 1, which were still under pressure. When the ship started breaking, these live steam mains from Boiler Room 1 would have let loose and the subsequent noise would have been thought to be 'boiler explosions'. The breakup of the hull happened through the engine room, so any of those brave engineers who were hard at work trying to save the ship – or merely standing at their stations on the platforms and cat walks waiting to die – would have been scalded.[7] A scald is a burn via something wet, including steam; scalding not only burns your skin but can damage your mouth, nose, windpipe and eyes. The men who sustained scalding injuries would have had three degrees of burn, depending on how close they were to the steam pipes and for how long. A first-degree burn only affects the epidermis, the skin's first layer, and does not do much damage beyond the superficial. Second- and third-degree scalding burns, however, are much more serious. A second-degree burn not only damages the first layer of skin but also the second, the dermis. The burn causes the skin to painfully separate, which results in fluid build-up and leads to inflamed blisters. The third-degree burn would have been the worst outcome. These burns penetrate all layers of skin and, rather than blisters forming, the skin would slough off entirely. Because it affects the deeper tissue, third-degree burns can make the skin appear dark red or even black.

Given the evidence that we have, we know that if the boilers were compromised or damaged, it would have been early enough during the sinking to avoid injuring or killing any stokers on board. Expeditions to the wreck have proved they are nearly intact. During the sinking, the boilers would've been cool enough to avoid steam pipes rupturing and, at any rate, most, if not all, of the stokers and engineering crew would have been away from the area by the time this could have happened. They would not have been able to work in the flooded boiler rooms and would have moved away from the danger via numerous routes, including going up the ladders to the funnel bases, out the engineers' lounge on the Boat Deck, or through Scotland Road – a crew alleyway that ran the entire length of *Titanic*, on E Deck's port side, nicknamed by the crew after the area in North Liverpool. However, most passengers would not have known that because they weren't experienced mariners or engineers.

The psychological impact of the noises the ship made during the sinking on passengers and crew should not be overlooked. While their eyewitness accounts are unreliable in their factual detail, Friedrich 'Rudi' Newman notes, '*Titanic*'s loss was a violent destruction of machinery, even if less so than other disasters. The sounds made as she sank were terrible enough to warrant description in newspapers and inquiries, staying with the survivors throughout their lives. In trying to explain them, they created some myths that have since been disproved, but the wreck still bears the scars of what they heard.'[8]

We do know that some of *Titanic*'s stokers,[9] coal trimmers and greasers managed to escape and survive the sinking – an estimated sixty-nine. One was Frederick Barrett, who kept the engines going for as long as possible before abandoning the task when the order came to leave, once it became clear the ship was beyond saving. Once he was on deck, he was put in charge of lifeboat no. 13 and was responsible for saving the lives of around seventy people. Another was Arthur John Priest, who happened to be off-duty and was catching some well-earned sleep between his shifts. Priest managed to make it to the upper deck with some of his fellow stokers, only to find that most of the lifeboats had already gone. The stokers did not have life jackets, so they had to swim for their lives in nothing more than the clothes on their backs. Priest suffered frostbite, as did many of those who survived after being in the water, and likely narrowly avoided suffering from hypothermia, but he survived the sinking. Priest had actually already survived two previous ship collisions – RMS *Asturias* in 1908 and White Star Line's own RMS *Olympic* in 1911 – and would go on to survive several sinkings, including HMS *Alcantara* and HMHS *Britannic*, alongside fellow *Titanic* survivor Violet Jessop, in 1916, and SS *Donegal* in 1917. While this earned him the nickname 'The Unsinkable Stoker', it did negatively impact Priest; after SS *Donegal* sank, he retired, supposedly saying that 'no one wished to sail with him after these disasters'.[10]

While the tables and chairs on the ship were bolted down, it is possible large items may have come loose and fallen (James Cameron's film depicts items falling, but this was more for dramatic effect than histori-cal accuracy – a big thanks is owed to Bruce Beveridge for his insight on this). Christopher Ward details one particular incident in D Deck's dining saloon, where a poor steward was crushed when one of *Titanic's* six grand pianos snapped its bolts and crashed into him.[11]

While that specific incident was unusual, death by injury from the ship's debris is very likely. Victims would have been crushed by the falling funnels (Jack Dawson's roommate Fabrizio in Cameron's film perished this way), and cables snapping from said funnels would have sliced people's heads from their necks or severed limbs, causing them to bleed out. Buoyant chunks of debris like wooden doors, furniture and beams would have shot to the surface as the ship descended, injuring and likely killing some of those who survived in the water. It is also likely that passengers died after falling into the belly of the ship as it broke in two: victims would have been impaled on wood or metal, or had their bones and or/skull crushed on a part of the ship as they plummeted.

Many would have died from falling off the ship and into, or more accurately *on* to, the water: the more the ship's stern rose out of the water, the greater the height people would have fallen from. Due to gravity, the speed of an object dropped from a height, including the human body, will increase at a rate of 10m/s every second as it falls. The higher you go, the faster you fall, and the more likely you are to die. Hitting water from a height is like hitting a concrete wall because the water molecules can't displace fast enough to create a soft landing. It can snap your bones like twigs because the water essentially becomes a solid surface. Even if you manage to fall completely vertically, the impact can still be strong enough to break your bones, compress your spine, give you a concussion, or even knock you unconscious. You aren't aware that you're in water when you're unconscious, so you'll breathe in the ice-cold water. If your body doesn't shut down from cold-shock response or hypothermia first, you'll likely drown before you ever wake up.

Life jackets were not the Hail Mary they were meant to be either. Life jackets are designed to stay atop the water, so you do not sink. If you hit water wearing one, it will push you to the surface and prevent you from succumbing to the waves, keeping your body afloat even if you are injured or lack the energy to continue swimming. The life jackets worn by *Titanic's* passengers and crew were made from canvas and cork. Cork is made from the bark of evergreen oak trees native to north-west Africa and south-west Europe, and was the ideal material for life jackets at the end of the nineteenth century and beginning of the twentieth for three main reasons. Firstly, cork is extremely buoyant and will therefore not sink. Secondly, it's highly incompressible, meaning that its buoyancy doesn't degrade in storage. And thirdly, it was the least likely material known at the time to waterlog (fill with water) and drag you down.

Cork, however, had disadvantages that people only became aware of in the direst of circumstances. Cork was buoyant, yes, but detrimentally so. In 1942, experienced seamen Phil Richards and John J. Banigan wrote *How to Abandon Ship*, a manual informed by lived experience, on how to ensure the maximum number of people survived when abandoning a ship. In their introduction, they state that their 'manual is the result of open boat experience in the time of stress, danger, and sudden death. It contains no armchair theory. It is a digest of the lessons learned by the survivors of torpedoed ship.'[12] Although the book was written within the context of the Second World War, many observations and practical advice it contains would have been highly beneficial to those fleeing the *Titanic*. They advised specifically against life jackets containing cork:

Do not trust your life to a cork preserver. Men have drowned in them. This type of preserver rides high on the wearer's back, and sometimes it actually forced the head under water. Men who have jumped overboard wearing cork preservers have had ribs, arms, and shoulders broken. The front of the preserver strikes the chin, knocking the wearer unconscious.

Albert Pfisterer, a wiper from the torpedoed *Gulf America*, reported: 'We saw bodies in the water, face downwards and feet up. This was the fault of the life preservers. The men could have been saved if it were not for the life preservers crawling up.'[13]

Cork life jackets were so buoyant that they could jerk the wearer's neck back so violently that it broke on impact. Only twelve of the 3,500 life jackets from *Titanic* survive and, notably, one recovered from the sinking's debris by *Mackay-Bennett* quartermaster Robert Edward has bloodstains on its collar, perhaps the result of an injury such as the ones mentioned by Richards and Banigan.

Life jackets can also be dangerous if you don't know how to properly use one, which many of the passengers and crew on board the *Titanic* did not. While lifeboat drills had taken place – with the crew, not the passengers – as far as I can find, no life-jacket-specific drill was carried out. Therefore, some of those who died but wore life jackets may have died in part because of their insufficient knowledge of how to properly enter the water wearing one. The correct way to enter water wearing a life jacket is to cross your arms across your chest/breast with your hands on the opposing shoulders (i.e., your right hand on your left shoulder, your left hand on your right shoulder). The buoyancy of life jackets, especially ones made from cork, can cause injury to the neck and/or spine if you jump into the water without following the proper procedure.

And even if you do follow it, you're still at risk of injury. Any height exceeding two metres, about the height of a standard door, will increase your risk of serious or even fatal injury. There was also a risk of strangulation with *Titanic*'s life jackets. Their design was flimsy at best and the strings of the jacket could wrap themselves around your throat and strangle you if not tied correctly. The passengers and crew who had time to ensure their life jackets were secure likely wouldn't have had this problem, but those who panicked as the severity of the situation became clear may not have had time to make sure their life jacket was fitted correctly. It is also entirely possible some life jackets fell off people altogether as they entered the water.

There are eyewitness accounts from several sinkings in which life jackets proved to be detrimental to survival – SS *Morro Castle*, for example. In 1934, a fire burned through the ocean liner's electrical cables during a journey from Cuba to New York, engulfing the ship in flames. Many passengers and crew were forced to jump into the water because the rescue effort by both the crew and nearby ships was not quick enough and the decks grew too hot to stand on, with thick smoke from the fire making it difficult to breathe.

Two men who jumped into the water wearing life jackets appeared to succumb to injuries caused by the buoyancy of their life jackets and their incorrect method of entering the water. The ship's doctor, Dewitt Vanzile of Brooklyn, New York, broke his neck when he jumped in, with witnesses claiming they saw his life jacket ride up under his chin as blood gushed from his nose and mouth before he rolled over in the water. Morton Lyon Junior, an insurance agent from Pennsylvania, broke his neck by jumping incorrectly into the water while wearing a life jacket, but he survived long enough to be pulled into a lifeboat. According to witnesses, Lyon moaned that he had 'done something' to his neck. He could not hold his head up with assistance and he had difficulty breathing. He died soon after.

If there had been adequate drills for both manning the lifeboats and how to properly use life jackets, more people would have survived. Richards and Banigan made a point of emphasising just how important these drills are at sea:

> Do not cheat yourself of life [the way this tragic seaman did]. Prepare yourself, which cannot be done simply by engaging in peacetime boat drills. You are not a lifeboatman unless you have had experience in lowering away. Swinging out is not sufficient. As a boat drill, the mere operation of swinging out has left men inadequately trained, resulting in the loss of many lives during emergencies. *The Comal Rico* crewmen were prepared. They held a boat drill every other day. When the ship was torpedoed, all survived except two who were killed by a direct hit. Do not ship out unless you have taken part in a complete abandon-ship drill. Insist on this drill. Joe Melendez from the torpedoed *Saber* reported: 'In the nineteen days since we left New York there had been no lifeboat drills.' Do not let this situation occur aboard your ships. Complete drills can take place in harbours and when coastwise ships lay-up at night and even at sea. Frank W. Ferguson reported: 'I was on the torpedoed *E.M. Clark* as A. B. There were 26 men in my lifeboat and of this number only three were completely familiar with handling a boat. Because of this fact we had a tough time getting clear of the ship. More drills, more survivors.'[14]

Suicide

Suicide is perhaps an unavoidable thing to discuss when talking about the sinking of *Titanic*. I was hesitant to include it at all, but I feel like it needs to be addressed. There is no concrete evidence that anyone died by suicide on *Titanic*, be that first-, second-, or third-class passengers, crew, or officers, but there is one prevailing story that seems to captivate storytellers for its tragic element. That is the supposed suicide of First Officer William McMaster Murdoch. I use the term 'supposed' very specifically here. His suicide – a gunshot to the head – is part of *Titanic* culture now, featured in several cinematic adaptations. The first depiction of Murdoch firing a gun but not shooting himself was in the clunky 1979 version, and the supposed suicide was depicted in both the highly inaccurate 1997 film version and the stage musical. But did the event in question actually happen?

William McMaster Murdoch was a Scottish naval officer who served as *Titanic*'s first officer. Following in his family's seafaring tradition, he apprenticed with William Joyce & Coy in Liverpool and was such a competent sailor that he passed his second mate certificate on his first try, one year before his apprenticeship was up. He became a White Star Line employee in 1900 and served on their ships for twelve years before perishing on *Titanic*. He was a man with a reputation for being 'canny and dependable' and had faced and triumphed over previous dangers and disasters at sea, including steering SS *Arabic* away from an approaching ship in 1903, using his professional judgement to disregard an order from his superior to 'hard-a-port'. Reportedly, the ships missed each other by mere inches, but it was thanks to Murdoch that a full-scale collision was avoided. This same quick thinking and professional judgement enabled Murdoch to save many on board the *Titanic*.

Following the sinking and the arrival of the survivors in New York, there were numerous reports of gunshots heard aboard that were communicated to the *New York Morning World* and *New York Herald*. Some claimed Captain Smith had shot himself, while others attested that it was Murdoch. Since Murdoch is the one commonly believed to have done the deed, he is the only one I am discussing here.

Eyewitness reports flooded in. Laura Francatelli, Lady Duff-Gordon's secretary, claimed she saw a 'dear brave officer [gave] orders to row away from the sinking boat at least 200 yards, he afterwards, poor dear brave fellow, shot himself. We saw the whole thing.'[15] However, as acknowledged in *On A Sea of Glass*,[16] the wording of this is unclear: Francatelli could be referring to either the shooting or the sinking, so it's not overly reliable. Another first-class passenger, George Rheims, wrote to his wife saying, 'I saw an officer with a revolver fire a shot and kill a man who was trying to climb into it [the last boat]. He gave a military salute and then fired a bullet into his head. That's what I call a man!'[17] Similarly, third-class passenger Eugene Daly claimed that a fellow passenger 'saw an officer trying to control the maddened rush by shooting two persons. The same officer shot himself two minutes later.' He later told his sister that 'they told me he shot himself, but I did not see him', and later again told his daughter that 'the officer who had shot the two men a few minutes before had put a gun to his own head and shot himself. I'm sure he did it in despair for what he had to do. My dad later saw his body on deck.'[18] Note that he was *told* of the incident but did not witness it himself.

Other third-class passengers, supposedly, stood by their testimony that an officer shot himself. One was Carl Jansson, who was quoted in several newspapers, stating he 'saw the Chief Officer [this was Henry Tingle Wilde, not Murdoch, so it's possible he confused the two men] place a revolver in his mouth and shoot himself. His body toppled overboard.'[19] (In *On A Sea of Glass*, the authors note, however, that not only was the quote *attributed* to Jansson, making it secondary and therefore unreliable, but Murdoch's name isn't specifically mentioned.) Anna Sjoblom also claimed she 'saw an officer shoot himself through the temple with a revolver'.[20] A saloon steward, Thomas Whiteley, backed up these speculations, adding that 'Murdoch shot one man – I did not see this, but three others did – and then shot himself'.[21] Whiteley also claimed he overheard the lookouts saying, 'no wonder Mr. Murdoch shot himself' while discussing the ice warnings that were allegedly ignored. Walter Lord also mentions Murdoch dying by suicide (and Captain Smith) in passing.

Eyewitness reports, as any historian knows, are notoriously unreliable, especially in a situation like the sinking of the *Titanic*. Emotions are high and things are in utter chaos. It is impossible to remember things verbatim, and it's possible that one may attribute what they overheard someone else claim they saw or heard as their own memory.

The surviving members of *Titanic*'s crew were quick to dispel any rumours of suicide. Second Officer Lightoller, in a letter to Murdoch's widow Ada, wrote that Murdoch was swept into the ocean by a wave washing over the boat deck while working to free Collapsible Lifeboat A. Murdoch's nephew, William, upon the release of James Cameron's 1997 film, asserted that his uncle did not die by suicide: 'From my own family connections and also from my father having spoken to various officers who survived, he didn't commit suicide. If someone says to you somebody in the family committed suicide when he hadn't, you take objection.'[22] Historian Susanne Störmer, who interviewed Murdoch's nephew for her book *Good-bye, Good Luck: The Biography of William McMaster Murdoch*, backed up Lightoller's claim, stating that 'Murdoch was swept off the deck of the *Titanic* by a wave he had his back to.[23] It took him by surprise, and he found himself plunged into the ice-cold water. He diligently tried to get back to the lifeboat he had started to launch.' This is also supported by Tom McCluskie, Michael Sharpe and Leo Marriott in their book *Titanic and Her Sisters Olympic & Britannic*, in which they stated:

> when the evacuation got under way, Murdoch took charge of lifeboats on the starboard side. He remained cool as the crush to escape became more chaotic, shouting, 'Stand back, stand back … it's women first' as his purser and sixth officer fired their sidearms into the air to prevent a stampede of anxious men. The epic film by James Cameron portrays Murdoch as a man who panicked, shot a passenger, and then put the gun to his own head. But those who were there say he was a five-star hero who gave his lifebelt and gun to another passenger to help them before being swallowed by the dark, icy waters.[24]

There are some historians who, while they admit that the evidence is circumstantial, argue that there is evidence an officer did die by suicide by gunshot and that the most likely candidate is Murdoch.[25] One such historian is Don Lynch, author of *Titanic: An Illustrated History*:

> Of all the *Titanic* issues that will never be resolved, the fate of First Officer Murdoch remains one of the most tantalizing. Various passengers and crew describe seeing Murdoch shoot a man who was trying to get into the last boat. Some claimed he then shot himself. Others such as Hugh Woolner, stated that the First Officer had only fired into the air to warn off a crowd just before the boat was lowered. Nellie Becker, who spent each day on the *Carpathia* discussing the sinking with other survivors, met no one who had actually seen anyone shot. And Second

Officer Lightoller testified that he saw the first officer still working at Collapsible A just before the bow began to plunge. Murdoch had been demoted from Chief Officer just before the *Titanic*'s maiden voyage, and it was he who stood on the bridge when the *Titanic* struck the iceberg, so it is tempting to imagine his anguished, suicidal state of mind as the ship sank. Certainly, Lightoller's testimony can be discounted – he may well have been attempting to protect the reputation of a fellow White Star officer, as well as that of his employers. It seems clear that some shots were fired, probably by Murdoch. Whether any were aimed and hit their mark, we will never know. First Officer Murdoch's body was not among those recovered, nor was any corpse found to have been shot.[26]

William McMaster Murdoch's body was never recovered, so we will never know his true fate. Eyewitness testimony is unreliable at the best of times, but the combination of bitterness, fear, lack of lighting, lack of legitimate proximity to the event, and lack of knowledge to identify each officer by just their uniform at the time of the supposed sinking means we'll never know for sure if a *Titanic* officer died by suicide, or if one did, whether or not it was Murdoch. Regardless of what happened to him, he was a hero on board the *Titanic* and deserves to be remembered as such.

Cold Water Shock and Hypothermia

Though one would assume with a shipwreck that the most obvious cause of death would be drowning, and that is not an unfair assumption to make, in the case of *Titanic*, a combination of cold water shock and hypothermia was the main cause of death for most of the victims. At the time of the sinking – between 11.40 p.m. when its starboard side struck the iceberg and the final submersion at 2.20 a.m. – the air around the Atlantic was 4°C (39°F), due to a high-pressure cold front from the east of Canada, and the water was -2°C (28°F), which is fairly average for that region of the Atlantic in April (the average temperature varies between -2°C and 2°C at that time of year). The water was so cold that if it had been fresh water as opposed to salt water, it would have been frozen solid.

Cold water shock triggers what is essentially a heart attack, which, compared to hypothermia, is probably the better option of the two because it does not take as long and is comparatively less painful. Not every victim who fell into the water would have experienced cardiac arrest – older victims and victims with health conditions or more body fat would have been the ones more likely to succumb to this fate. Anyone who falls into freezing cold water likely dies from cold water shock before they even get the chance to die from hypothermia because they rarely live long enough for their body to reach the critical point at which hypothermia sets in. When a person enters cold water – anything colder than 15°C – their body goes into shock almost immediately. In their panic, they inhale involuntarily, and some people can drown this way if their first breath is underwater and they hyperventilate once they break the surface, inhaling more and more water until their lungs can't take any more.

If they survive long enough not to drown and put pressure on their lungs from lack of oxygen, they will feel a throbbing pain that shoots up their arms and legs as their blood rushes to protect their internal organs. But as this process is happening, the cold causes blood vessels to violently and quickly contract, which leads to a rapid heart rate and a major increase in blood pressure, causing cardiac arrest. Various studies have found that most people, immersing even one hand in water that is just above freezing, can tolerate only a few minutes at the most. Now imagine it's your entire body.

For anyone who survived long enough to overcome the initial intense pressure of cold water shock, a phenomenon present in all mammals, including humans, called the Dive Reflex, would have been triggered. This natural response enables the body to preserve oxygen by lowering blood pressure and removing resources (blood flow) from non-essential functions (the extremities – i.e., your limbs) to your essential organs in your torso and head.

There are four parts to this process:

1. Bradycardia: your heart rate falls by up to 25 per cent.
2. Splenic contraction: your spleen stores a reservoir of blood in case of emergencies. When the body enters a level of low oxygen, your spleen releases red blood vessels to increase your blood oxygen capacity.

3. Peripheral vasoconstriction: the walls of your blood vessels contract to narrow them, thus reducing blood flow and redirecting blood from non-essentials to vital organs.
4. Blood shift: similar to splenic contraction, your heart will push a substantial amount of blood to your lung's blood vessels to prevent them from collapsing.

Those who did not drown from shock or cardiac arrest, triggered by cold water shock, but survived long enough for the Dive Reflex to kick in, would have died from hypothermia.

Hypothermia, in its simplest terms, is what happens when the body loses heat faster than it can generate it. Human bodies have a regular internal temperature of between 37°C (98.6°F) and 37.2°C (99°F). If it falls below 35°C (95°F), hypothermia will set in. It is therefore unsurprising that being in a freezing environment means hypothermia sets in quickly, especially in cold water. Compared with hypothermia brought on by cold air, cold water drives heat away from the body up to twenty-five times faster.

Cold water life expectancy is measured by a range of six temperatures, the warmest being 27°C (80.6°F) and the coldest 0°C (32°F). The water at the time of the sinking was actually below the coldest temperature: a debilitating -2°C (28.4°F). According to Jess Bier in her article 'Bodily Circulation and the Measure of a Life: Forensic Identification and Valuation after the Titanic Disaster', people who are immersed in freezing water can expect to survive, at most, for forty-five minutes.[27] Even in relatively warm temperatures, such as the sea surrounding the Caribbean, which averages between 75°F (23°C) and 85°F (29°C), people can still die within two hours of entering the water. But for most people who entered the freezing water of the Atlantic during the sinking, they would have lost consciousness after fifteen minutes and been dead in another ten. As we know, the lifeboats did not return within forty-five minutes, so the victims in the water had an almost 0 per cent chance of surviving in the water that night. We know of a small number of people who survived after being pulled out of the water, but that was before hypothermia had a chance to sink in, and the number is a measly forty-four to forty-eight. Second Officer Charles Lightoller was one of the officers who fell into the freezing cold water and was quickly rescued by one of the lifeboats.

He described the feeling of entering the water as 'a thousand knives being driven into one's body',[28] which is where the famous line from Jack Dawson in James Cameron's film comes from: 'I fell through some thin ice and I'm telling ya, water that cold, like right down there, it hits you like a thousand knives stabbing you all over your body. You can't breathe. You can't think. At least not about anything but the pain.'[29]

There are three stages to hypothermia.

The first involves you losing all feeling in your arms and legs as the Dive Reflex kicks in, your internal body temperature plummeting, your pupils dilating, and the onset of intense shivering that causes your teeth to chatter uncontrollably. Understandably, your first instinct would be to swim, as you would assume that movement would help, but that is not the case. The reason so many of the *Titanic* victims succumbed to hypothermia as quickly as they did is because they were desperately swimming away from the ship to avoid being sucked down into the water or falling victim to debris. If you swim during the onset of hypothermia, you actually shorten your chances of survival because you lose body heat up to 50 per cent faster. Ideally, the best thing to do is not move at all, but that is a difficult thing to do when you're surrounded by a sinking ship and hundreds of equally terrified people. One of the reasons cited for the lifeboats not being turned around to rescue people sooner was the fear that those stuck in the water would attack the boat in a frenzy and capsize it, but the victims would have been too weak to do anything of the sort. If the crew had known this, it's likely they could have saved more people.

The final part of stage one hypothermia is that, paradoxically, you will start to feel warmer, and you may assume that this is a good thing. It's not. Your body temperature is still plummeting rapidly and the more you move, the faster it drops. The reason you feel warm is because of the Dive Reflex – you can feel your blood moving from your arms and legs to your essential organs, which creates a false sensation of warmth. There are documented cases of a phenomenon known as hypothermia-induced paradoxical undressing, in which sufferers become convinced that they are now *too* warm and start stripping their clothes off for relief – one famous example of this is the Dyatlov Pass Incident of 1959, when nine young hikers died in the northern Ural Mountains under mysterious circumstances – but since this sensation of warmth is false, if you undress you are doing nothing more than hastening your own death.

Stage two is arguably the scariest part of hypothermia. You know you are about to enter stage two when you are no longer able to touch your thumb with your little finger as all your blood has rushed to your internal organs and the cold has constricted your muscles. Your hands, lips, ears and toes turn blue, your movement becomes slower as your body tightens, and you lose strength faster and faster. While your pulse rate drops, your heart rate increases. Breathing becomes more laboured, sometimes shallow, and it becomes difficult to think, leading to confusion and panic.

Once the body's internal temperature drops below 32°C (89.6°F), you have entered stage three. Shivering stops as you lose consciousness, caused by your internal cellular metabolic processes shutting down, and major organs fail as less and less blood is being pumped into them. Clinical death usually occurs at 26°C (78.8°F), but brain death does not occur until later.

Not a soul in the Atlantic that night would have been alive after 3 a.m.

One of the saddest things I learned during my research was that people could have been revived after succumbing to hypothermia. In his study *Drowning, Near Drowning and Ice-Water Submersions*, J.P. Orlowski found seventeen cases of survival from hypothermia.[30] Someone who has suffered from hypothermia can be revived with the appropriate resuscitation measures, which include cardiopulmonary resuscitation and rewarming of the body to jumpstart the brain and internal organs. In his paper, Orlowski asserts that patients should not be considered dead until they have returned to a near normal internal temperature, because if the proper measures are conducted, they still have a chance of surviving. It is entirely possible that some of the victims in the water were still alive and could have been saved, but their external appearance made them look as if they were dead. This paper was written in 1987, so the crew who returned to the victims in 1912 would have been unaware of this possibility, but it is still heartbreaking to consider that some could still have been saved if they had known this.

I would also like to address one *Titanic* myth that continues to prevail to this day, and that is the story of Charles Joughin. Joughin was the chief baker on board *Titanic* and he survived the sinking of the ship. His story has become somewhat legendary in *Titanic* scholarship and fandom, because for many years it was theorised that he was able to survive for as long as he did in the freezing water because he was drunk. Joughin had had a drink at the time of the sinking, but he was not fully inebriated. After assisting the officers with getting women and children into the lifeboats, he went below decks to have 'a drop of liquor', which he later specified was a tumbler half-full of booze, in his quarters. As the ship went down, Joughin managed to hold on to the outside of the safety rail of the stern and was dragged into the water by the force of the suction, though he insisted that his head did not go fully beneath the water at any point. Joughin was a strong swimmer and when he spotted Collapsible Lifeboat B upturned in the water, with about thirty men standing on top of it, he and Second Officer Lightoller swam towards it. There was no room for him, but Isaac Maynard, a fellow cook, recognised him and helped Joughin hold on to the side of the boat, with his legs still in the water. He was eventually pulled into another lifeboat and survived the sinking with only swollen feet.

The key thing to note here is that while Joughin had drank the night of the sinking, he was not in the water for long and when he was, it was mostly his legs. He was briefly submerged under water when he swam from the taffrail to the lifeboat. Many have incorrectly attributed his survival to him being intoxicated, believing that the alcohol in his system warded off the hypothermia long enough for him to be retrieved from the water. While the alcohol likely helped numb the initial shock, the reason Joughin did not suffer from hypothermia was because his torso, where his vital organs were, was not submerged in the water for a sustained period of time. It had very little to do with the alcohol.

In fact, alcohol increases the likelihood of hypothermia. According to the director of clinical pharmacology at the University of Iowa, Dr William Haynes, 'consumption of alcohol undoes many of the human body's healthy reflexes, one of which is keeping the core body temperature warm in cold weather'.[31] One drink is enough to start this process. The reason we feel cold is because our blood flows away from the skin and into our vital organs to increase our core temperature. Alcohol reverses this process. Alcohol is a vasodilator – vasodilation being a process that prevents muscles from tightening and the walls of our veins from narrowing, meaning blood flows more easily through the vessels. This increased blood flow to your skin creates a false sensation of warmth and stops your body from shivering, which is the body's way of creating warmth. So, if you drink and succumb to hypothermia, you may feel that you are warm and therefore safe, but that is rarely the case. Joughin survived by keeping his vital organs out of the water – that is the best thing you can do in a freezing water situation. Another *Titanic* survivor, Fang Lang (real name Wing Sun Fong), a transport passenger of White Star Line who was travelling to America to work on the company's facilities on the West Coast, kept himself alive the same way. He managed to keep himself afloat on a piece of wreckage (some sources say it was a door, others a table, but according to Bruce Beveridge it was in fact a piece of first-class lounge panelling, which is currently in a museum in Halifax) by balancing on his fingers and feet before being rescued by Fifth Officer Lowe in Lifeboat 14.

One of the most harrowing parts of the *Titanic* story is the accounts from survivors about what they heard while the victims died. One survivor, Jack Thayer, who plunged into the water but was rescued by Collapsible Lifeboat B, along with Second Officer Charles Lightoller and first-class passenger Archibald Gracie, described it as 'locusts on a Summer night',[32] while Lawrence Beesley testified that he heard 'every possible emotion of human fear, despair, agony, fierce resentment and blind anger mingled – I am certain of those – with notes of infinite surprise, as though each one were saying, "How is it possible that this awful thing is happening to me? That I should be caught in this death trap?"'[33] He went on to say that the cries of the dying 'came as a thunderbolt, unexpected, inconceivable, incredible. No one in any of the boats standing off a few hundred yards away can have escaped the paralyzing shock of knowing that so short a distance away a tragedy, unbelievable in its magnitude, was being enacted, which we, helpless, could in no way avert or diminish.'[34] Another survivor, George Rheims, described it as 'a dismal moaning sound which I won't ever forget; it came from those poor people who were floating around, calling for help. It was horrifying, mysterious, supernatural.'[35]

When recounting his memories of the sinking, Gracie said that he admired those in the water because he did not hear one rebuke from anyone if assistance was not granted. One refusal, he said, was followed by an authoritative voice that said, 'All right boys. Good luck and God bless you.'[36] One of the firemen, Walter Hurst, believes this man was Captain Smith. He claimed that the man cheered the occupants of the lifeboats on, shouting, 'Good boys! Good lads!' Hurst was moved by the swimmer's valour and support, but when he reached out to him with an oar to help him, the man was already dead. We cannot be sure if the man in question was Captain Smith, but knowing what we do about Smith's character, I would not be surprised. Regardless of who the man was, he deserves to be remembered for his courage.

The screams and cries from the dying subsided after about twenty minutes as hypothermia took the last of them. Lady Lucy Duff-Gordon recalled after the sinking that 'the very last cry was that of a man who had been calling loudly: "My God! My God!" He cried monotonously, in a dull, hopeless way. For an entire hour, there had been an awful chorus of shrieks, gradually dying into a hopeless moan, until this last cry that I speak of. Then all was silent.'[37] It was not until this silence that the crew decided to attempt to rescue those in the water. Fifth Officer Lowe, who commanded Lifeboat 14, testified that he 'waited until the yells and shrieks had subsided for the people to thin out' before attempting rescue.[38] But they were too late. While Lowe, his crew and one survivor who volunteered to help did find four men alive, one who died afterwards, he testified that all they could see was 'hundreds of bodies and lifebelts'; the dead seemed as 'if they had perished with the cold as their limbs were all cramped up'.[39]

Decomposition

According to the findings of the US inquiry, the bodies of *Titanic*'s victims were not immediately visible directly following the sinking. They noted:

> Captain Rostron, of the *Carpathia*, although four hours in the vicinity of the accident, saw only one body, and that Captain Lord, of the *Californian*, who remained three hours in the vicinity of the wreckage, saw none. The failure of the captain of the *Carpathia*, of the captain of the *Californian*, and of the captain of the *Mount Temple* to find bodies floating in that vicinity in the early morning of the day following can only be accounted for on the theory that those who went down with the ship either did not rise to the surface or were carried away or hidden by the extensive ice floe which during the night came down over the spot where the ship disappeared, while those bodies which have been found remote from the place where the ship went down were probably carried away from the scene by the currents or by the movement of the ice.[1]

But we know for a fact that the bodies were in the vicinity of the sinking. The body recovery effort did not begin until the first recovery ship, the *Mackay-Bennett*, reached the wreck site six days after the sinking, so the bodies of those left behind had time to drift, decompose, and be subject to scavenging by surrounding animals and seagulls.

Bodies would have been in one of three places: floating on top of the ocean, floating beneath the ocean's surface, or trapped within the ship itself (though probably not as many as people theorise). Many of the bodies without life jackets would eventually drift downwards towards the wreck itself. Robert Ballard described it as 'hundreds and hundreds of bodies came like rain and landed all across the debris field of the *Titanic*'.[2]

Regardless of where the bodies of the victims were, they would decompose. Decomposition has three main stages: bloat, active decay and skeletonisation:

1. Bloat: this stage, known as autolysis or self-digestion, happens immediately after death. Once the heart ceases to beat, blood circulation and respiration stops. The body cannot get rid of the oxygen left in its system, nor can it remove internal waste, so carbon dioxide builds up, which causes your cells to rupture and break down. The membranes within these cells eat the other cells, starting in your intestine and working their way to your other internal organs. Your body essentially eats itself from the inside out. Your skin also begins to discolour as the sulphur-heavy compounds in the bacteria trapped within your body break down. The enzymes – proteins that speed up our body's chemical reactions and metabolism – leak and produce gases, such as methane and ammonia, causing bodies to bloat. This is known as putrefaction and, in dry environments, causes the pungent smells one associates with a dead body.

2. Active decay: in dry environments, the fluids within your body leak from every available orifice and your soft tissue – organs, muscles, and skin – liquefy. This is why bodies sometimes appear smaller in death than they did when they were alive. After this stage, only bones, hair and cartilage remain. Nails and teeth can fall out during the later part of this stage.

3. Skeletonisation: the final stage. Once your soft tissue has completely deteriorated, your body will have lost its flesh, muscle and organs, meaning that the only remaining part of you is your skeleton. There is no set timeframe for skeletonisation, as it varies depending on how quickly you lose your organic components.

This is the normal process for decomposition. Bodies decompose differently, however, in water than they do on land. The bacterial process that causes a body to bloat with methane and ammonia gas – the putrefaction part of active decay – happens more slowly in a cold and anaerobic environment (meaning lacking oxygen or very limited oxygen). Your body will eventually bloat as it would on land, which leads to the skin tearing and sloughing off the muscle and tissue beneath. Air sacs in your lungs absorb water, which increases your density and drags you down – this would have been the case for those without life jackets. Your skin also slowly absorbs water, the outer layer blistering and turning a greenish-black, and peels away from the underlying soft tissue, which is advanced by the sea current bringing in sea scavengers, such as fish, crabs, shrimps, and sea lice, to feast upon it.

Please note, to dispel another *Titanic* myth, that it is very unlikely that any of *Titanic*'s victims were eaten by sharks. While there are sharks found in that part of the Atlantic – the great white shark, the tiger shark, and short and longfin sharks – they do not have the physical tolerance for the freezing water *Titanic* sank in. The only species of shark that would have been anywhere near the sinking would have been the Greenland shark, but as they prefer depths of 600–2,400ft, the bodies that sank to the seafloor, a depth of 13,200ft, would not be at risk of being eaten by this kind of predator. It's possible, but highly unlikely.

Moving on.

The decomposition process can take longer in cold water because it encourages adipocere to form. Adipocere, also known as grave or corpse wax, is a yellow-brown wax-like substance that formulates in anaerobic environments and is made from the fatty parts of your soft tissue. It inhibits bacterial growth, so bodies in water take longer to decompose. They will decompose, just a lot slower than if they were on land.

Skeletons on dry land can be preserved for hundreds of thousands of years, but the deep underwater environment is not skeleton-friendly. Deep-sea scavengers feed on bone like they would any other tissue, and because the ocean has a low level of calcium carbonate minerals, the building blocks for the skeletons, bones dissolve, and dissolve fast. In fact, Robert Ballard himself has stated that the bones of *Titanic* victims would have disappeared in as little as five years, the only thing left behind being their clothes and shoes.

Anyone interested in *Titanic* will have likely seen the famous photographs of the remains of the trousers and shoes of *Titanic* victims. These are still preserved in and around the wreck, as leather and various other items of clothing are treated with tannic acid, which deters bacteria and deep-sea scavengers from eating them. While there are some who argue that the shoes, in particular, do not indicate where someone's body landed after death – examples of arguments include two left shoes beside each other, two shoes with different types of buckles, or even the way the shoes are positioned not being a realistic way for someone's feet to lie – it's likely that some of the shoes *are* indicative of where a victim came to their final resting place. There is one particularly compelling story told by Robert Ballard in *Titanic: 20 Years Later with James Cameron*.[3] He and his crew came across a deteriorated cabin and in the centre lay two pairs of shoes: one belonging to a woman and one to a little girl, more than likely a mother and a daughter.

I appreciate that some of the clothing items would have been stored in wardrobes and various luggage carriers, and the material they were made from has likely disappeared over the last 100 years, leaving the clothing itself behind. I do also believe that some of these clothing items were worn by the victims during their time of death, particularly the third-class passengers, as many of them would have only owned two or three pairs of shoes. Some may have only had one pair and that is what they wore for the entirety of what was supposed to be a short journey to New York.

One of the biggest controversies within the *Titanic* community is whether there are preserved bodies trapped deep within the ship, the boiler room being a major site of contention for those who argue that there could be bodies there. One such victim that could be used as a potential example is Junior Assistant Second Engineer Jonathan Shepherd, who likely perished in Boiler Room 5 (it's important to note that his death in this room cannot be confirmed, however, and is therefore open to dispute). The usual line of argument is that there is no oxygen and no scavenger animals, so their bodies would not be subject to the processes that speed decomposition along. In fact, Ballard firmly believes that bodies may still be down there: 'I would not be surprised if highly preserved bodies were found in the engine room. That was deep inside the ship.'[4]

James Cameron disagrees. Having been down to the wreck numerous times himself – thirty-three times so far – he asserts that he has 'never seen human remains'.[5] Yes, there are items of clothing and shoes, which indicate victims coming to rest there, but there are no bones. Parts of *Titanic* may be anoxic, meaning there is a low level of oxygen, which would slow decomposition greatly, but as the ship itself continues to deteriorate and rust away, any bodies trapped within it would have been subjected to oxygenated currents and deep-sea scavengers, just like the other bodies. It may have taken longer, but it happened regardless. If any preserved bodies were going to be discovered, it was in 1985 when the wreck was first discovered, certainly not forty years on. As Cameron says, 'ocean currents blow through the ship like a drafty house with all the windows open'.[6]

In a situation like the sinking of SS *Kamloops*, a freighter that sank in Lake Superior in the US, it is entirely possible there are bodies preserved within its wreck because the lake is cut off from the open ocean, thus preventing fresh oxygenated currents from disturbing any bodies trapped within its depths. Lake Superior is also freezing, which rapidly slows down the decomposition process. Bodies trapped within SS *Kamloops* will eventually decompose; it will just take a lot longer. The wreck of *Titanic* is unlikely to have tangible remains such as the famous victim Old Whitey within the wreck of SS *Kamloops*, but the presence of the victims is still felt, even if their bodies are no longer there. And that can't be ignored.

The possible presence of bodies, or the obvious remains of bodies such as the items of clothing surrounding the *Titanic* wreck, brings a multitude of ethical considerations to the table. This is discussed at length in chapter eleven.

PART TWO

The Body
Recovery Effort

The First Recovery Ship:
Mackay-Bennett

The cities, towns and villages on the shores of Nova Scotia are no stranger to tragedy. In fact, just fifty years prior to the *Titanic* disaster, the people of Prospect Bay had cared for the victims of White Star Line's own SS *Atlantic*, a transatlantic ocean liner built at Harland & Wolff, which struck rocks and sank off the cost of Nova Scotia. The ship had been travelling from Liverpool to New York, its nineteenth Atlantic Ocean voyage, with some 975 passengers and crew on board (stowaways too). By 31 March 1873, the ship was running low on coal, so it was diverted to Halifax to refuel; Captain James Williams had feared they would not make it to New York otherwise. Captain Williams was unfamiliar with Halifax and was therefore 'unaware of the strong currents of the Western Atlantic caused by the 50-foot tides of the Bay of Fundy'.[1] Rather than being close to Halifax, as he believed, Williams and his crew were 20km to the west and at 3.15 a.m., the SS *Atlantic* smashed full speed into the shores of lower Prospect Bay. Some 550 people were killed, including every woman on board and almost all the children (only one survived). It was the worst disaster White Star Line faced prior to the sinking of *Titanic* and is known colloquially as the 'first' *Titanic*. The people of Prospect Bay and the surrounding villages stepped up: they rescued and sheltered the survivors, providing them with food, tea and blankets, and helped recover over 300 bodies.[2]

The biggest port in Nova Scotia, Halifax, is filled with kind people who have a deep respect and reverence for the sea. It has been a prominent seaport since the mid-1700s, and its people have borne witness to more than 10,000 ships wrecked on its shores. They are always willing to help should tragedy strike, and help they did when the news of *Titanic* reached them.

Before the reality of what had happened reached White Star Line officials in New York, they were convinced that *Titanic*, which they thought was only damaged – not at the bottom of the Atlantic – would sail to Halifax, where it would be docked and repaired, and any survivors would be transported to New York via other ships or the secure rail network in the city. This was not helped by the newspaper reports that were flooding in: the *Oakland Tribune* reported that the ship was floundering, 'limping toward Halifax after all on board are rescued';[3] the *Press and Sun-Bulletin* that the 'vessel was still afloat and under control';[4] and the *Elmira Star-Gazette* that the passengers were safe, the vessel in tow, and that passengers were transferred 'from the damaged ship without accident'[5]. The *Evening World* in New York, the day after the sinking, published several quotes from Philip A.S. Franklin, vice-president of the International Mercantile Marine Company and White Star Line's representative at their New York office, including that he was certain that 'absolutely no fear is entertained for the safety of the passengers', and that the ship was 'unsinkable':

No one need fear that the *Titanic* will go down. Even though all her former compartments and bulkheads were stove in by the iceberg, she would still float indefinitely. She might go down a little at the bow, but she would float. I am free to say that no matter how bad the collision with an iceberg, the *Titanic* would float. She is an unsinkable ship ... we feel certain that all of the passengers will be landed safely in Halifax. Their relatives and friends need entertain no fears. From our revised lists we find that there are 325 saloon passengers, 300 second cabin passengers, and 800 steerage passengers.[6]

To make matters worse, the *Liverpool Courier* published a fake photograph of *Titanic* being towed to New York by Allan Line's RMS *Virginian*.[7]

Obviously, none of this was true. Families of passengers and crew members flocked to the White Star Line offices in Southampton and

Liverpool to demand news, and soon there were enormous crowds storming its London office on Cockspur Street. According to Christopher Ward, a chant of 'murderers' echoed throughout the streets of London.[8] Though Bruce Ismay called for a strategic news media blackout until the survivors of the sinking reached New York, the damage had been done.

When it became clear that *Titanic* had indeed sunk and that there was no saving the ship, and the priority became retrieving the bodies of the 1,500 passengers and crew left behind, the people of Halifax were quick to lend a hand. The first ship to be chartered for *Titanic's* body-recovery effort was CS *Mackay-Bennett*. Bruce Ismay, from the safety of New York, issued the following message from White Star Line:

> The cable ship *Mackay-Bennett* has been chartered by the White Star Line and ordered to proceed to the scene of the disaster and do all she could to recover the bodies and glean all information possible. Every effort will be made to identify bodies recovered and any news will be sent through immediately by wireless. In addition to any such message as these, the *Mackay-Bennett* will make a report of its activities each morning by wireless, and such reports will be made public at the offices of the White Star Line. The cable ship has orders to remain on the scene of the wreck for at least a week, but should a large number of bodies be recovered before that time she will return to Halifax with them. The search for the bodies will not be abandoned until not a vestige of hope remains for any more recoveries. The *Mackay-Bennett* will not make any soundings, as they would not serve any useful purpose, because the depth where the *Titanic* sank is more than 2000 fathoms.[9]

Built in 1884 by John Elder & Co. of Govan for the Commercial Cable Company, the *Mackay-Bennett* was, like *Titanic*, made of steel. It had a sheeting of greenheart wood (common in boatbuilding, as it's highly resistant to the decay caused by aquatic organisms), was 270ft long and registered at around 1,700 tonnes. Its name came from two directors of the Commercial Cable Company: mining magnate John W. Mackay and *New York Herald* owner James Gordon Bennett Junior. Throughout its career, *Mackay-Bennett* served as a cable ship, whose crew were responsible for laying and repairing transatlantic cables that connected Europe and the United States.

At the time of the sinking of the *Titanic, Mackay-Bennett*'s crew and their captain for the last five years, Frederick Harold Larnder, were preparing to repair a cable break near Cape Cod. During its preparation on 16 April 1912, Larnder was unexpectedly called into the office of Commercial Cable Company, his direct employer, where he was introduced to White Star Line's Halifax representative, A.G. Jones. Larnder was informed that his ship had been chartered by White Star Line to retrieve the bodies of *Titanic*'s victims. While other vessels docked in Halifax at the time had been considered, including the steamers *Seal* and *Florizel*, and the coastal ship *Lady Laurier*, Larnder's ship was chosen because it was the largest. The ship was also ideal for the task. Purpose-built as a cable ship, it was equipped with grappling hooks and grapnels, powerful steam winches (mechanical devices shaped like drums that are used to handle sheets and control lines) and a capstan (a vertical-axled rotating machine to increase the pulling force of the crew when hauling ropes and cables). It was also designed to be able to drift comfortably, so the crew could install the cables without worrying about the ship moving too far away from its intended location. The ship was also manned by a crew who were experts in what they did and were widely respected for it within the Halifax shipping community.

Mackay-Bennett was chartered at a rate of $550 per day, and Larnder was told that his men would receive double pay should they sign up to the task. The gruesome task was also, in no small part, motivated by a $100,000 reward offered by J.J. Astor's son Vincent for the recovery of his father's body. Larnder and his crew readily agreed, keen to help in any way they could. Jones handed Larnder a piece of paper with the coordinates 41.46N, 50.14W, the last known location of the ship radioed in by *Titanic*'s wireless operator Jack Phillips before it went down. Knowing the bodies would not be in stasis, Larnder was informed that he would have to make calculations based on sea currents and wind to determine where they would most likely be once *Mackay-Bennett* reached its destination.

Larnder set to work immediately. He and his crew removed all non-essential equipment from the ship to make room for what their essentials were to become: over 100 coffins,[10] stacked so high on the ship that they threatened to topple into the ocean; sheets upon sheets of sailing canvas to wrap the bodies in; wooden cases of embalming fluid (enough for around seventy bodies); 10 tonnes of iron bars for any bodies that would need to be buried at sea rather than brought back to Halifax; and ice – tonnes and tonnes of ice. This had been Larnder's idea: decades of experience had taught him that ice was the only effective method of keeping fish fresh until you returned to port. Ice would keep the bodies fresh. Well, as fresh as they could be. The ice was stored in three enormous drums beneath the ship, which were normally used to house the ship's cables.

Larnder and his crew recruited extra men for the journey by visiting Halifax's inns – anyone who was sober enough and had the stomach for the work was brought on board. Larnder was also joined by a makeshift mortuary team who had been contracted by White Star Line. John R. Snow Junior was the chief embalmer of John Snow & Co., the largest undertaking firm in Nova Scotia. He was accompanied by George P. Snow, an undertaker-stonecutter who worked at the George A. Sanford & Sons Nova Scotia Steam Marble and Granite Polishing Works next door. Snow knew this would be no small task, so he asked for assistance from every available undertaker and embalmer in the surrounding areas, which included Nova Scotia, Prince Edward Island and New Brunswick. More than forty members of the Funeral Directors' Association of the Maritimes came to his aid and made their way to Halifax, including Elizabeth Walsh – wife of the owner and manager of O'Neill Funeral Home, Arthur Walsh – and her sister Annie F. O'Neil, whom Snow made responsible for embalming the women and children (he hoped there would be mercifully few). Snow instructed his team to bring their own equipment and soon they were on board *Mackay-Bennett*, awaiting departure. Canon Kenneth O. Hind of All Saints Cathedral in Halifax also joined the crew. He was there to conduct any burials at sea. According to Alan Ruffman, the local newspapers, alongside representatives from New York and Boston, hovered about the docks during the ship's preparations with 'kodaks slung on their shoulders and ready at a moment's notice for human interest pictures'.[11]

17 April 1912

By Wednesday 17 April, two days after the sinking, *Mackay–Bennett* was ready. It departed at 12.28 p.m. from 155–157 Upper Water Street, Halifax. It was, as funeral historian Todd Van Beck described, the 'largest floating embalming facility on earth'.[12] Larnder took his preferred route – the east channel past George's Island and McNab's Island – and was prepared for the heavy fog (the fog cleared by the evening, leaving them with cold and clear weather) and potential risks, including icebergs, pack ice and growlers, which are smaller fragments of ice that have broken away from large icebergs. These can be around the size of a grand piano and only rise about 3ft out of the water, making them harder to spot but no less hazardous. The name comes from the sound air makes when it escapes melting icebergs, which explorers likened to the growl of an animal. To avoid facing the same fate as *Titanic*, Larnder called for a 24/7 watch for ice almost immediately. Crew members would take turns, undertaking one-hour watches.

According to Larnder's calculations, it would take *Mackay–Bennett* three days to reach the wreck site. In the meantime, the crew made whatever preparations they could. Under instruction from Snow, the ship's carpenter made an operating table for Snow and his team, which was strong enough for a 20 stone (280lb, 127kg) man. He also made three screens, at Snow's request, to maintain privacy and dignity when he was embalming the victims. Crew members were assigned the grim task of preparing the canvas sailcloth into small bags, into which any identifying items belonging to the deceased would be placed.

18–19 April 1912

The survivors from *Titanic* arrived in New York. A cable engineer on board *Mackay–Bennett*, Frederick Hamilton, kept a diary during his time at sea (his diary is now at the National Maritime Museum, in Greenwich, England). There was little to report on over the next two days. Larnder doubled the crew's rum ration to lift their spirits and he doubled the ice watch. According to Hamilton, *Royal Edward* lay to their east, and they were reporting icebergs and growlers.[13] The weather, which had been clear and crisp, turned to rain and fog. Hamilton recorded in his diary that at 6 p.m. on the night of the 19th, while the favourable weather turned to rain and 'very dense' fog, the crew lowered the ship's cutter and retrieved an Allan Line lifebelt.[14]

20 April 1912

Mackay-Bennett sent two messages to the offices of White Star Line, addressed to Ismay. Noted in Larnder's log, the first read, 'Steamer *Rhein* reports passing wreckage and bodies 42.10 north, 49.13 west, eight miles west of three big icebergs. Now making for that position. Expect to arrive 8 o'clock tonight.' The second read, 'Received further information from (steamship) *Bremen* and arrived on ground at 8 o'clock. Start operation tomorrow. Have been considerably delayed on passage by dense fog.'[15] A first-class passenger on board *Bremen*, Johanna Stunke, later told press:

> We saw one woman in her night dress, with a baby clasped closely to her breast. Several of the women passengers screamed and left the rail in a fainting condition. There was another woman, fully dressed, with her arms tight around the body of a shaggy dog that looked like a St. Bernard. The bodies of three men in a group, all clinging to one steamer chair, floated close by, and just beyond them were a dozen bodies of men, all of them encased in life-preservers, clinging together as though in a last desperate struggle for life.[16]

She also asserted that numerous passengers urged that the *Bremen* stop and retrieve the bodies, but they were assured by the crew that *Mackay-Bennett* was only two hours away from the wreck site and would be equipped to do just that.

Mackay-Bennett passed several icebergs, which Larnder recorded in his log. One of them, he reported, was about 200ft high. Hamilton noted in his diary on the same day: 'a large iceberg, faintly discernible to our north, we are now very near the area where lies the ruins of so many human hopes and prayers.' He adds, rather grimly, 'The embalmer becomes more and more cheerful as we approach the scene of his future professional activities, tomorrow will be a good day for him.'[17]

Mackay-Bennett stopped for the night, with the crew deciding to commence their operation in the morning come first light.

21–25 April 1912

No one on board, the captain included, knew how many bodies they would find, and come the following morning, the reality of the task became quite clear. Two icebergs floated nearby and Hamilton described them, with romantic awe, in great detail:

> Two icebergs now clearly in sight, a solid mass of ice, against which the sea dashes furiously, throwing up geyser-like columns of foam, high over the topmost summit, smothering the great mass at times completely in a cascade of spume as it pours over the snow and breaks into feathery crests on the polished surface of the berg, causing the whole ice-mountain, which glints like a fairy building, to oscillate twenty to thirty feet from vertical.[18]

The water was littered with wreckage – woodwork and chairs, mostly – an overturned lifeboat, and bodies, so many bodies. Larnder said later that the scene before him was 'like nothing so much as a flock of seagulls resting upon the water … all we could see at first would be the top of the life preservers. They were all floating face upwards, apparently standing in the water.'[19] An unsettling sight for any man to witness. The crew got to work quickly, cutting the engines and lowering the ship's cutters. Some of the crew manned the cutters and retrieved five or six bodies at a time before returning to *Mackay-Bennett* and passing them to the crew on deck.

As experienced sailors, a dead body was no strange sight. In fact, one crew member commented, 'The first ten bodies are difficult – after that it's just work.'[20] That may sound harsh, but if they had not been able to separate themselves from the horrors they witnessed, they might not have been able to continue. Finding the bodies of women and children was unpleasant enough, but the fourth body retrieved would be the most heartbreaking of them all: a 2-year-old boy without a lifebelt. On 1 May, the *Morning Chronicle* reported, 'The little body floated up alongside the searchers' boat and it was tenderly taken on board. The sight of this little form floating face upwards on the deep brought tears to the eyes of many of the hardy sailor men.'[21]

According to a press interview Larnder gave after the ship returned to Halifax, he and his crew recovered fifty-one bodies on the first day (forty-six men, two children and three women) and twenty-six the next. The current had shifted overnight and bodies were scarce, despite *Mackay-Bennett* searching 15 miles in and along the wreck site. By the next day, however, the bodies were numerous. Larnder reported that they picked up ninety before noon. It was physically demanding work, too, as all the bodies wore waterlogged clothing. When asked about how the bodies were found, Larnder said, 'The bodies were floating some near together, some far apart. There seemed no order among them – none were hand-in-hand or had embraced.'[22] This contradicts what Johanna Stunke of SS *Bremen* observed, but that doesn't necessarily mean she was mistaken: it's possible Larnder and his crew did not come across the same bodies the passengers of *Bremen* witnessed.

Once the bodies were safely on board *Mackay-Bennett*, the undertaker took over. Each body was given an identification number. The bodies were undressed to aid identification, allowing the purser, Frank Higginson, and the ship's surgeon, Dr Armstrong, to note any distinguishing marks, such as scars or tattoos. Body no. 6, for example, an unidentified male, had a blue tattoo. Body no. 36, another unidentified male, had tattoos all over his left arm, clasped hands and a heart on his right arm, and Japanese fans on his breast. The clothes were stored in bags in the ship's hospital, and would be burned on arrival at Halifax to stop them being snapped up by souvenir hunters, who would either sell them to make a profit or keep in a private collection. A description of their physical appearance was noted down, and a bag had the corresponding number stencilled on. This was for placing their personal effects in, which would also aid identification once the bodies returned to Halifax. It would also help return personal items to the correct kin. The items did not always aid identification, particularly if the victim was lower class and had no survivors on board who recognised them or kin able to travel to Halifax to identify them. A body might also be too decomposed or damaged – mostly from knocking against other bodies or wreckage and falling prey to seagulls – to be embalmed or brought back to port.

This method of identification would prove to be so effective that it would be used again during the Halifax Explosion of December 1917. SS *Imo*, another White Star Line ship originally built by Harland & Wolff in Belfast as a cattle-ship named *Runic* (its name was changed again in 1895 to *Tampican* before being changed to *Imo* in 1912), was leaving Halifax Harbour for New York to provide war-relief supplies when it collided with the bow of SS *Mont-Blanc*, which was carrying fifteen types of high explosives, at 8.45 a.m. While the captain and the crew (all but one man) managed to abandon ship, SS *Mont-Blanc* exploded at 9.05 a.m. It killed almost 2,000 people and injured at least 9,000. According to the Maritime Museum in Nova Scotia, 'A roiling cloud of hot gas rose high above the blast. Chunks and shards of the ship fell across an 8km range. Vaporised fuel and chemicals from the explosion fell as rain, coating people and wreckage with an oily film. Richmond and the Mi'kmaw community of Turtle Grove were struck by the full force of the blast.'[23]

The items retrieved from *Titanic*'s bodies varied depending on the class of the victim, what they were able to grab during the sinking, and what they already had on them when the ship went down. This is just a snippet of the items found on the bodies:[24]

- Gold ring with 'Madge' engraved (Body 36, unidentified male)
- A chemise marked 'B.H.' in red on front (Body 8, unidentified female)
- Shoes marked 'Parsons Sons, Athlone'; medallion round neck marked 'B.V.M.'; wore wedding ring, keeper and another gold ring; locket and photo; one jet and one bead necklace (Body 12, unidentified female)
- Addresses found on body: 'Mr. Freyer Lawrence Villa, Stephenson Road, Cowes'; also 'G. R. Barnes, 22 Sidney St., Cambridge' (Body 26, unidentified male)
- A gold watch marked on back 'C.K.S.,' pinned on left breast. Opal and pearl rings, also garnet ring, engraved 'H.N. to D.S.' Wedding ring engraved 'A.L. to C.S., April 21st, '09.', all worn on the left hand (Body 55, unidentified female)

- A purse with miniature photo of a young man and a photo locket (Body 63, unidentified female)
- Empty purse; crucifix; snuff box and medallion; 4 rings; 2 pieces of silver; 1 turquoise, 1 garnet and pearl; 1 gold ear-ring (Body 5, unidentified female)
- Pocket book; 1 gold watch and chain; silver sov. Purse containing £6; receipt from Thos. Cook & Co. for notes exchanged; ticket; pipe in case; revolver (loaded); coins; keys; etc.; bill for Charing Cross Hotel (Room 126, April, 1912) (Body 15, identified as Louis M. Hoffman)
- Lady's handbag; locket; gold watch; chain; and badge; £63 10s in gold; 13s 7d in silver and copper; $2 in paper and silver, etc.; letter; baggage receipt; keys; tie clip; pipe; nail cleaner; baggage insurance; marriage certificate. (Body 17, identified as John H. Chapman)
- Gold watch and chain; keys; knife; 2 books; Freemason's book; photos; papers; lodge badge 'Natl. Union Ship's Steward's, Butcher's and Baker's.' (Body 34, identified as H. W. Ashe)

In 1912, bodies were required by Canadian law to be embalmed if they were to be brought to shore. This law was influenced by the belief that unembalmed bodies posed a health risk to the living (which we now know to be untrue) and also by the desire to preserve the victims so families could say a proper goodbye to their loved ones without being traumatised by the sight of their decomposing bodies. This was particularly important for bodies that would be transported elsewhere, via railway, once they arrived in Nova Scotia.

Embalming, in its simplest terms, is a process of delaying decay. It has been practised for a millennium, particularly in ancient Greece and Egypt. Our modern method of embalming originated in England during the late eighteenth century, spearheaded by the English physiologist William Harvey, but it did not become a common practice in the Western world until the American Civil War (1881–65). The standard process for preserving bodies before this was by keeping them cool in ice, but it did not always work.

The horrors of the Civil War left thousands of men dead and miles from home; those in the south were at risk of decomposing exceptionally quickly due to the high temperatures. An emerging group of American businessmen-turned-undertakers saw an opportunity: they offered the new mortuary practice of embalming to preserve the soldiers until they could be returned home. The 'father of modern embalming', Thomas Holmes, embalmed 4,000 soldiers alone, at $100 per body. Embalmers began to travel to battlefields with the soldiers, setting up tents close to the sites and even offering soldiers the option to pre-pay for their own embalming should they die in battle. Although there was resistance initially, with people believing the practice to be barbaric, predatory and invasive, it became an almost patriotic act after President Abraham Lincoln was embalmed so his body could be put on display and mourned by the people he had served.

The process of embalming in 1912 was not far from the process we use today. *Encyclopedia Britannica* explains it thus:

The blood is drained from one of the veins and replaced by a fluid, usually based on Formalin (a solution of formaldehyde in water), injected into one of the main arteries. Cavity fluid is removed with a long hollow needle called a trocar and replaced with preservative. This fluid is also based on Formalin mixed with alcohols, emulsifiers, and other substances (like embalming fluid) to keep the body temporarily from shrivelling and turning brown.[25]

Whether or not the bodies on board *Mackay-Bennett* were embalmed came down to two things: whether they were first-class passengers and whether their body was considered to be in a decent enough condition to warrant it. First-class passengers were given preference when it came to coffins, which they quickly ran out of, and anyone below that was sewn into a canvas bag and stacked on deck. One body that was embalmed and given a coffin (in fact, a coffin was laid aside specifically for this man, should he be found) was that of J.J. Astor, the 124th body to be recovered. Astor was easy to identify by the silk initials sewn on the inside of his collar and his various effects, including gold cufflinks with diamonds, a gold watch, and a diamond ring with three stones. He was also carrying $3,000 in cash. Astor was one of the few victims White Star Line confirmed had been found while *Mackay-Bennett* was on its recovery mission.

Following the insistence of Ismay's media blackout, other victims' names were kept out of any correspondence between White Star Line and the public. Despite this, newspapers in and around Halifax were speculating as to who had been found and positively identified. Families of victims, who had travelled to Halifax in the hopes of gaining some semblance of information about their loved ones, were understandably outraged at the respect and precedence being given to the wealthy passengers of *Titanic* at the seeming expense of those deemed of lower importance. The families demanded answers but received very few. According to Christopher Ward, White Star Line claimed that the reason it had no information to give was because of difficulties transmitting so many names via Morse code, but in reality it was 'reluctant to admit that almost half the bodies that had been identified had already been buried and sea and would not be returning to Halifax'.[26]

In an attempt to satiate the outcries from victims' families, White Star Line created an information bureau, which it operated out of Halifax Hotel on Hollis Street. It provided two bulletins, the first of which mentioned only Astor and Isidor Straus by name, which just served to further ignite the rage of the public. The second bulletin read: 'when bodies are ready for shipment, friends may take them on the same train in the baggage car on payment of the regular first-class fare … bodies may also be sent by express on payment of two first-class fares. The offices of the Canadian Express Company are prepared to render every assistance.'[27] Every assistance *at a price*. It would have cost families an exceptional amount of money to travel to Halifax at all, never mind the added financial pressure of shipping their loved ones back home. White Star Line was not handling the situation well.

Meanwhile, the crew of *Mackay-Bennett* were having their own difficulties. They retrieved more bodies than they had anticipated – 306, over the course of a few days – so they quickly ran out of embalming fluid and canvas bags. The remaining bodies deemed in good enough condition to return to shore were stored in amongst the ice in *Mackay-Bennett*'s hold, but the ship itself was running out of room. The difficult decision to bury some of the victims at sea was made. The crew had hoped it would not come to this, but this was discussed back in Halifax just in case, which is why they equipped the ship with iron bars to weigh bodies down should they need them. They did need them, and, in fact, they needed more than they thought. Of the 306 bodies retrieved from the Atlantic, 116 were buried at sea – more than a third of the bodies recovered. Burial at sea, according to Jess Bier, was, while not without its moral reservations, fairly common in the North Atlantic. She notes that 'it was widely viewed as being an appropriate expedient for any who died at sea, as long as no other options were available – such as in cases where a ship was a long way from port and there was no way to preserve a human body'.[28]

It's no coincidence that most of the bodies buried at sea were those of a lower class, no matter how historians dress it up. First-class bodies were prioritised, as per the social hierarchy of the Edwardian era. Any body with characteristics such as tattoos or piercings, wearing a crew uniform, or that possessed 'foreign' physical traits was far more likely to be buried at sea than a first-class passenger. While it's argued that these bodies happened to be beyond the point of preservation, it seems suspicious that very few of the first-class passengers were buried at sea. Their belongings were sent to the White Star Line's New York office when the recovery ships docked, as there was no one immediately available to claim them. There did appear to be some communication or agreement between White Star Line, Larnder and the undertakers after body 201 was buried at sea, as no other bodies were buried at sea after that, but the details surrounding that are unclear.

On 22 April, alongside more bodies that were smashed and badly bruised, the crew found an enormous amount of wreckage and a lifeboat with its side smashed in. Larnder recorded a detailed description of what he saw that day:

Everybody had on a lifebelt and bodies floated very high in water in spite of the sodden clothes and things in pockets. Apparently, the people had lots of time and discipline must have been splendid, for some had on their pyjamas, two or three shirts, two pairs of pants, two vests, two jackets and an overcoat. In some pockets, a quantity of meat and biscuits were found, while in the pockets of most of the crew quite a lot of tobacco and matches besides keys to the various lockers and stateroom doors were found.[29]

Having gotten wind of the reports coming in from *Mackay-Bennett* and various accounts from other passing ships, the *San Francisco Call* reported that day that 'masses of wreckage, accompanied here and there by swollen bodies, rising and falling in the water, mark the grave of the *Titanic* for miles around the actual spot where the huge liner foundered'.[30]

The first burial service took place on the night of 22 April. The bodies to be committed to the sea – those too disfigured to be embalmed and those, quite frankly, not deemed important enough to embalm (mostly unidentified third-class passengers and lower-ranking crew members) – were sewn up in canvas and weighed down with the iron bars, which weighed 50lb (22.7kg) each, according to Larnder's log. Canon Hind was responsible for the service, which Hamilton detailed in his diary:

The tolling of the bell summoned all hands to the forecastle where thirty bodies are ready to be committed to the deep, each carefully weighted and sewn up in canvas. It is a weird scene, this gathering. The crescent moon is shedding a faint light on us, as the ship lays wallowing in the great rollers. The funeral service is conducted by the Reverend Canon Hind, for nearly an hour the words 'For as much as it hath pleased ... we therefore commit his body to the deep' are repeated and at each interval comes, splash! as the weighted body plunges into the sea, there to sink to a depth of about two miles. Splash, splash, splash.[31]

Like many tragic situations, there were some amusing incidents, which the crew later revealed. One such incident was recalled by 22-year-old Arminias Wiseman, a fireman on board *Mackay-Bennett*. The incident, which Wiseman did not discuss until he was in his late 50s, is as follows:

One such occurrence happened while I was on duty, the 4 to 8 watch, when the second engineer sent one of the oilers with a message to watch the officer on the bridge. As he came up from the engine room and stepped out on the passageway, a body slid by him and almost knocked him down. He retreated to the engine room in a hurry with a report saying that a body had become alive and was going up and down the passageway. He was pretty scared. The engineer asked me to go up and investigate. I did and discovered a body had become dislodged from a pile that was in the passageway and due to the pitching of the ship, had slid down in front of the engine room door. The desk crew was notified and the body was secured.[32]

Though the crew did find small moments like this amusing, it was clear that Captain Larnder needed help. He contacted White Star Line's offices in New York to inform them of the situation and soon A.G. Jones & Company chartered another ship, *Minia*, to assist Larnder and his crew.

5

Remaining Recovery Ships: *Minia, Montmagny* and *Algerine*

Like *Mackay-Bennett, Minia* was a cable ship. It was owned by the Anglo-American Telegraph Company and chartered by White Star Line to assist with the body-recovery effort. Captained by William George Squares de Carteret, *Minia* and its crew were joined by Reverend Henry Ward Cunningham of St George's Church in Halifax, embalmer William H. Snow, and assistant undertaker and surgeon Dr Byard William (Will) Mosher. Dr Mosher, in a letter to his sister, Agnes, wrote: 'We have been chartered by the White Star to hunt for bodies, body snatching we call it ... This place [Halifax] has been nothing but an undertaker's establishment for this last month.'[1] After a short delay waiting on more coffins to be built (they took 150 in total) and more embalming equipment to be gathered, *Minia* left Halifax at midnight on 22 April.

The following day, 23 April, 128 more bodies were brought on board *Mackay-Bennett*. Larnder noted in his log that 'the sea was dotted with bodies as far as one could see'.[2] Recovery had begun at 6.30 a.m. and lasted over twelve hours. Another burial service took place that night, seeing seventy more bodies committed to the deep. Hamilton commented on the atmosphere on the ship the next day, saying that 'the hoarse tone of the steam whistle reverberating through the mist, the dripping rigging, and the ghostly sea, the heaps of dead, and the hard weather-beaten faces of the crew, whose harsh voices join sympathetically in the hymn tunefully rendered by Canon Hind, all combine to make a strange task stranger' and that 'even the most hardened must reflect on the hopes and fears, the dismay and despair, of those whose nearest and dearest, support and pride, have been wrenched from them by this tragedy'.[3] An Allan Liner, *Sardinia*, was able to provide additional supplies, as it was passing the wreck site the following day, but it still wasn't enough.

26 April 1912

Minia reached the wreck site and joined *Mackay-Bennett* on the body-recovery effort by 26 April. It was two miles westward of *Mackay-Bennett* and, according to Hamilton, the first body they recovered was that of Charles M. Hays, president of the Grand Trunk Railway Company, who Mosher wrote in another letter to his sister was the 'star corpse' of the day.[4] Like J.J. Astor, he had been easy to identify; in a letter to his mother, a telegraphist on board *Minia*, 20-year-old Francis Rickards Dyke wrote, 'It was no trouble to identify him as he had a lot of papers on him and a watch with his name on it.'[5]

Minia stayed at the wreck site to continue with the recovery effort, but *Mackay-Bennett* had run out of equipment and room, so it was time to return to Halifax. Hamilton wrote in his diary that it had been 'an arduous task for those who have had to overhaul and attend to the remains. The searching, the numbering and identifying of each body, depositing the property found on each in a bag marked with a number corresponding to that attached to the corpse, the sewing up in canvas and securing of weights, entailed prolonged and patient labour.' He added, not for the first time, that 'the embalmer is the only man to whom the work is pleasant, I might add without undue exaggeration, enjoyable, for to him it is a labour of love, and the pride of doing a job well'.[6]

Mackay-Bennett recovered 306 (some sources say 305, others 307) and of those, 116 were committed to the sea. The ship sailed back to Halifax with a total of 190 bodies, all ready to be taken care of, identified and buried. In his logbook, Larnder, under the heading 'TOWARDS HALIFAX', wrote 'moderate breeze. Hands stowing corpses on bridge deck and securing coffins on poop deck.'[7]

27–28 April 1912

Minia recovered ten more bodies, mostly waiters and sailors, according to Dyke. Though only 20 years old at the time, Dyke possessed a strong sense of compassion. He noted that although none of the crew particularly liked the job they'd been given, it was 'better to recover them and bury them properly than let them float about for weeks'.[8]

Mosher's second letter to his sister detailed the task: 'it was blowing a gale and foggy, and it was several days before we could get a sight ... Bodies were all scattered, never came on two together. We picked up some 150 miles east and north from the scene of the wreck.' The wreckage that day was particularly noticeable. Mosher wrote:

Picked up any amount of wreckage. Deck chairs, doors, chests of drawers, cushions, two of the steps of the grand stairway some beautiful carved panels (oak) and cords of painted wood, molding, boards, etc., I am having a picture frame made from some wreckage and am looking for a picture of the ship to put in it. Also am making a cribbage board and a paper weight, making the paper weight out of the leg of a table (oak) and am having a silver plate put on top with *Titanic* engraved on it. I found a card signed by Ismay in the pocket of one of the stewards whose body we picked up and am keeping it as a chief souvenir. This ship is full of souvenirs at present, everyone is making checkerboards, cribbage boards or paper weights.[9]

Dyke also commented on the wreck site, noting that 'the *Titanic* must have been blown up when she sank, as we have picked up pieces of the grand staircase ... most of the wreckage is from below deck, it must have been an awful explosion, too, as some of the main deck planking 4ft thick was split and broken off short'.[10]

Back on land, twelve memorial services in churches all around Halifax took place in honour of the victims. Reportedly, at All Saint's Cathedral, a special hymn composed by Hall Caine, an English novelist, was sung by the congregation. The song, titled simply 'The Titanic', was sung to the tune of 'O God, Our Help in Ages Past'.

While these memorial services were being conducted, White Star Line was under fire for its handling of the body-identification process. They held a meeting, with the main agenda of conclusively deciding how best to identify the victims who would cause the least amount of pain and confusion for their friends and family. Already it had been reported that 'certain gentlemen' (identities unconfirmed/unknown) had tried to bribe undertakers to speed up the embalming of their friends. According to White Star Line, the attempt had failed, and the company asserted that it wouldn't stand for such behaviour.

But that wasn't White Star Line's main issue. Its main issue was its statement that disfigurement of some of the corpses would make identification impossible, which would be highly distressing to those waiting around to find the bodies of their loved ones. White Star Line decided that when the embalmers had finished with their embalming procedure, the body would be brought into the main room of the Mayflower curling rink on Agricola Street, which was to serve as a makeshift morgue, where the rest of the victims could be embalmed and identified before burial. The name of the deceased (if known) would be called out, and those wishing to claim said body could approach and confirm identification. From there, the appropriate burial arrangements would be made. To make the process as seamless as possible for the embalmers and the family and friends of victims, anyone wishing to claim a body had to register with A.G. Jones and Company at Halifax Hotel, where White Star Line's victim information bureau was operating from.

Though no photographs were meant to be taken on board, there exists a shot of Mosher with a crewman and an undertaker preparing a body on board the ship.

30 April–18 May 1912

Minia's Captain de Carteret reported to White Star Line that bad weather hampered the *Minia*'s search efforts, with many bodies being pushed out into the Gulf Stream. However, they managed to recover a total of seventeen bodies, two of which were unidentified firemen, who were buried at sea. *Minia* returned to Halifax on 6 May. After being quarantined in Halifax Harbour pending inspection, the crew soon transferred all their unused ice, coffins, canvas bags and embalming equipment to the third ship that assisted in *Titanic*'s body-recovery effort, *Montmagny*.

Montmagny had left its home port of Sorel, Quebec, three days prior. It was primarily a lighthouse supply and buoy tender ship, which also delivered construction materials, but, like *Mackay-Bennett* and *Minia*, it had been chartered by White Star Line for this harrowing task. It was selected, in no small part, because of its immense speed, its working deck being almost at water level, and booms that enabled it to recover items on and in the water. It had two captains – Peter Crerar Johnson and François-Xavier Pouliot – and its crew were joined by two church representatives –Reverend Samuel Henry Prince of St Paul's Church and Father Patrick McQuillan of St Mary's Basilica – and John R. Snow Junior, who had departed from *Mackay-Bennett* after it docked. He was accompanied by another undertaker, one Cecil E. Zink from Dartmouth. The bad weather hindered *Montmagny* as it had *Minia*, with the crew sighting more wreckage than they did bodies by the time they arrived at the site on 9 May.

In the end, they were able to recover four more bodies from the Atlantic. The first was recovered the afternoon of 9 May: a bedroom steward who was found still wearing his life jacket, with nothing upon him to aid identification. The following morning, the crew spotted a life ring in the water. As they approached, they realised that a frozen hand was still grasping it, the victim's wrist tangled in its rope. After bringing the body on board, the crew quickly found an address on a small piece of paper and were able to identify the victim as 21-year-old Harold Reynolds, a third-class passenger. He had been a baker who had lived in London and had been aboard *Titanic* so he could join a friend in Toronto. That afternoon, another body was spotted and brought on board: a young girl, around 15 years of age, believed to be a Syrian immigrant (possibly Hileni Jabbur/Zabour). She wore a lace-trimmed red and black overdress, a black underdress, a green-striped underskirt, a black woollen shawl and black slippers. Her features were described as refined and her 'very dark skin' and golden-brown hair was noted. The final body, that of Charles Smith, was found later that day.

The crew held a funeral service for the unidentified bedroom steward, whom they buried at sea. Captain Pouliot would later tell his children and grandchildren that the weather was calm that day, but as they memorial service ended, a gust of wind, seemingly out of nowhere, rushed through the ship and rang the ship's bell. The captain was moved by the incident and spoke of the story with great emotion. The three remaining bodies were delivered to Louisbourg, Nova Scotia, upon *Montmagny*'s return on 13 May. They were shipped to Halifax for burial via the Sydney & Louisbourg and Canadian National Railways. After retrieving more supplies, *Montmagny* returned to the scene of the disaster but was unable to find any more bodies.

It is interesting to note that following his experience in the *Titanic* body-recovery effort, Captain Johnson put forward his own theory for what had happened to *Titanic* on the night of the sinking. Speaking with the *Dundee Evening Telegraph* in June 1912, he asserted that a change within the Gulf Stream's usual current caused a cold pocket in a part of the ocean that is usually warmer, which, he argued, may have accounted for why Captain Smith of the *Titanic* did not heed the ice warnings as he should have:

In approaching the 'cold pocket' from the eastward, I found the temperature of the water 62 degrees. Close by the pocket of cold water I found a temperature of 60 degrees and between the cold and warm water of the Gulf Stream a well-defined line was shown evidenced by froth stretching as far as the eye could reach. Directly after crossing this line we found a temperature of 48 degrees, and ten miles within the line was an iceberg, the water being 42 degrees within 100 yards of it. My contention is that Captain Smith some distance east of the position where he struck the iceberg, found the temperature of the water 60 degrees, and as he was steering a course directly opposite to the usual current that he expected to be there, never dreamed that there was an iceberg ahead and he took what he considered ample precautions to clear the ice reported to him by wireless. In crossing into the cold water from the Gulf Stream Captain Smith would get a temperature of 60 at the stern and 48 at the bow of his ship. The surface currents in this pocket I found very uncertain, but the tendency was east-north-eastward. I found bodies that had drifted only about sixty miles from the scene of the disaster after being in the water twenty-five days, whereas the Gulf Stream in this vicinity was running at the rate of about thirty miles a day.[11]

There remain *Titanic* scholars today who view this theory as not only credible, but highly likely.

There are several photographs from *Montmagny*'s expedition, taken by Reverend Prince, which he used later in life when lecturing on *Titanic*. The photographs show the crew and the gruesome task to which they were subjected. They also show the state of decomposition of the victims when they were recovered; the young Syrian girl is particularly emotive. The original photographs were kept by Captain Pouliot, who also kept the life ring Harold Reynolds had clung to for survival. It is now in the care of his grandchildren, who, according to one of them, Michelle, used to play with it during their childhood, pretending their grandfather's shed was a ship and flinging the life ring to his siblings to rescue them.

19 May–8 June 1912

Montmagny met with the fourth and final ship chartered by White Star Line, *Algerine*, around 6 p.m. on 19 May to report its findings before returning to Halifax and resuming its regular duties. The search for *Titanic* victims had been officially called off by White Star Line, but *Algerine* was to finish its search before returning. *Algerine* was a steamer originally built by Harland & Wolff, but served most of its career in Newfoundland under Bowring Brothers of St John's as a cargo and passenger ship. Its captain, John Jackman, and its crew were joined by Chief Officer Richard B. Giles and two undertakers, Andrew Carnell and Lawrence (first name unknown/unconfirmed). Unlike the previous three recovery ships, *Algerine* did not have any church representatives on board. *Algerine* searched the waters of the Atlantic for three weeks but was only able to recover one body, that of First-Class Saloon Steward James McGrady, the 330th body found. McGrady's body was brought to St John's and transferred to Halifax via the steamer *Florizel*, a passenger liner and flagship of the Bowring Brothers' Red Cross Line, where he was buried almost two months after his death. *Algerine* returned to its regular duties shortly after.

Other bodies were recovered from the ocean, though not by White Star Line chartered ships. RMS *Oceanic* found the bodies of three passengers in the still-floating Collapsible Lifeboat A over a month after the disaster. The identities of these men remain unconfirmed, but it is believed that one body was that of Thomson Beattie, a first-class passenger wearing his dinner jacket, and the other two were unidentified firemen.

Shane Leslie, who was on board the *Oceanic* when the lifeboat was found, later recalled:

> The sea was calm at noon when the lookout shouted that you could see something floating ahead. The ship slowed down and it was evident that the object was a ship's lifeboat floating in the open sea in the middle of the Atlantic. What was horrifying is that it contained three decomposing corpses. A lifeboat was sent with an officer and a doctor. What followed was appalling. Two sailors could be seen seated, their hair bleached from exposure to the sun and salt, and a third body, dressed in a tuxedo, lying on the floor. All three were dead and had been on the surf and under the open sky since they had seen the largest ocean liner sink. The three bodies were stuffed into duffel bags with a steel bar at the bottom each. Then, one after another, they were wrapped in the Union Jack, a sermon was read, and they were thrown into the sea.[12]

SS *Ottawa* found the body of William Thomas Kerley, a saloon steward, on 6 June and buried him at sea. William Frederick Cheverton, one of *Titanic*'s victualling crew, was found two days later by SS *Ilford*, and was also buried at sea.

2 March 1912. *Titanic* alongside the Fitting-Out Wharf. (Steve Hall collection)

Lifeboat with survivors from RMS *Titanic*, 1912. (World History Archive / Alamy Stock Photo)

The cable ship *Mackay-Bennett*, which recovered over 300 bodies from the scene of the *Titanic* disaster before heading for Halifax, Nova Scotia, April 1912. (Chronicle / Alamy Stock Photo)

The captain and crew of the *Mackay-Bennett*. (George Grantham Bain Collection / Library of Congress)

CS *Minia*. (George Grantham Bain Collection / Library of Congress)

Captain William Squares de Carteret of the CS *Minia*. CS *Minia* was involved in the recovery of bodies after the *Titanic* sinking, *c.* 1912. (Image History Collection / Alamy Stock Photo)

April 1912: anxious relatives gather around the White Star offices in London as they await the list of survivors from the sinking of *Titanic*. (De Luan / Alamy Stock Photo)

Crowd awaiting *Titanic* survivors. (George Grantham Bain Collection / Library of Congress)

Recovered bodies from *Titanic* arriving at the Mayflower Curling Club in Nova Scotia, which was set up as a temporary morgue in 1912. (Photo by Gauvin and Gentzel. ARCHIVIO GBB / Alamy Stock Photo)

Sidney Leslie Goodwin, who was established to be Unknown Child no. 4.

Halifax Harbour, where the *Titanic* victims were taken. (New York World-Telegram and the Sun Newspaper Photograph Collection / Library of Congress)

Hearses lined up on Halifax wharf to carry *Titanic* victims to funeral parlours, Halifax, Nova Scotia, 6 May 1912. (Historic Collection / Alamy Stock Photo)

Titanic graves in Halifax, Nova Scotia. (Adwo / Alamy Stock Photo)

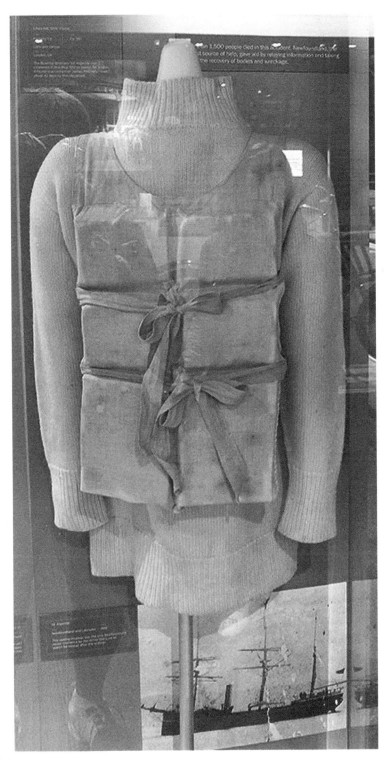

Above and overleaf: The life jacket of James McGrady, the last victim to be recovered. (Courtesy of Dee Ryan-Meister, Titanic Society of Atlantic Canada)

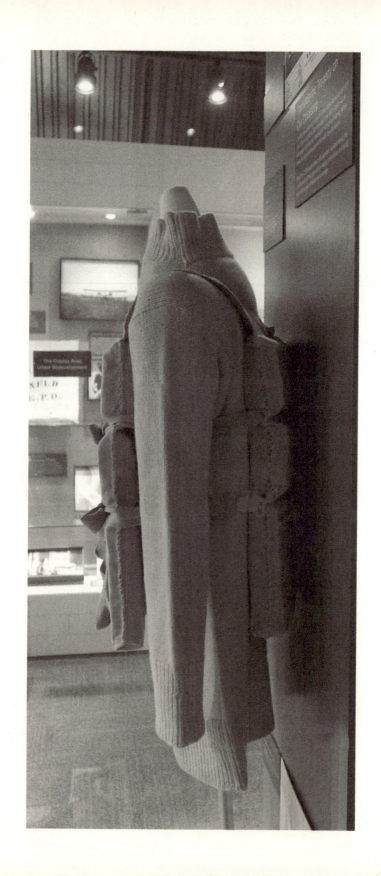

Return to Halifax:
Caring for the Dead

Mackay-Bennett reached the shores of Halifax on the cold, misty morning of 30 April 1912. It solemnly sailed the three miles into Halifax Harbour, as the bells of forty of the city's church towers tolled at one-minute intervals in a 'deafening chain of grief'.[1] Ships cut their engines and flew their flags at half-mast. Stores 'draped their windows in black and placed in them pictures of the *Titanic*'.[2] *The Washington Times* reported that thousands of Halifax residents flocked to vantage points along the harbour to watch the ship return with its 'cargo of woe'.[3] People stood on the roofs of their homes and local businesses, and flooded the streets in and around the waterfront, hoping to, respectfully, catch a glimpse of the tragic scene their city was playing host to.

An area of the harbour had been quarantined to ensure *Mackay-Bennett*'s cargo had privacy. At 9 a.m., the ship was approached by *Monica* and *Scotsman*. On board *Monica* was Dr Norman E. Mackay, who was there to adhere to Canada's legal requirement of having a doctor on board when a ship docked at a harbour with one or more dead body. On board *Scotsman* was Halifax's chief of police, John A. Rudland, who boarded *Mackay-Bennett* alongside detectives Francis Hanrahan and Horace Kennedy, and White Star Line representative P.V.G. Mitchell.

As the ship docked at the Canadian navy's anchorage point at Coaling Wharf No. 4, known as Flagship Pier, it was reported that spectators fell and some even fainted when they saw *Mackay-Bennett's* 'afterdeck piled high with coffins and on her forward deck a hundred unshrouded bodies'.[4] Crew from other boats, clad with mourning bands around their sleeves and their caps, towed their vessels out of the way to give *Mackay-Bennett* ample space. The dock itself was littered with the crew from the HMCS cruiser *Niobe* and members of the Canadian army, who had taken it upon themselves to guard the gates to ensure spectators, especially reporters with press cameras from New York, Boston and Halifax, did not intrude on or disturb *Mackay-Bennett*. One reporter managed to slip through the cracks but was quickly caught; his camera was confiscated under direct orders from John A. Rudland.

Once they were sure no one was able to get through to the ship, the crew set up a white marquee awning that covered the entirety of the deck appointed to *Mackay-Bennett*. *The Washington Times* reported that the 'atmosphere of a morgue pervaded the pier'.[5] That said, they also reported some rather amusing incidents from the spectators as they waited for *Mackay-Bennett* to dock: a uniformed naval man accidently sprayed disinfectant on himself when he turned his nozzle the incorrect way, dousing himself from head to shoulders, and two undertakers turned a spare rope into a jump rope, with which a grey-haired man skipped. Nervous anticipation makes you do odd things.

Awaiting the bodies were more coffins – 500 in total, ordered by White Star Line from Ontario – sitting beneath the marquee that had been lined up and opened by a team of undertakers, embalmers, and ambulance crew. Thirty horse-drawn carriages manned by formally uniformed undertakers from all over Nova Scotia stood not far away, ready to transport the dead. The hearses were to take the bodies to the Mayflower Curling Club's ice rink, which was to serve as a makeshift morgue, where the rest of the victims could be embalmed and identified before burial. The curling rink was the ideal venue for the task because it was large and had ice on hand, which would help preserve the bodies long enough for them to be embalmed. Any bodies that were unclaimed and/or unidentified would be buried in one of three Halifax cemeteries, where White Star Line had purchased plots: Fairview Lawn, Baron de Hirsch and Mount Olivet.

From 9.40 a.m., the bodies were transferred from *Mackay-Bennett*, from least cared for to most. Bodies were transferred at a fast rate of one per minute. This was a difficult job and an undertaker, Russell Hilchey, actually broke his leg while transporting a victim from the hold.[6] Anyone on the foredeck, mostly crew and steerage passengers who hadn't been embalmed, went first, followed by second-class and any third-class passengers who were wrapped in canvas. The bodies that were not covered appeared to be a grotesque spectacle. Christopher Ward noted that many were naked, 'their arms and legs frozen grotesquely or kicking at their moment of death', and that 'shoulders and hips of some of these dead had to be broken or dislocated to fit them into the narrow coffins'.[7] The last to leave *Mackay-Bennett* were the first-class passengers, most of whom were not only embalmed and placed in coffins but were identified too. Their coffins were described as darkened, dirty-white pine boxes.

J.J. Astor's coffin was reopened before being removed from the ship. There had been a mix-up on board *Mackay-Bennett* with the identification of fellow millionaire George D. Widener – his body was never found but his manservant was; they had mistakenly assumed him to be Widener, which caused a great deal of trauma and stress to his family – so Astor's son Vincent wanted to be certain the man *Mackay-Bennett* claimed was his father was, in fact, the correct man. Vincent had travelled to Halifax as soon as news of the disaster circulated, accompanied by the Astor's family lawyer, Nicholas Biddle, and the captain of Astor's private boat, Richard Roberts. It was Roberts who positively identified Astor on Vincent's behalf. Of the body, he said, 'the features were perfect, the face only being slightly discolored, which would be the result of the action of icy waters of the Atlantic upon a human body'.[8] Astor was handed directly over to John Snow & Co., who took his body straight to its facilities rather than to the Mayflower curling rink. Vincent had, a week previously, selected a coffin for his father, as well as a floral display, inside which he would be transferred to New York via his private train, *Oceanic*, so he could be interred in the Astor family vault.

Relatives awaiting their loved ones arrival were disappointed when they were informed that they could not see the bodies until the following day, as it would take up to four hours to embalm the bodies that still required it. The bodies that had been embalmed and identified already could be viewed that day but not until that evening, as the undertakers needed time to organise the victims in a way that would be efficient and avoid any more emotional discomfort than necessary.

At 11.15 a.m., once the last of the bodies had been transferred from the ship and were on their way to the Mayflower curling rink (it had taken over three hours to transport all the bodies: identified bodies went to Snow's and unidentified ones went to the curling rink), Captain Larnder invited the press on board. He led them to *Mackay-Bennett*'s dining saloon, where, using his log, he recounted the experience of retrieving and bringing the bodies home. Canon Hind expressed his admiration and gratitude for the crew, highlighting how 'earnestly and reverently the work was done, and how nobly the crew acquitted themselves'.[9]

The following was reported in *The Washington Times* in its 30 April 1912 feature 'Morgue Ship in Halifax; Captain Gives Dramatic Story of Finding Bodies':[10]

We arrived on the scene at 8 o'clock Saturday night, stopped and let ship drift. In middle watch, wreckage and a few bodies were sighted. At daylight the boats were lowered and, although a heavy sea was running, fifty-one bodies were recovered that day. Night closed down on us Sunday with bodies still around us. We commenced work again on Monday morning at daylight, but bodies were scarce. We got only twenty-six that day. We searched fifteen miles in and out along the line of wreckage. At night we marked the floating wreckage with a drifting buoy, so we could find it readily in the morning.

Tuesday morning bodies were numerous again. We picked up ninety before noon. Then the weather came on and in the afternoon we recovered only twenty-nine. We found no two bodies together, all floating separately. No two were clasped in each other's arms or anything like that. In one place we saw them scattered over the surface, looking like a flock of seagulls. They looked like gulls with the white ends of the life belts fluttering and flapping up and down with the rise and fall of the waves.

A great many of those recovered were injured when the *Titanic* went down. When the water swept her decks many must have been rushed before it and carried against stanchions, against spars, and other parts of the vessel. All of those we picked up wore life belts and they rode upright in the waves, the belts carrying them high above the water.

All day Wednesday we were in thick fog, and it was blowing hard from the southwest. We saw nothing all day. About midnight the weather eased up and we shaped our course back for the bodies. At 5.30 o'clock Thursday morning we found one drifting near us. We let her drift until daylight and then commenced work. We picked up eighty-seven bodies that day. Thursday I got a message saying the *Minia* was coming out to assist us. She arrived about forty-five minutes after midnight Friday.

At daylight the two ships started searching together. At noon I picked up fourteen more bodies and then started for Halifax, because we had as many on board as we could look after. We experienced bad weather all the way in. We had five men in each small boat. When they went to look for bodies they kept within sight of the bridge of the *Mackay-Bennett*, and we signaled them by wigwag. When the weather was heavy, we would bring them in. If the weather was calm they could handle seven or eight in a boat. The bodies were hoisted on board and when they were searched, the contents of the pickets and their valuables were placed in canvas bags, having on them the same number as that on the body. In this way we made some identifications long after the bodies were taken aboard.

We brought in the bags of all who were buried at sea, and some of those committed to the deep may yet be identified by the contents of those bags. We covered a square of sea about thirty miles long and thirty miles wide, about sixty miles northeast of the scene of the disaster. All of the bodies found were in the cold waters north of the gulf stream.

We had three burial services at sea. One Tuesday night, one Wednesday night, and one at noon on Thursday. The bodies were sent over the side three at a time. No bodies that we found contained any bullet wounds. I feel certain that all of the passengers picked up have already been identified, and that the unidentified were members of the ship's company. I feel sure that those buried at sea were practically all either seamen, stewards, or other employees of the White Star Company. I think that there were about eighteen or twenty women among the bodies picked up. We have quite a lot of jewelry taken from both men and women. I don't know how much cash we took from the bodies.

When asked about the decision to bury bodies at sea, Larnder said:

Most of them were members of the crew and we couldn't care for them. When we left Halifax we took on board all of the embalming fluid in the city. That was only enough to care for seventy bodies. It wasn't expected that we would find bodies in such great quantities. The undertaker didn't think these bodies would keep more than three days at sea, and as we expected to be out more than two weeks we had to bury them. They received the full services for the dead before they were put over.[11]

In another, admittedly problematic, account, Larnder supposedly said:

No prominent man was recommitted to the deep. It seemed best to embalm as quickly as possible in those cases where large property might be involved. It seemed best to be sure to bring back to land the dead where the death might give rise to such questions as large insurance and inheritance and all the litigation. Most of those who were buried were members of the *Titanic*'s crew. The man who lives by the sea ought to be satisfied to be buried at sea. I think it is the best place. For my own part I should be contented to be committed to the deep.[12]

This quote was attributed to Captain Larnder by sensationalist journalist and biographer of US President Theodore 'Teddy' Roosevelt Jay Henry Mowbray, who wrote his book *Sinking of the Titanic: Thrilling Stories Told By Survivors* less than a month after the tragedy.[13] It was produced exceptionally quickly to take advantage of the public's interest in *Titanic*. It's a unique resource filled with first-hand accounts from survivors and commentary on newspaper reports (mostly tabloids) and investigations into the sinking, but it should be acknowledged that the speed of its publication means one should take it with a pinch of salt. It is likely Captain Larnder did say the above, or at least something of similar sentiment, but there is no way to prove he said it, as this particular quotation only appears in Mowbray's book and not in other newspaper reports from the impromptu press conference.

The press conference was called to an end when the table Larnder was sitting at collapsed, which was considered a bad omen by those in attendance.

The last of the bodies left Halifax Harbour at 11 a.m. and were taken to the Mayflower curling rink. When the bodies arrived, they were taken into private partitions at the west end of the rink to be embalmed. The team of undertakers had constructed sixty-seven canvas-enclosed cubicles, each of which could fit three coffins; once a body was ready, it was taken to one of these cubicles and placed into a coffin. The embalmers worked through the night to ensure as many bodies as possible would be available for viewings and identification the next day. This was a long and gruelling process, and many of the bodies that had been kept on ice – steerage and crew, mostly – were beginning to thaw and rapidly decompose. Many were beyond the point of embalming and so they were placed into the coffins as they were. And over the following days, more and more bodies, those found by *Minia*, *Montmagny* and *Algerine*, were being brought to the rink, which put the embalmers under a lot of pressure. One harrowing incident involved a poor embalmer by the name of Frank Newell, who collapsed from shock after unexpectedly finding the body of his relative, one Arthur W. Newell.

When bodies were ready to be identified, members of the public claiming to be relatives of the victims were allowed to enter the makeshift morgue, but only ten people at any one time. If a body went unidentified, and therefore unclaimed for two weeks, they were taken off the morgue floor and other preparations for their remains were made. Mourners waited in an observation room to see their loved ones when they arrived, and a registered nurse, Nellie Remby, stood by with smelling salts to help restore anyone who fainted at the sight of them.

Identified relatives were transported from Halifax to their places of burial while others remained in the city, due to transportation costs being too much for some families, even with free aid offered by the Canadian Express Company. One example is *Titanic*'s band. Their leader, Wallace Hartley, was able to be transported home but Jock Hume, Christopher Ward's grandfather, was buried in Halifax and remains there to this day.

On the second floor of the Mayflower curling rink was a makeshift coroner's office. Keen to follow Nova Scotian law regarding disposition of bodies, the city's Registrar of Vital Statistics John Henry Barnstead and the city's provincial coroner and medical examiner Dr W.D. Finn established this office. Having the provincial medical examiner present at the morgue meant fully formal inquests would not be necessary, which sped up the administration process regarding the issuing of death certificates and burial permits, making it quicker for families to view their deceased loved ones and have them either taken elsewhere for burial or buried in Halifax. It was here that staff processed all the information provided by *Mackay-Bennett*'s crew.

The identification method was devised by Barnstead himself and remains in use to this day; in fact, it was so meticulous that it was used to aid modern DNA methods to identify *Titanic* victims almost 100 years after the disaster. This information was documented on small crimson-coloured squares and placed with the appropriate body; it included a detailed description of the body's height, weight, appearance and estimated age. Any valuables found on the victims were labelled and kept in a safe. Photography studio Gauvin & Gentzell was engaged to take photographs of the dead to assist in identification. Gauvin agreed to take the photos himself. According to Christopher Ward, the glass negatives were destroyed to prevent them from falling into the hands of macabre collectors, but it is possible that two or three survived and exist now in private collections.[14]

There are some discrepancies within the historical records as to the condition of the bodies. The *Halifax Evening Mail* reported that John R. Snow Junior had witnessed mutilated bodies and quoted him in a feature the day after the bodies were brought to the Mayflower, saying that he found 'arms and legs shattered, faces and bodies mangled, many still in evening dress, their watches stopped at ten past two' and that 'there was awful evidence of the fierce struggle for life, hands clutching wildly at clothing, faces distorted with terror … ours was a sickening task'.[15] One such body that had supposedly been mutilated was that of J.J. Astor himself. It was reported that Astor's body had been found covered in soot, completely crushed, which led people to believe that he had been crushed by one of the ship's funnels as it crashed down into the water. Archibald Gracie, a fellow millionaire and acquaintance of Astor's, wrote about this description in his memoir. Other accounts offer a different picture. Gerald Ross, one of *Mackay-Bennett*'s electricians, claimed that Astor's face was swollen and one side of his jaw was injured but nothing much beyond that. The man who identified Astor, Captain Roberts, said Astor's features were perfect. Snow would later claim that he had said nothing of the sort. The bodies, with the exception of ten or so, were actually in fairly good condition, given the circumstances. The *Morning Chronicle* asked *Mackay-Bennett*'s doctor, Thomas Armstrong, for his insight, and he said that the victims' 'looks were calm and peaceful. In fact, so peaceful it was difficult to realise that they were dead.'[16]

The bodies were to be interred at one of three cemeteries in Halifax, all chosen by the city's Registrar of Vital Statistics John Henry Barnstead and the provincial coroner and medical examiner Dr W.D. Finn. The burial plots were purchased by White Star Line's representative P.V.G. Mitchell: $846.75 for 3,600ft.[217] Fairview Lawn Cemetery, established in 1894, is a non-denominal cemetery and is the final resting place of 121 *Titanic* victims, the largest number of the three cemeteries. There are three lines of graves there, three single trenches into which the bodies were interred; and as the process of creating gravestones took so long, wooden crosses (some sources say slabs) were placed at each with a corresponding number until the proper arrangements could be made. The burial plots were laid out by land surveyor F.W. Christie, who, whether intentionally or not, laid them out in such a way as to evoke a sense of *Titanic*'s 'bow with its starboard side sheared away' when you stand at the bottom of the gravesite.[18] Today, most of the headstones are small black gabbro grave markers with bevelled tops, upon which is engraved 'Died April 15, 1912' and the number to which they were assigned, if they remain unidentified. Those who have been identified since have had their grave markers updated by their remaining family members. White Star Line paid for the upkeep of these graves until the 1930s (it ceased operations in 1934) and then a trust fund was established to maintain that upkeep.

One grave at Fairview Lawn Cemetery has received significant attention since James Cameron's *Titanic* was released in 1997. By sheer coincidence, the body of a young Irish man named Joseph Dawson is buried there and his grave marker reads 'J. Dawson'. He was a coal trimmer in *Titanic*'s boiler room and is in no way connected to the fictional Jack Dawson we see in the film. Cameron claims that he was unaware of the grave when he and his team worked on the film, but it has nonetheless made a massive impact on people: when *Titanic* was in cinemas, visitors used to leave their tickets stubs at his grave and, for some time after, many young women left love letters, trinkets and teddy bears, as they cried at the grave. To this day, visitors leave flowers.

Nineteen *Titanic* victims are buried in Mount Olivet Catholic cemetery. They occupy a small part of the cemetery's third section and have
the same small black gabbro headstones as those in Fairview Lawn
Cemetery. The graves of the victims form two lines: one of nine graves
and one of ten. During the body-recovery effort, it was important to
not only the crew of the recovery ships but also to White Star Line that
victims be given a burial suited to their faith. Positive identification and
personal items found on the bodies, such as Bibles or crucifixes, enabled
victims to be sorted by their religious beliefs and buried as such.

Ten of *Titanic*'s victims, eight of whom remain unidentified (some
sources claim seven), are buried in the Jewish Baron de Hirsch Cemetery.
Also known as the Beth Israel Synagogue Cemetery, it has been the
official burial ground for the Jewish congregation of the synagogue
since 1893 and it seemed only fitting, to Halifax Rabbi Jacob Walter,
for Jewish victims of the *Titanic* to be buried there (there are theories
that the bodies aren't actually Jewish at all).

While every effort was made to ensure that those of the Jewish and
Catholic faiths were buried in the correct cemeteries, issues did occur.
A passenger named Michel Navratil, the fifteenth body to be recovered,
was travelling with his two sons, Michel M. and Edmond Roger, under
the fake name Louis Hoffman (some sources claim he used the name
Charles rather than Louis). Navratil was a Catholic man born in Slovakia
who had lived most of his life in France. At the time of *Titanic*'s departure, he had been having business difficulties and was estranged from his
wife Marcelle (some sources assert she had an affair, but it is unclear what
the real reason for the estrangement was). Marcelle had taken their sons
to live with her, but he decided to take them with him to make a new
life in America. They boarded at Southampton with three second-class
tickets and listed their name as Hoffman, a Jewish surname that derives
from the Yiddish word *hofn*, which means hope. It is unclear whether
Navratil chose that particular surname because of its meaning, but it is
bittersweet in hindsight that he chose that name knowing he was going
to start a new life, only to have it torn from him in the most tragic of
circumstances. His sons survived but he did not. When his body was
recovered, the crew of *Mackay-Bennett* were able to identify him by his
personal effects, which included a pocketbook, a gold watch and chain,
a silver purse containing £6, a receipt from Thos. Cook & Co. for notes

exchanged, his *Titanic* ticket, a pipe in its case, a loaded revolver and a bill for Charing Cross Hotel, dated April 1912. They assumed, with the surname Hoffman, that he was Jewish, so he was interred at Baron de Hirsch Cemetery when his wife refused to claim his body. It was only after he was buried that his real name, and therefore real religious affiliation, was discovered. As Jewish law states that bodies cannot be exhumed once buried, Michel Navratil and Frederick Wormald, who was of the Church of England denomination, were unable to be moved to Mount Olivet and Fairview Lawn, respectively.

Another issue occurred when Rabbi Jacob Walter removed several of the bodies destined for Fairview Lawn Cemetery. He believed that the bodies in question were Jewish and therefore meant to be buried at Baron de Hirsch Cemetery (he believed, in fact, that forty-four of the bodies recovered by *Mackay-Bennett* were Jewish, but this could not be proved). These bodies were already en route to Fairview Lawn, so he commissioned several members of the Jewish congregation to move them back to the mortuary without telling anyone. It did not take long, however, for White Star Line and Halifax's provincial authorities to learn of this unauthorised move when they arrived at Fairview Lawn and realised several coffins were missing. Rabbi Walter was not permitted to be involved with any more *Titanic* burials after this.

Burial Services

The first burial service was a small and private affair. W.H. Harrison, Ismay's private secretary, was recovered by *Mackay-Bennett*, alongside Ismay's favourite deck steward, Ernest E.S. Freeman. On the evening of 1 May, a short service at All Saints Cathedral was held in their memory. Most of the attendees were representatives from White Star Line. Ismay himself did not attend, likely due to his commitments to the American and British inquiries into the disaster and to avoid more negative (and unfair) media attention.[1] Ismay was greatly affected by the loss, and on 19 April he telegraphed Harrison's widow Anne: 'Words fail to express my sorrow at your terrible loss. Am overwhelmed by this frightful calamity, heartfelt sympathy with you in this dark hour, Ismay.'[2] Harrison was buried at Fairview Lawn cemetery that night (Freeman was buried several days later, on 10 May).

Some of the bodies that were brought back to Halifax were more decomposed than others due to the thawing of the ice used to keep them preserved. The Evangelical Alliance, after being contacted by White Star Line, agreed to arrange for the unidentified and severely decomposed to be buried first; it did not make sense to use the limited embalming resources on these bodies. Their burial service took place on 3 May at Brunswick Street Methodist Church in Halifax. It was also a relatively small affair, conducted with the utmost respect and dignity for the victims – every victim buried that day was unidentified, and they were referred to as the 'unidentified many' during the memorial service. The service was attended by representatives from White Star Line and several senior officers from HMCS *Niobe*. The church was draped in black and purple, and the pulpit was covered with a Union Jack and the USA's Stars and Stripes flag.

The church was also covered in hundreds of pink and white carnations. These were provided by Mrs Rood, who had travelled from Seattle to Halifax in the hopes of identifying the body of her husband, Hugh, who was on board *Titanic*. His body was never found but Mrs Rood attended and donated flowers to every memorial service during her time in Halifax. She dedicated the flowers to the memory of 'the dear ones who died so bravely'.[3] Indeed, this bravery was also acknowledged by Principal Clarence MacKinnon in his sermon. He stated, 'In Halifax these graves will be kept forever green. All we know is that they heard the order: "All men step back from the boats," and they stepped back and they shall sleep in a hero's grave.' Before the service concluded with a moving rendition of Hall Caine's *Titanic* hymn, sung by the congregation in companionship with the Royal Canadian Regiment Band, MacKinnon also added that 'they shall rest quietly in our midst under the murmuring pines and hemlocks but their story shall be told to our children and to our children's children'.[4]

During the service, the bodies in question – thirty-six in total – were transported to Fairview Lawn Cemetery and a short service was also conducted there by several clergymen of various denominations to ensure as many faiths as possible were catered for. The bodies were interred at 3 p.m. in a large trench, side by side, under the watchful eyes of hundreds of mourners, including 100 men from *Niobe*. According to Alan Ruffman, the Royal Canadian Regiment Band played again, this time in accompaniment to the sorrowful singing of 'Nearer, my God, to Thee'. Each grave was given a wooden slab with their corresponding identification number to aid any future exhumations.[5] Similar services were conducted for the remaining unidentified bodies – there were too many to bury on the same day – the following Monday.

The burial service on 4 May, perhaps the most heartbreaking of all the burials, was dedicated to one person: Unknown Child #4, the 2-year-old found by the crew of *Mackay-Bennett*. The boy went unclaimed and White Star Line was unsure what to do, especially given the numerous offers of help it was getting, but Captain Larnder stepped up: he asked for permission for he and his crew to be responsible for laying the boy to rest. White Star Line agreed. Larnder and his crew, out of their own pockets with the reward money for finding J.J. Astor, paid for the service and the child's little white coffin, in which he rested at the Mayflower curling rink on a bed of roses. Alan Ruffman made a simultaneously heartwarming and heartbreaking observation about the Unknown Child's time at the makeshift morgue. He was placed in the middle of the unclaimed women, which Ruffman said was 'as if they were his caregivers in death'.[6] During the service, *Mackay-Bennet*'s crew placed a copper pendant on top of his coffin that read 'Our Babe', and six crew members served as the child's pallbearers. The service was fittingly conducted by Canon Kenneth Hind, who had been on board *Mackay-Bennett* when the child was recovered.

The service was held at St George's Anglican Church on Brunswick Street and it was filled with hundreds of mourners, including the entire seventy-five-man crew of *Mackay-Bennett*, and just as many flowers, all touched and heartbroken at the sight of this little boy's coffin. The congregation was so packed, in fact, that it spilled out onto the street. As the pallbearers carried the coffin to the horse-drawn hearse that transported the Unknown Child to Fairview Lawn Cemetery, hundreds gathered in the streets leading to the cemetery to pay their respects to the lost soul. The hearse was packed with flowers from mourners, including 'White Star Line, the coroner, the undertaker John R. Snow Junior, and his wife, Mrs Hugh R. Rood, the children of Bloomfield School, the Novia Scotia Nursery, and a bouquet of flowers signed only, "The boys from the morgue"'.[7] At his gravesite, the crew, again out of their own pockets, erected a black marble obelisk grave marker for him with an inscription reading: 'Erected to the Memory of an Unknown Child Whose Remains Were Recovered after the Disaster of the Titanic, April 15th 1912.'

The child's little leather shoes survive to this day. The policeman in charge of burning the victims' clothing to ensure it did not fall into the hands of macabre souvenir collectors, Clarence Northover, couldn't bring himself to burn them so he kept them in his personal desk drawer at the police station until he retired in 1918 and moved to Ontario. On the bottom of one shoe, Northover wrote, 'Shoes of the only baby found. SS *Titanic* 1912.' His grandson, Earle, deciding that the shoes belonged in Halifax, donated the shoes to Halifax's Maritime Museum of the Atlantic in 2002.

In fact, it was these shoes that helped confirm the identity of Unknown Child #4. For years, the child was believed to be either 2-year-old Swedish boy Gösta Pålsson or 2-year-old Irish boy Eugene Rice until a 2002 documentary investigated the remains within the grave – three teeth and a small bone – and found DNA that was linked to a Finnish woman named Maria Emelia Panula, a *Titanic* victim and mother of 13-month-old Eino Viljami Panula, who also perished. However, when the Northover family came forward with Unknown Child #4's shoes, it was immediately clear that the shoes would have been far too large for a 13-month-old child. Researchers tested and investigated the shoes in 2007 and discovered that they had been made in England, not Scandinavia, making it incredibly unlikely that Eino Viljami Panula was the true identity of the child. Using the child's HVSI, a mitochondrial DNA molecule, researchers at Canada's Lakehead University confirmed that the DNA did not match any surviving relatives of Panula. Eventually, through testing at the US Armed Forces DNA identification laboratory in Maryland, researchers were able to trace Unknown Child #4's DNA and find a positive match.

The child is Sidney Leslie Goodwin, the 19-month-old son of Frederick and Augusta Goodwin. The Goodwins were travelling to America so they could relocate to Niagara Falls, where Frederick's brother Thomas had already moved and found work. Frederick was set to take a job at a new hydroelectric power station, most likely the Schoellkopf Hydroelectric Power Station (Station A), which was due to open later in 1912. Sidney, along with his five older siblings – Lillian, Charles, William, Jessie and Harold – were packed up and ready to begin their new lives. The Goodwins originally booked a passage on SS *New York* from Southampton but changed to *Titanic* at the last minute. Some historical sources claim they changed their ship so Lillian, their eldest child, could join them and the family could travel as one unit, while others claim it was due to delays caused by a coal strike. Whatever the reason, the entire family boarded *Titanic* and perished together. Sidney was the only member of the Goodwin family to be recovered.[8] It was agreed that Sidney's grave would not be altered to include his name, as he has come to represent the lives of all the children who died in the sinking. A small black marker that identifies Sidney was placed near the base of the original marker.

Congregations filled the churches of Halifax in droves to pay their respects, regardless of the number of victims being buried that day. For example, four unidentified Roman Catholic women were given a solemn service at St Mary's Basilica. The church was full of mourners, many with 'tear filled eyes',[9] and the burial itself was attended by representatives from White Star Line.

On 5 May 1912, the first Sunday since *Mackay-Bennett*'s return, a large memorial service was conducted for all the victims at St Paul's Anglican Church in Halifax. The congregation was enormous, filled with all manner of Halifax residents and high-ranking representatives, including the mayor, Supreme Court judges and the lieutenant-governor. Representatives from the Charitable Irish Society, Nova Scotia Historical Society, the North British Society, St George's Society and the YMCA also attended. Among the congregation sat Captain Larnder and his crew, who had requested that their next voyage be postponed so they could attend the service (*Mackay-Bennett* resumed its usual responsibilities after the service, setting sail on 6 May).

To mark the solemn occasion, the holy table, lectern and pulpit were draped in black. A prayer given by Reverend Samuel Prince opened the service:

We are met solemn in memorial today. Over the whole of the civilised world there rests the shadow of a great sorrow. Dare we do aught but drape our churches and mourn the memories of those whose bodies now lie in that place of death beneath the seas, but whose souls have passed into the presence-chamber of the king of kings. Some have been spared. Please God there may be more. We rejoice with them that do rejoice and we weep with them that weep.

Smaller, more humble services were also held. Two of the bodies recovered by *Montmagny* – Harold Reynolds and a man identified as J. Smith – were among the bodies held at the Mayflower curling rink in the hopes that someone would claim them. When no one came forward, they were eventually buried with smaller services at Fairview Lawn cemetery. A similar modest service was held for Hileni Jabbur/Zabour, the young Syrian girl recovered. Her burial at Mount Olivet was overseen by Dean Crawford of All Saints Cathedral.[10] James McGrady, the final body recovered and the last of the 150 bodies buried in Halifax, was shipped from St John's to Halifax and given a modest memorial service by All Saints Cathedral on 11 June, and buried at Fairview Lawn the following day.

8

Memorials and Monuments
Around the World

The *Titanic* tragedy was mourned by people around the world and continues to be recognised and remembered today. There are dozens of memorials and monuments scattered around the globe.

In Northern Ireland, where *Titanic* was built, a memorial garden sits on the east side of Belfast City Hall. Opened in April 2012 in honour of the 100th anniversary, the garden features a plinth with fifteen bronze plaques engraved with the name of every victim who perished on the ship, amongst them twenty-eight men from Belfast, including the ship's chief designer Thomas Andrews. It was also the first memorial to list everyone who died – passengers and crew alike – it is known as 'The Belfast List'. The plants were carefully selected to reflect the colours of the water and ice of the North Atlantic (blues, greens, whites and silvers), encouraging contemplation and a sense of peace. Flowers were chosen based on their visual aesthetic (magnolia stellatas that blossom into white; star-shaped flowers, representing White Star Line) and on their symbolic value (forget-me-nots and rosemary, which symbolise remembrance). These particular plants bloom spectacularly in the spring, flowering every year in April as a reminder of when *Titanic* sank.

In Thomas Andrews's hometown of Comber, Northern Ireland, there stands Andrews Memorial Hall. Founded by his widow, Helen, Andrews Memorial Hall took two years to complete (1913–15), the work beginning when his daughter Elizabeth broke ground at the site and finished when his mother Eliza set the foundation stone. It is a beautiful building designed by Young & McKenzie, a prominent Belfast architectural firm. It features a gabled façade, lattice glazing, Tudor arches and beautiful decorative panels on the first floor that feature a heraldic shield motif accompanied by the Andrews' family motto 'Always faithful'. The spandrel of the arched central doorway is inscribed with 'Thomas Andrews Jr Shipbuilder Memorial Hall', with cherubs playing musical instruments on each side. The building also features a memorial plaque dedicated to Andrews, with a medallion portrait of him, which reads:

> This hall was erected and endowed in memory of Thomas Andrews, Junior. By the inhabitants of the town and district of Comber and other friends. Born 7th, February, 1873, at Ardara, Comber. He entered at the age of sixteen years upon his apprenticeship with Harland & Wolff, Ltd. shipbuilders. Through his industry and ability he became successively Work Manager, Head of the Repair Department, and Chief of the Designing Staff, and ultimately in 1902 he was appointed one of the managing directors of the company. He took a prominent part in the designing and construction of all the leviathan ships built by the company between the years 1899 and 1912, including the '*Cedric*', '*Baltic*', '*Adriatic*', '*Oceanic*', '*Amerika*', '*President Lincoln*', '*President Grant*', '*New Amsterdam*', '*Rotterdam*', '*Lapland*', '*Olympic*', and '*Titanic*'.
>
> He was lost on 15th April 1912, in the foundering of the '*Titanic*' which collided with an iceberg in mid-Atlantic during her maiden voyage from Southampton to New-York. His manly character and lovable disposition won for him in his brief life the affection and esteem of all who knew him. When with tragic suddenness the call came he died as he lived, faithful to duty and gave his life that others might be saved.[1]

Thomas Andrews was and is widely respected by Northern Ireland and is considered one of the greatest heroes of the *Titanic*; several eyewitnesses claimed he was quick to help others, refusing to even put on a life jacket. Though his body was never found, he is not forgotten.

Ireland has several modest *Titanic* memorials in honour of the victims, including Addergoole *Titanic* Memorial Park. Cobh, previously known as Queenstown, was the *Titanic's* last port of call before sailing into the North Atlantic, so it has several memorials dedicated to those they lost. The most famous one was erected in 1998 in Pearse Square. It is a large rectangular stone with two brass plaques, one depicting Irish emigrants, including couples and families with young children, boarding the ship that would take them across the water to *Titanic*; the other a short inscription dedicated to the memory of the victims:

> Commemorating R.M.S. *Titanic* and her last port of call on her maiden and final voyage, April 11, 1912. In special memory of the Irish emigrants and all those who lost their lives in this great tragedy. Ah dheis dé go raibh an anmacha [Gaelic for 'at God's right hand are the souls']. Memorial erected by the *Titanic* Historical Society, the Irish *Titanic* Historical Society, and the people of Cobh.[2]

A very modest and easily missed memorial is one commemorating the Rice family. One of the bodies recovered by *Mackay-Bennett* was that of Margaret Rice, a widow from Athlone in County Westmeath. The bodies of her five children were never found. Rice was the twelfth body found by *Mackay-Bennett* and she was identified by what she carried on her person: a pill box with 'Margaret Rice' engraved on it, her wedding ring, a locket and photo, a jet bead necklace, a gold brooch in a bag, £3 in gold, £4 in Irish notes, a pair of plain gold earrings, a charm around her neck, distinctive false teeth in her upper jaw, a medallion marked 'B.V.M.', and shoes marked 'Parsons Sons, Athlone'. Her body never returned to Ireland – she was buried in Mount Olivet Catholic Cemetery in Halifax – but her hometown memorialised her and her family with a plaque on the building where the Rice family lived. There is also a big focus on Margaret Rice in the Cobh Museum in County Cork.

One of the most recent memorials was established in 2011. St Patrick's Church in Lahardane, with funding from surviving descendants, installed two stained-glass windows, designed by local artist Michael Coleman of Whitethorn Studios, in memory of the eleven people from Lahardane who perished on *Titanic*. Situated on either side of an existing marble memorial plaque erected in 2002 is one window entitled 'Emigration' and one 'The *Titanic* Rescue'. The design was inspired by *Titanic* survivor and Lahardane local Annie Kate Kelly's memories of the sinking (Kelly stayed in America after the sinking, settling in Michigan and becoming an Adrian Dominican Sister). Kelly recalled waiting in line to enter a lifeboat. Beside her, two women refused to enter them, both stating that they refused to leave their loved ones. These women, according to Kelly, were Catherine and Mary Bourke from Addergoole. Kelly eventually stepped into the boat and she vividly remembered looking up to see her cousin Pat, who was holding his rosary beads and waving at her. He did not survive.

There are several *Titanic* memorials in England. A 'Memorial to the Engine Room Heroes of *Titanic*' stands at Pier Head in Liverpool city centre, close to where Liverpool's White Star Line headquarters was. Although the ship never docked in Liverpool, many of the crew members were from the city and the engineers' skeleton crew played a vital role in the sinking, especially in keeping its lights on up until ten minutes before it went beneath the waves (most of the engineers were released from their duties around 1.30 a.m. and proceeded to the upper deck). Not a single engineer survived the disaster. The memorial, designed by Welsh sculptor Sir William Goscombe John, is enormous and features life-sized sculptures of engineers and stokers, all of which are incredibly realistic. The memorial, which stands on granite footings and has a pedestal mounted by a granite obelisk, has four allegorical figures representing water, earth, air and fire. According to Historic England, the memorial is 'one of the most artistically significant memorials to the *Titanic* disaster on either side of the Atlantic'.[3] Though the memorial was intended solely to be in memory of those lost on *Titanic*, by the time it was erected many engineers and stokers had been lost in the First World War, so it was agreed that no specific mention of *Titanic* would be made. Liverpool also has a modest plaque in the Philharmonic Hall on Hope Street dedicated to the ship's musicians.

No city was hit harder by the *Titanic* disaster than Southampton. Of the more than 900 crew members on board *Titanic*, over 700 of them were from Southampton, and with only 213/14 crew members having survived, the town of Southampton suffered a great and heartbreaking loss. The town remembers the victims with several plaques in local churches and graveyards, a memorial to the postal staff at the council chambers of the town's guildhall, a memorial to the ship's musicians on the corner of Cumberland Place and London Road (this is a replica of the original memorial – the first was destroyed during the Second World War), and a memorial dedicated to the restaurant workers at St Joseph's Church. Southampton also honoured the memory of *Titanic*'s band with two memorials. One is a white marble memorial in Cumberland Place. Located on the side of a building, the memorial was commissioned in 1913 by the Amalgamated Musicians' Union and lists all members of the band in a circle: W. Hartley, C. Krins, R. Bricoux, W.T. Brailey, J. Woodward, J.F. Clarke, J.L. Hume, P.C. Taylor. A short inscription accompanies it: 'They died at their posts like men.' The other is a large, brass plague in St Mary's Church. The plaque reads:

> Erected to the memory of that heroic band of musicians of the S.S. *Titanic* who, in their last hour of this mortal life by their self-sacrificing devotion, sought to inspire and sustain in others the assurance of life eternal. April 15th 1912. W. Hartley. R. Bricoux. F.C. Clarke. J.W. Woodward. G. Krins. P. C. Taylor. J. Hume. W.T. Brailey.[4]

The most impressive memorial Southampton has is a large *Titanic* engineers' memorial in Holyrood Church. This memorial is dedicated to Joseph Bell, the chief engineering officer, and his twenty-four staff of engineers, boilermakers, plumbers and clerks who perished in the disaster. It features a large bronze statue of the goddess of victory, Nike, standing on the prow of a ship with her arms outstretched, a wreath in both hands. Beside her stand two panels depicting the engineers. Upon it is the following inscription:

> Greater love hath no man than this. That a man lay down his life for his friends St. John 15th Ch. 13th V. To the memory of the engineer officers of the R.M.S '*Titanic*' who showed their high conception of duty and their heroism by remaining at their posts. 15th April 1912. Erected by their fellow engineers and friends throughout the world.[5]

On each side of the central platform, inscribed on the back, are the names of each individual engineer. On the right panel are the names

Robert Millar, Alfred P. Middleton, William Y. Moyes, Albert G. Ervine, William McReynolds, William Kelly, Henry P. Creese, George A. Chishall, Thomas Millar, Hugh Fitzpatrick, Peter Sloan, Arthur A. Rous, Alfred S. Allsop, William L. Duffy, Herbert Jupe; and beneath are three more names: Thomas Andrews, Archibald Frost and Robert Knight. On the left are Joseph Bell, Jonathan Shepherd, Wm E. Farquharson, Charles Hodge, John Hesketh, Francis E.G. Coy, Norman E. Harrison, James Fraser, George F. Hosking, Henry R. Dyer, Edward C. Dodd, Renny W. Dodds, Leonard Hodgkinson, Arthur Ward, James M. Smith, Thomas H. Kemp, Bert Wilson, Frank A. Parsons, Herbert G. Harvey and William D. Mackie.

The memorial was unveiled on 22 April 1914 by Sir Archibald Denny Bt, LLD, the then president of the Institute of Marine Engineers in front of an impressive 100,000 people. During the service, as he unveiled the statue, Sir Archibald said:

> By the manner of their deaths [the engineers] carried out one of the finest traditions of our race. They must have known that pumping could do no more than delay the final catastrophe, yet they stuck pluckily to their duty. Driven back from boiler room to boiler room, fighting for every inch of draught to give time for the launching of the boats, not one of those brave officers was saved.[6]

There are memorials to specific individuals in England. In Beacon Park, Lichfield, there is a statue of *Titanic*'s Captain Edward Smith, which was unveiled by his daughter in 1914. Though Smith was not from the area (he was born in Hanley, Staffordshire, and lived in Southampton), the decision to erect the statue in Lichfield was made because it was the cathedral city of the district in which Smith had been born. There is also a plaque in Hanley Town Hall, which reads:

> This tablet is dedicated to the memory of Commander Edward John Smith RD, RNR. Born in Hanley, 27th Jan 1850, died at sea, 15th April 1912. Be British. Whilst in command of the White Star SS *Titanic* that great ship struck an iceberg in the Atlantic Ocean during the night and speedily sank with nearly all who were on board. Captain Smith having done all man could do for the safety of passengers and

crew remained at his post on the sinking ship until the end. His last message to the crew was 'Be British'.[7]

Though there was some controversy surrounding Captain Smith's character following the inquests into the sinking – with the statue, according to some sources, being placed in Lichfield rather than his hometown because of this – both the statue and the memorial plaque have become incredibly popular with tourists. It should be noted that the controversy, while not as intense as it was 100 years ago, is still ongoing and far from being resolved.

In Colne, Lancashire, there is a monument to band leader Wallace Hartley. Hartley was one of the bodies recovered by *Mackay-Bennett*, with his violin case still strapped to his back,[8] and after he was positively identified, he was transported home and buried at Keighley Road Cemetery. His funeral was attended by over 1,000 people and it is estimated that 30,000 to 40,000 witnessed his coffin being transported to the cemetery. His headstone, which stands at 10ft high, features a carved violin and the opening bars to 'Nearer My God to Thee', the song played by *Titanic*'s band as the ship went down. A memorial bust to him sits outside what was then Colne's library. The bronze bust is mounted on a plinth and features two female figures, both caped, holding lyres. The memorial's inscription reads: 'Wallace Hartley Bandmaster of the R.M.S *Titanic* who perished in the foundering of that vessel April 15th 1912. Erected by voluntary contributions to commemorate the heroism of a native of this town.'[9]

Eastbourne in East Sussex is home to a memorial dedicated to John Wesley Woodward, the band's cellist. Unlike Hartley, Woodward's body was never recovered but he is remembered in Eastbourne, where he was part of the Eastbourne Municipal Orchestra, the Duke of Devonshire's Orchestra and the Grand Hotel Eastbourne Orchestra before joining *Titanic*'s musicians. The memorial was unveiled in 1914, installed within the seafront's bandstand. In the centre is a likeness of Woodward's face, beneath which is his beloved cello. On the right is *Titanic* with its stern out of the water, the iceberg in the background and several lifeboats; on the left is an inscription above a small cherub. It reads:

This tablet is erected as a tribute to the self-sacrifice and devotion of John Wesley Woodward (Formerly a member of The Eastbourne Municipal

Orchestra, The Duke of Devonshire's Orchestra and the Grand Hotel Eastbourne Orchestra), who, with others of the hero-musicians of the ship's band, perished in the Atlantic through the sinking of the White Star liner '*Titanic*' on April 15th 1912. 'Faithful unto death'.[10]

London has several memorials to individuals who were lost on *Titanic*. A modest memorial to British newspaper editor and journalist William Thomas Stead hangs at Temple Place at the Victoria Embankment. Stead was a fascinating character. He was a prolific journalist who, when he became editor of the *Pall Mall Gazette*, helped transform the newspaper industry as we know it. He moved away from the incessantly formal archetype of traditional newspapers by adding subheadings, illustrations, maps and diagrams, and pioneered modern interview techniques, including incorporating his own opinions into the features he wrote. He understood that journalism could have a positive impact and influence legislative change – one of his campaigns, 'The Bitter Cry of Outcast London', featured descriptions and reports of London's slums that were so shocking, and true, that it led to a Royal Commission recommending that the government should clear the slums and build low-cost housing in their place to help those who were in need.

Stead was, however, controversial in his journalistic methods, even when his heart was in the right place. In 1885, he published a series of articles entitled 'The Maiden Tribute of Modern Babylon' in a radical crusade against child prostitution in England. The investigation involved undercover journalists posing as prostitutes and pimps, but it wasn't enough for Stead. He wanted to show how easy it was to elicit a prostitute in London, so, using various connections, he purchased the daughter of a chimney sweep, 13-year-old Eliza Armstrong. Nothing untoward came out of the relationship; it was purely to highlight just how easy it was to purchase a child for the sole purpose of sexual gratification and exploitation. Stead spent three months in prison for the act, but his investigation helped further the passing of the Criminal Law Amendment Act 1885, otherwise known as 'An Act to make further provision for the Protection of Women and Girls, the suppression of brothels, and other purposes', which raised the age of consent for girls and women from 13 to 16.

Stead boarded *Titanic* in 1912 at the request of President William Taft, who wished him to speak at a peace conference in New York. There were some fascinating coincidences that connected Stead to *Titanic* prior to sailing. In 1886, Stead wrote *How the Mail Steamer Went Down in Mid Atlantic*, a short story involving a liner sinking with a great loss of life due to insufficient numbers of lifeboats, much like the ill-fated *Titanic*. In fact, he further laboured the point in an editorial comment in which he said: 'This is exactly what might take place and will take place if liners are sent to sea short of boats.'[11] In 1892, he published another short story in his journal *Review of Reviews*. *From the Old World to the New* tells the tale of a clairvoyant sailing on White Star Line's *Majestic*, who senses a ship has collided with an iceberg nearby. *Majestic* was able to rescue the survivors, much in the same way as RMS *Carpathia*. Mrs Irwin, the clairvoyant in the tale, described a vision eerily similar to that of *Titanic*:

> I was saying that last night, as I was lying asleep in my berth, I was awakened by a sudden cry, as of men in mortal peril, and I roused myself to listen, and there before my eyes, as plain as you are sitting there, I saw a sailing ship among the icebergs. She had been stove[d] in by the ice, and was fast sinking. The crew were crying piteously for help: it was their voices that roused me. Some of them had climbed upon the ice; others were on the sinking ship, which was drifting away as she sank. Even as I looked she settled rapidly by the bow, and went down with a plunge. The waters bubbled and foamed. I could see the heads of a few swimmers in the eddy. One after another they sank, and I saw them no more. I saw that there were six men and a boy on the iceberg. Then, in a moment, the whole scene vanished, and I was alone in my berth, with the wailing cry of the drowning sailors still ringing in my ears.[12]

Stead was an avid believer in spiritualism, and it quickly became the opinion of many that Stead's short story was not fictitious at all, but a premonition or prediction of what was going to happen to *Titanic*. What made it all the more compelling was that Stead himself was aboard the ship and lost his life on the night of the sinking.

Stead's body was never found but his hometown of London held a memorial service for him at Westminster Chapel on Buckingham Gate on 25 April. At his service, Stead was described by the Reverend Dr Clifford as, first and foremost, 'a journalist – brilliant, gifted, unconventional, rapid, accomplished, as a fountain of fresh and original ideas ... always a prophet'.[13] His memorial, though humble, remains in London today. The small, bronze tablet depicts a side profile of Stead surrounded by a garland of laurel leaves and features the following inscription:

> W.T. Stead. 1849–1912. This memorial to a journalist of wide renown was erected near the spot where he worked for more than thirty years by journalists of many lands in recognition of his brilliant gifts fervent spirit & untiring devotion to the service of his fellow men.[14]

The inscription is accompanied by a male figure of St George to represent fortitude and a female figure to represent sympathy, with the figure holding a wreath in one hand and a globe in her left. There is an almost identical memorial to Stead in New York, too, which was erected in tribute to him by his friends and admirers across the water. There is also a memorial stone for Stead outside Darlington Library in Darlington, County Durham, across the road from the old *Northern Echo* headquarters, where he worked as an editor from 1871–80. Behind the large stone is a plaque that reads:

> This stone, originally in possession of Mr. W.T. Stead when resident at Grainey Hill & to which he tethered his dogs & pony, is probably the only Monument in Granite to his memory in Darlington. The Boulder is a fitting symbol of his indomitable courage & strength of character & may keep green the memory of one of England's Greatest Men. His Body perished on the *Titanic*, when she sank April 15th 1912. His spirit still lives.[15]

London also has a memorial to Charles Melville Hays, the president of The Grand Trunk Railway, whose body was recovered by *Minia*. Hays was travelling on *Titanic* to get back to Canada as quickly as possible; his daughter Louise was having a difficult pregnancy and his presence was required at a gala opening for the Château Laurier Hotel in Ottawa on 25 April. Though he was buried in Montreal, there was an additional memorial service for him in London and a memorial plaque was commissioned. While it is unclear why the directors of the Grand Trunk Railway chose to place this plaque in London, it is a touching one. The small brass plaque, located on the interior western wall of the Church of St Edmund the King in the City of London, where his memorial service was held, is set behind glass and is now part of the church's wooden panelling. Its inscription reads:

In memory of Charles Melville Hays. President of the Grand Trunk and Grand Trunk Pacific Railway Companies of Canada, who lost his life on April 15th 1912, by the foundering in mid-Atlantic, of the steamship '*Titanic*' through collision with an iceberg, while on her maiden voyage from Southampton to New York. A memorial service was held in this Church simultaneously with one at Montreal, on Thursday, April 25th 1912. This tablet with the kind permission of the Rector and Churchwardens was placed here by the Directors of the Grand Trunk Railway Company of Canada in recognition of Mr Hays's great services to the company, and of his high character in public and private life.[16]

In Cadogan Square Gardens in central London stands a memorial to first-class passenger Christopher Head, a former mayor of Chelsea and a man much respected in the city. His body was never recovered. The memorial is in the form of a stone sundial, surrounded by greenery. A bronze plaque sits beneath the sundial. Its inscription reads: 'To the memory of Christopher Head, for some years Hon. Secretary of these gardens, who perished on the *Titanic* April 15th 1912.'[17] It is a humble but moving memorial.

London is also home to a small *Titanic* memorial garden at the National Maritime Museum, Greenwich, which was opened by Edith Haisman in 1995. At the time, she was one of the oldest living survivors. There is also a plaque in Coleman Street's Marine Engineers headquarters. It lists thirty-eight names and is topped by a figure of Triton, the Greek god of the sea, driving a team of polar bears.

In the small town of Scarborough, there stands a memorial plaque dedicated to Sixth Officer James Paul Moody, the only junior officer, aged just 24, to perish during the disaster. Moody was the officer who answered lookout Frederick Fleet's telephone call on the bridge, warning of the incoming iceberg. He relayed Fleet's message, 'iceberg, right ahead', to First Officer Murdoch. He was responsible for preparing the lifeboats to be launched and was directly responsible for saving dozens upon dozens of women and children that night. Moody was last seen helping launch Collapsible Lifeboat A just before the ship began its final descent. The lifeboat was washed off *Titanic* while the officers, including Moody, were attempting to attach it to the falls. The lifeboat was completely engulfed by the wave, likely dragging Moody out to sea. His body was never recovered. He is memorialised by a plaque affixed to the south wall of St Martin on the Hill Church's nave, on Albion Road in Scarborough. Its inscription reads: 'To the Glory of God And in affectionate memory of James Paul Moody 6th Officer of R M S *Titanic*. Born at Scarborough On the 21st August 1887. Went down with the ship On the 15th April 1912' and features the Biblical quote from Revelation 2:10: 'Be thou faithful unto death and I will give thee a crown of life',[18] highlighting Moody's bravery, consideration and care for *Titanic*'s passengers and his fellow officers, and the reward that awaits his serving Christ unto death.

In Godalming, Surrey, is a memorial to Jack Phillips, *Titanic*'s Senior Wireless Operator. Although his body was never found, his hometown decided to commemorate him by erecting a headstone in the shape of an iceberg in Godalming's Old Cemetery. The townspeople also built a cloister and garden in his memory, adjoining St Peter and St Paul's church, alongside a fountain that was donated by the Postal Telegraph Clerks' Association. Upon the cloister is an inscription that reads:

> This cloister is built in memory of John George Phillips. A native of this town. Chief wireless telegraphist of the ill-fated SS *Titanic*. He died at his post when the vessel foundered in mid-Atlantic on the 15th day of April 1912.

There is also a memorial plaque dedicated to Phillips in Farncombe church, where he was a choir member in his youth. The plaque's inscription features a similar sentiment to that above, with the additional line of 'faithful to his duty till the last'.[19]

Broadway, a small village in Worcestershire, has a memorial to first-class passenger Francis Davis Millet. Millet was an American and a man of many talents. He served in the Civil War as a drummer boy and then a surgeon, attended Harvard, where he earned a Master of Arts, and then became a prolific journalist and artist specialising in murals, portraits, and sculptures. Millet was a close friend of Archibald Butt, an American army officer who served as the military aide for both President Roosevelt and President Taft. Millet settled in Broadway with a small commune of fellow artists, where he had a wife named Lilly and three children, despite also living with Butt and having what some scholars have characterised as a 'don't ask, don't tell' relationship. After a short vacation, Butt was returning to New York and wanted Millet to accompany him on his travels; he readily agreed. Millet boarded *Titanic* at Cherbourg, in France, which was its first port of call after leaving England; Butt boarded at Southampton. Both Millett and Butt died the night of the sinking. Millet's body was recovered and cremated in Boston, but Butt's body was never found. Twenty years later, Millet's son, Jack, donated £120, the equivalent of almost £9,000 today, to St Eadburgha's Church for the construction of lychgates that were to be dedicated to his father's memory. The lychgates mark the entrance to the village's lower cemetery on Snowshill Road and bear a touching tribute to Millet:

In tribute to Francis Millet, a man of excellence in the Arts and Literature. He met his death with fortitude as the ship *Titanic* sank whilst still giving hope to those who feared for their lives. His dear friends sought the dedication of this memorial in fond memory of his treasured fellowship.[20]

Scotland also has a *Titanic* memorial. In Glasgow there is a memorial to thirty-six engineers that was erected by the Institution of Engineers and Shipbuilders in Scotland. It stands at Elmbank Crescent, the former site of the institution's headquarters. It features a marble plaque mounted by two female nudes carrying a wreath. Its dedication outlines the memorial's purpose: 'To keep alive the memory of the engineers of the *Titanic* who all died at their duty on the fifteenth day of April 1912 when the ship was lost in mid-Atlantic.'[21]

A small memorial resides in Guernsey, the second-largest of the Channel Islands, just west of Normandy. Nineteen people from its small-knit community boarded *Titanic* but only five survived the disaster. Those who were lost are remembered with a fourteen-sided blue stone tablet, each side representing one soul, with their names engraved. The memorial was unveiled in April 2012, the 100th anniversary of the sinking of the *Titanic*, and was funded by descendants of one of the victims, Laurence Gavey.

Cherbourg, France, has a wealth of *Titanic* material, among it a memorial stone and plaque, which were erected in April 1996 close to the Quai de l'Ancien Arsenal, where the *Titanic* passengers boarded *Traffic* and *Nomadic* to transport them to *Titanic*. Cherbourg and the Titanic Historical Society funded the memorial and it was unveiled by French *Titanic* survivor Louise Laroche. Translated from its original French, the memorial's inscription reads:

> R.M.S. *Titanic*. During her maiden cruise, the liner *Titanic* made its only stopover in Cherbourg on April 10, 1912. It was to sink in the night of April 14 to 15, off Newfoundland. The *Titanic* Historical Society at Indian Orchard (Massachusetts U.S.A.) and the City of Cherbourg commemorated this tragic event April 19, 1996.[22]

The United States, *Titanic*'s intended destination, is home to many memorials to the victims of the disaster. In New York, there is a *Titanic* memorial lighthouse that stands 60ft high, commissioned by the 'Unsinkable Molly Brown' in remembrance of those who died. It was originally constructed on the Seamen's Church Institute Headquarters' roof above the East River before being moved to Fulton and Pearl Streets in the financial district of downtown Manhattan in 1968. In memory of Isidor and Ida Straus, Straus Park was established in the Upper West Side district of Morningside Heights. The couple were highly respected by their fellow New Yorkers, so they added a centrepiece to the park, the Isidor and Ida Straus Memorial, in 1915, to remember them. The dedication to them reads: 'Erected by voluntary contributions from many fellow citizens and accepted for the City of New York by Mayor John Purroy Mitchel and Cabot Ward, Commissioner of Parks. AD MCMXV.'[23] There is also a memorial to them in the original Macy's store, unveiled in 1913. Isidor, in particular, was especially kind to his employees, providing them with health insurance and hot meals, and greeting each individual by name. The loss hit them hard so they memorialised Isidor and Ida with a beautiful plaque that includes the inscription, 'Their lives were beautiful and their deaths glorious' and 'a voluntary token of sorrowing employees'.[24]

There are two *Titanic* memorials in Washington D.C. One is a 13ft-high male figure in a loose robe with his arms outstretched. Erected by the Women's Titanic Memorial Association, it was designed to represent the brave men who stepped aside to let the women and children on to the lifeboats. It was unveiled in May 1931 by Helen Herron Taft, the widow of President Taft, who was the president in office during the disaster. The inscription honours the men:

To the brave men who perished in the *Titanic* April 15 1912. They gave their lives that women and children might be saved. To the young and the old, the rich and the poor, the ignorant and the learned, all who gave their lives nobly to save women and children.[25]

President Taft also had a direct connection to *Titanic* and erected his own monument to Archibald Butt, who has been previously mentioned. The Butt–Millet Memorial Fountain in President's Park was established in 1913 and commemorates the loss of Archibald Butt and Francis Davis Millet. Upon hearing the news of the *Titanic* disaster and Butt's death, President Taft was left utterly devastated, as he considered Butt to be like a member of his own family. Of his lost friend, Taft said, 'I knew that he would certainly remain on the ship's deck until every duty had been performed and every sacrifice made that properly fell on one charged, as he would feel himself charged, with responsibility for the rescue of others.'[26]

Smaller, more modest memorials exist too. A plaque for Edith Evans, a wealthy socialite who gave up her seat in the lifeboats in favour of married women with children, was fitted under a stained-glass window inside Grace Church in New York, where her memorial was held on 22 April 1912. One line stands out: 'Love is strong as death.'[27] A plaque in the Boston Symphony Hall commemorates the musicians of *Titanic*, reading: 'In memory of the devoted musicians who were drowned still playing as the *Titanic* went down, 15 April 1912.'[28] A park bench near Audubon, Pennsylvania, stands in memorial to 106 passengers whose intended destination had been Pennsylvania.

A small town in Maryland, Libertytown, is believed to be the home of the first ever *Titanic* memorial. At the time of the disaster, Libertytown was in the process of renovating the cemetery of St Peter the Apostle Catholic Church. Upon hearing the news, the townspeople of Libertytown dedicated a monument of a calvary crucifixion scene to the victims. This was on 19 April 1912, just one day after the confirmation that the *Titanic* had sunk.

Halifax, the final resting place of the recovered victims, does not have a singular memorial for all those who were lost (yet). It does, however, have a memorial for George Wright, a Halifax-born businessman and philanthropist who was a well-respected and much-loved member of the community. He has a grave marker in the Christ Church cemetery in Dartmouth, donated by his brother, and his home remains a fundamental part of Halifax's historic homes. Halifax also has a spool yard at Queen's Marque, installed in 2022, which highlights Halifax's role in the history of transatlantic cable, paying homage to key ships like *Mackay-Bennett*.

Interestingly, and quite unexpectedly given that it has no direct connection to the disaster, Australia also has *Titanic* memorials. In the mining city of Broken Hill, New South Wales, a group of bandsmen erected the Titanic Musicians' Memorial in 1913 in a gesture of solidarity with their fellow bandsmen. Its inscription reads:

> Erected by the Citizens of Broken Hill as a memorial to the heroic bandsmen of the steamship *Titanic* who, playing to the end, calmly faced certain death whilst women, children and their fellow men were being rescued from the wreck of that ill-fated vessel off the coast of Newfoundland on the 15th April 1912.[29]

There is also a bandstand dedicated to them in Ballarat, Victoria. This memorial was erected in 1915 and stands in front of the Mechanics' Institute in its Struct Street Gardens. It cost £150 to build, which is the equivalent of £15,000 in today's money.

These are but a few of the memorials dedicated to *Titanic* victims around the world. Eugene Nesmeyanov, author of several *Titanic* books and articles, including the fascinating *The Titanic Expeditions: Diving to the Queen of the Deep: 1985–2021*,[30] recommends an illuminating project by the Swiss Titanic Society called *TitanicMap*,[31] which lists the hundreds of memorials and their numerous locations.

PART THREE

The Aftermath: *Titanic*'s Legacy

The Inquiries: Proposed Legislative Changes

The sinking of *Titanic* changed maritime law almost immediately. The British Wreck Commissioner's inquiry into the sinking of *Titanic* (2 May to 3 July 1912) and the United States Senate inquiry into the sinking of the *Titanic* (19 April to 25 May 1912) brought several issues regarding safety on the seas to light,[1] and it quickly became apparent that while the disaster was a tremendous tragedy, it was one that more people would have survived if stricter and more thorough measures and procedures had been in place.[2] That is not to say that Captain Smith and his crew were in any way incompetent – far from it – or that the existing legislation was inefficient, only that such a tragedy could have been evaded. The two inquiries approached the disaster differently. The British inquiry focused more on the technical aspects of the sinking and on changing things for the better in the future, while not attributing any concrete blame to White Star Line, the British Board of Trade (except in the case of the lifeboats) or Captain Smith to, arguably, protect the reputation of its members. Charles Lightoller defended the inquiry in his book, arguing that the British Board of Trade and White Star Line did the best they could with the knowledge and 'the ever-present possibility of just such a disaster'. He believed:

A washing of dirty linen would help no one. The Board of Trade had passed that ship as in all respects fit for the sea ... Now the Board of

Trade was holding an inquiry into the loss of that ship – hence the whitewash brush.[3]

In contrast, the US inquiry, while arguably poorly managed, was driven by what Stephanie Barczewski in her book *Titanic: A Night Remembered* characterised as a 'righteous indignation' and a 'passion to right the wrongs' done to the victims of the tragedy. She emphasises that their proceedings were bristled with 'criticisms of established seafaring traditions and of the conduct of the *Titanic*'s builders, owners, officers and crew'.[4] This righteous indignation is no better demonstrated than in Senator Isidor Rayner's concluding speech:

> The sounds of that awe-inspiring requiem that vibrated o'er the ocean have been drowned in the waters of the deep, the instruments that gave them birth are silenced as the harps were silenced on the willow tree, but if the melody that was rehearsed could only reverberate through this land 'Nearer, My God, to Thee', and its echoes could be heard in these halls of legislation, and at every place where our rulers and representatives pass judgment and enact and administer laws, and at every home and fireside, from the mansions of the rich to the huts and hovels of the poor, and if we could be made to feel that there is a divine law of obedience and of adjustment, and of compensation that should demand our allegiance, far above the laws that we formulate in this presence, then, from the gloom of these fearful hours we shall pass into the dawn of a higher service and of a better day, and then, Mr. President, the lives that went down upon this fated night did not go down in vain.[5]

The inquiries themselves, including their motives, their approach to the proceedings, how the testimonies were conducted and their subsequent findings are not without their critics, and rightly so in some respects, but their recommendations were taken on board and incorporated into new and existing legislation, and the culture of the shipbuilding and seafaring communities. The *Titanic* disaster prompted four main changes in maritime legislation: the number of lifeboats aboard vessels; the extensive and compulsory use of wireless radio; more thorough procedures regarding ice; and building ships optimised for safety at every possible opportunity. It is important to note that the legislative changes passed were proposed mostly by lawmen, governmental employees and politicians who had very little on-sea experience. They were not officers or sailors. They were not mariners. What follows are the *proposed* changes.

Lifeboats

Both the British and US inquiries acknowledged that while the lifeboats had been lowered correctly, there had been too few lifeboats available, and they had not been filled to capacity in the way they should have been. This was in no small part due to inadequate lifeboat drills – part of which would have informed the crew that they could fit sixty-five to seventy persons in some of the boats, which should have prepared the crew to conduct the procedure thoroughly.

The British inquiry asserted that the number of lifeboats should be based on the number of persons, both passengers and crew, that the ship could accommodate and not based on the tonnage of the ship, which, up until this point, it had been. The sizes and types of these boats would depend upon the ship's method of storing them, and this decision would be made at the discretion of the Board of Trade. The British inquiry recommended that each boat should have the capacity number clearly marked upon it, and that it be fitted with a protective fender – a cushion-like device, either inflatable or non-inflatable, that would prevent the boat from being damaged by colliding with another boat or hitting the ship itself – to lower the risk of damage as the lifeboat was lowered. It also recommended that each boat should be fitted with a mechanical propulsion device to aid in power and navigation. In a case such as *Titanic*, this would enable the lifeboats to get as far away from the suction of the ship and the rough waves it caused as it sank.

The members of the British inquiry argued that more thorough inspections of lifeboats should be conducted by the Board of Trade, and that stricter regulation regarding the storage of the appropriate equipment one would need on a lifeboat should be enforced. The equipment would include the likes of compasses, provisions, lamps and pyrotechnic lamps for signalling other lifeboats or passing vessels that may aid in rescue. As one of the biggest issues with the sinking of *Titanic* was a lack of thoroughly trained men to man the lifeboats, every member of the crew should be trained and drilled – in lifeboats, fires and watertight door drills – before the ship set sail and, when possible, no less than once a week during the voyage. These drills would be recorded in the ship's log. They also recommended that crew members should be tested in boat work and pass before being signed off, and that a sufficient communication plan be developed and approved by the Board of Trade before the ship left port.

The US inquiry generally agreed, but it was highly critical of the British Board of Trade and what Barczewski refers to as its perceived arrogance and complacency regarding the disaster.[6] In the final report, the US inquiry found that the lack of emergency preparations and inadequate drills had left *Titanic*'s crew and passengers in 'a state of absolute unpreparedness' and criticised their response: 'no general alarm was given, no ship's officers formally assembled, no orderly routine was attempted, or organised system of safety begun.'[7] They also found that although no third-class passengers had been kept below or purposely prevented from reaching the lifeboats that night, the lack of organisation inadvertently led to a higher number of deaths amongst the third-class passengers. The US inquiry further argued that *Titanic*'s lifeboats themselves had not been properly tested and that the lack of lifeboats was the fault of the British Board of Trade, upon whom they placed most of the blame. They argued that this 'awful tragedy' was the direct result of their 'laxity of regulation and hasty inspection'.[8]

In its final report, the US inquiry recommended, like the British inquiry, that there should be sufficient lifeboats to accommodate everyone on board, and that boat drills should be carried out not only by the crew, but by passengers as well. They recommended that no fewer than four crew members should be assigned to each boat, and that they should be well drilled in lowering and rowing the boats no less than twice a month (considerably less than the British inquiry recommended). They agreed that these drills should be officially recorded in the ship's log.

They, like the British inquiry, recommended that crew should be assigned to lifeboats before the ship left port and that every crew member should know to which boat they had been assigned. They recommended this procedure be applied to passengers too, and that their assigned boat should be chosen based on the location of their rooms to maximise convenience and speed, and to minimise confusion and reduce the risk of chaos. These assigned boats, and the shortest route to them, they argued, should be posted in every stateroom.

The findings of the British and US inquires were incorporated into the International Convention for the Safety of Life at Sea (SOLAS) treaty of 1914. This treaty was the final result of a conference held in London in January 1914, attended by sixty-five countries. Several officials involved with *Titanic* were present, and it was evident that 'the ghost of *Titanic* hovered near, and the convention felt her influence'.[9] Although the treaty was not entered into force because of the outbreak of the First World War, it would provide the blueprint for the updated version that was drafted in 1929 and put into force in 1933, and has remained in force to this day, with updates made as and when required. With regards to lifeboats on board vessels, the International Convention for the Safety of Life at Sea outlined that:

- A vessel mustn't carry any more passengers than it can accommodate in its lifeboats
- Each lifeboat should be strong enough to be safely lowered into the ocean when fully loaded with passengers, crew, and the appropriate equipment
- A vessel must be issued with a safety certificate after a thorough investigation to determine if it meets all the safety requirements

Wireless Radio | The Radio Act 1912

One of the most important expert witnesses at both the British and US inquiries was Guglielmo Marconi, the Italian physicist and inventor who was responsible for transforming radio waves into wireless telegraph. During *Titanic*'s construction in Belfast, his company, Marconi's Wireless Telegraph, fitted the ship with its most powerful and modern wireless equipment and appointed two of its employees, Jack Phillips (Senior Wireless Operator) and Harold Bride (Junior Wireless Officer), to operate it during the maiden voyage. The radio proved extremely popular amongst the crew and passengers, and the two men operated it practically non-stop throughout the entire voyage.

The radio system on board *Titanic* played a crucial part in its story. It was via radio that Jack Phillips received ice warnings from several ships throughout the day on 14 April and another from *Mesaba* that night, which Lightoller told the British inquiry was accidently placed under a paperweight and forgotten about. It should be noted, however, that research by various historians dispute the accuracy of this claim, and it was fervently discredited by Harold Bride in a letter to Lightoller in 1936 in response to a snippet of his book published in the *Dundee Evening Telegraph*. In the letter, he said, 'Jack Phillips, the senior telegraphist of the Titanic, was one of the most skilful and experienced operators then in the service of the Marconi Company' and that:

> At the Board of Trade inquiry, which is recognised for all purposes as being officially correct, no proof was available that the *Mesaba* message was ever received aboard the *Titanic*. Had it been received, I say with all sincerity that Jack Phillips would have realised its importance and immediately communicated it to the bridge, for the mysteries of latitude and longitude were not confined to navigating officers.[10]

Regardless of the specifics of the situation on board *Titanic*, we can say with certainty that radio technology in 1912 was advancing but it was not perfect. Nearby ships jammed each other's signals, which was made all the more irritating by amateur radio operators clogging up the airwaves with meaningless nonsense that got in the way of important messages. When Phillips was in the middle of trying to send messages around 11 p.m., Cyril Evans, the wireless operator from *Californian*, called to warn him of ice but Phillips used a Marconi code – constant hitting of the letter D – to explain he had an emergency transmission and that the air had to remain clear so he could send his own messages out first. Some argue that Evans was told to shut up or keep out, but this is not true – a big thank you to Bruce Beveridge for providing clarification on this. The 'shut up', 'keep out', etc. description is related in the 1912 testimony and interviews with the people present at the time – it is not new. That is how the attitude of the transmission was described, but it is not to be taken as the *literal* communication transmitted – only that the continuous D means to keep the air clear for an emergency transmission so he could send his own messages out first. Evans went to bed shortly after this, leaving *Californian*'s wireless equipment unattended. Phillips was unaware of any real danger at this point, but missing the ice warning from *Californian* would prove to be another catastrophic factor in the *Titanic* tragedy.[11]

Around thirty-five minutes after the collision with the iceberg, with the damage and subsequent inescapable fate of *Titanic* confirmed by Thomas Andrews, Captain Smith commanded Phillips and Bride to send the distress call – 'CQD', a Marconi code whose powerful sound bled through lesser companies' signals – and read out the ship's position. A Newfoundland telegraph station heard the distress call but could not make sense of it due to chaos on the airwaves, so they were unable to assist. Nearby ships were alerted to the tragedy, including *Carpathia*, and raced towards *Titanic*, but they were too far away to get there in time. With water quickly flooding the ship, Bride told Phillips to try a new distress call that had been suggested at the 1906 International Convention on Wireless Telegraphy. Phillips and Bride continued to send out the distress calls until around 2.10 a.m., when *Titanic*'s electricity finally gave out. Released from their duties, the pair fled in hopes of survival. Bride reached Collapsible Lifeboat B and was eventually rescued, alongside crewmates and passengers, by *Carpathia*. Phillips did not survive and his body was never recovered.

Although the efforts of Phillips and Bride were clearly heroic, it was felt by both the British and US inquiry committees that more could have been done to save more people that night. Guglielmo Marconi was brought to both inquiries as an expert witness to verify if this was true or not. Marconi was questioned on day twenty-six of the British inquiry and days one, six and ten of the US inquiry. He was cooperative and answered their questions to the best of his ability, assuring them that the equipment on board was modern and up to date, and that his employees had done the best they could under the circumstances. Marconi's role in the radio communication on board the *Titanic* did not go unnoticed by the survivors, who presented him with a gold medal in gratitude for his invention saving as many as it did.

The main concern of both inquiries after this line of questioning became the confusion that resulted from the mixed communication received by those on land while the survivors were on board *Carpathia*. Nearby ships, smaller boats and amateur radio operators along the coast received conflicting and confusing messages from the wireless communications being sent out. One of the most devastating interpretations that was passed on was that *Titanic* was safe and was being towed to Halifax for repairs, with no casualties. Part of one of the messages that was sent out was worded: 'passengers will probably land there Wednesday all safe.'[12] It is probable that the sender, likely a White Star Line employee, meant that the rescued passengers on board *Carpathia* were safe, but this was not made clear within the message. Newspapers in the US and the UK quickly got wind of this and began reporting that *Titanic* had not sank and that everyone on board was safe. The US inquiry committee was furious about this inaccurate reporting and condemned the individual who passed on the miscommunication to the press, stating that 'whoever sent this message under the circumstances, is guilty of the most reprehensible conduct'.[13] The identity of the sender was never confirmed.

Once this confusion was cleared up and it was confirmed that *Titanic* had indeed sank, *Carpathia*'s sole wireless operator, Harold Thomas Cottam, was inundated with hundreds of messages enquiring about the fate of loved ones. Cottam was so exhausted by the end of that first night that Bride actually assisted him – despite having spent most of the day in the infirmary with frostbitten feet – in responding to as many personal messages as possible, ignoring governmental messages, including one from President Taft.

This combination of the wireless equipment's role in the sending of distress signals during the sinking of *Titanic*, and the sending and receiving of confusing and misleading communication, as well as prioritising which messages to respond to, led the British and US inquiries to conclude that more thorough procedures and regulation for wireless technology on board ships needed to be enforced.

The British inquiry insisted that all ships should be installed with wireless telegraphy and that trained operators, the number of which depended upon the size of the vessel, should work to ensure a continuous service day and night. They also supported the suggestion of the International Conference on Wireless Telegraphy, which recommended that a silent chamber for receiving messages should form part of the installation to minimise confusion and miscommunication.

The US inquiry went even further, incorporating their suggestions into what would become the Radio Act of 1912. All wireless operators, they asserted, should be officially licensed and adhere to particular band-widths. They recommended that an operator be on duty at all times to receive any messages coming through, regardless of the time of day, and that additional auxiliary power sources should be installed wherever practical to ensure the wireless was working at all times. Direct communication, particularly that relating to the safety of the vessel, should be conducted via telephone, a messenger, or a voice tube to the crew on the bridge, depending on the size of the vessel and the equipment available. Ships should maintain contact with nearby vessels at all times, alongside any coastal ones in their vicinity. They also recommended that legislation regarding the security and privacy of messages be enacted to prevent amateur operators from clogging up the lines, communicating falsities and gaining access to sensitive information. Amateurs would be permitted to listen to messages but not broadcast their own.

Further aiding the Radio Act of 1912 was the Wireless Telegraphy Convention, which took place in London at the close of 1912. The findings of the inquiries helped the convention develop its own internationally agreed regulations, which included:

- 500kc/s frequency being made compulsory for all vessels equipped with wireless technology
- All ships having emergency transmitters and receivers powered by batteries rather than electricity, so in the case of an emergency where the electricity was cut, messages were still possible
- The establishment of formal working hours for the wireless operators to ensure no messages were missed and to prevent miscommunication
- The reinforcement of 'SOS' as the international signal for distress
- Formal certification of wireless operators to ensure they were sufficiently trained and understood their responsibilities
- Silent periods: ships had to cease wireless operations and listen only for distress signals
- Having at least one lifeboat carry emergency wireless equipment

These measures were also incorporated into the International Convention for the Safety of Life at Sea, which stated that vessels with fifty or more on board should be fitted with radiographic installation (except those whose regular journeys did not exceed 150 miles from its home coast) and that the radiographic installations should be capable of transmitting clearly perceptible messages and signals over a range of at least 100 sea miles, under normal conditions.

International Ice Patrol

The British inquiry concluded that *Titanic* sank from colliding with an iceberg at a dangerously fast speed, and that Captain Smith had been negligent in his decision to not slow down or change course, despite being warned of ice in *Titanic*'s vicinity several times. The report noted that given the:

> … knowledge of the proximity of ice which the Master had, two courses were open to him: The one was to stand well to the southward instead of turning up to a westerly course; the other was to reduce speed materially as night approached. He did neither. The alteration of the course at 5.50p.m. was so insignificant that it cannot be attributed to any intention to avoid ice. This deviation brought the vessel back to within about two miles of the customary route before 11.30 p.m. And there was certainly no reduction of speed.[14]

When considering why this had been the case, the writer of the report explained:

> It was shown that for many years past, indeed, for a quarter of a century or more, the practice of liners using this track when in the vicinity of ice at night had been in clear weather to keep the course, to maintain the speed and to trust to a sharp look-out to enable them to avoid the danger. This practice, it was said, had been justified by experience, no casualties having resulted from it. I accept the evidence as to the practice and as to the immunity from casualties which is said to have accompanied it. But the event has proved the practice to be bad. Its root is probably to be found in competition and in the desire of the public for quick passages rather than in the judgment of navigators. But unfortunately experience appeared to justify it.[15]

While the British inquiry did agree that Captain Smith had done what any other man in his position would have done, it concluded that it was a catastrophic mistake that cost the lives of 1,500 people. The inquiry recommended in its final report that:

Instruction should begin in all Steamship Companies' Regulations that when ice is reported in or near the track the ship should proceed in the dark hours at a moderate speed or alter her course so as to go well clear of the danger zone.[16]

In the section of the report entitled 'Account of Ship's Journey Across the Atlantic / Messages Received / Disaster Action That Should Have Been Taken', Lord Mersey defended Captain Smith's actions,[17] justifying why he did what he did on the night of the sinking. He also expressed hope that a similar situation would not reoccur:

In these circumstances I am not able to blame Captain Smith. He had not the experience which his own misfortune has afforded to those whom he has left behind, and he was doing only that which other skilled men would have done in the same position. It was suggested at the bar that he was yielding to influences which ought not to have affected him; that the presence of Mr. Ismay on board and the knowledge which he perhaps had of a conversation between Mr. Ismay and the Chief Engineer [Bell] at Queenstown about the speed of the ship and the consumption of coal probably induced him to neglect precautions which he would otherwise have taken. But I do not believe this. The evidence shows that he was not trying to make any record passage or indeed any exceptionally quick passage.[18] He was not trying to please anybody, but was exercising his own discretion in the way he thought best. He made a mistake, a very grievous mistake, but one in which, in face of the practice and of past experience, negligence cannot be said to have had any part; and in the absence of negligence it is, in my opinion, impossible to fix Captain Smith with blame. It is, however, to be hoped that the last has been heard of the practice and that for the future it will be abandoned for what we now know to be more prudent and wiser measures. What was a mistake in the case of the *Titanic* would without doubt be negligence in any similar case in the future.[19]

The British inquiry also argued that the ship's officers were at fault in their complacency, including Second Officer Lightoller, who was sure he would see ice in time to avoid any complications. He recalled a conversation he had on the night of the sinking, revealing that he 'judged [he] should see [an iceberg] with sufficient distinctness', and that despite the flat calm, he was sure there would be 'a certain amount of light from the bergs' and that they would be able to make out the iceberg's outlines in enough time to divert any danger. Lightoller relayed a message to the lookouts in the crow's nest to 'keep a sharp look-out for ice, particularly small ice and growlers' until daylight, and stayed on the bridge until the end of his watch at 10 p.m. to look for ice himself.[20]

Despite Lightoller passing on the possibility of ice to William Murdoch when their watch switched, and Murdoch being aware of the possibility even more commencing his watch, the ship still struck a large iceberg and sank as a result. While the British inquiry did acknowledge that not seeing the iceberg from a distance may have been possible even with competent look-outs at the crow's nest and bridge, which was supported by evidence given by *Carpathia*'s Captain Rostron, the British inquiry still felt that the officers could have done more to prevent the collision with the iceberg. The US inquiry agreed, finding that:

... no general discussion took place among the officers; no conference was called to consider these warnings; no heed was given to them. The speed was not relaxed, the lookout was not increased, and the only vigilance displayed by the officer of the watch was by instructions to the lookouts to keep 'a sharp lookout for ice'.[21]

While the legislative changes discussed above were just the proposals, not what ultimately became law, the findings and conclusions of the both the British and US inquiries were crucial factors in how the issue of ice was approached in the International Convention for the Safety of Life at Sea treaty of 1914. Article 8 of the treaty stated that:

The master of every vessel which meets with dangerous ice, or a dangerous derelict is bound to communicate the information by all the means of communication at his disposal to the vessels in the vicinity, and also to the competent authorities at first point of coast with which he can communicate. Transmission of messages respecting ice and derelicts is free of cost to the vessel concerned.[22]

Article 10 stated, 'When ice is reported on, or near, his course, the master of every vessel is bound to proceed at night at a moderate speed, or to alter his course so as to go well clear of the danger zone'.[23] In a letter to the then US president, Woodrow Wilson, Chairman J.W. Alexander explained that Article 10, in particular, was 'a most important rule' and would 'result in greater safety to navigation than prescribing fixed Governmental trans-Atlantic lanes, because, no matter where the ice may suddenly appear, the master of every vicinity must either go at moderate speed or leave the vicinity at once'.[24]

The conclusions drawn from the inquiries into the *Titanic* disaster and the subsequent new legislation that was passed concerning ice led to the founding of the International Ice Patrol in 1912. The following information was kindly provided by Dee Ryan-Meister:

When the international patrol was formed in 1912, ships were relied on heavily to navigate the waters with regard to locating icebergs. After the Second World War, planes were used to monitor the icebergs in Iceberg Alley (during ice season when the risk of iceberg collisions is greatest, 1 February–31 July). In recent years satellites have been used more frequently, with a vision to rely mainly on satellites to monitor the North Atlantic for icebergs in the near future. The US Coast Guard-International Ice Patrol was located in Connecticut, but moved to Maryland, USA, in 2021.

Every year, except for during the Second World War and in 2020 due to the COVID 19 pandemic, a ceremony is held by the Ice Patrol each Spring when schedule allows (late March to late April), alternating between US Home Base and Halifax, Nova Scotia, in memory of the *Titanic* victims. After the formal ceremony, in which wreaths are blessed, the wreaths are transported by air and released over the wreck site. Wreaths have been provided by the Titanic International Society, the Titanic Society of Atlantic Canada and the Titanic Historical Society, as well as historical organisations and descendants.

The dates below, except for one, represent ceremonies held in Halifax, NS (2016 and 2018: Fairview Lawn Cemetery; 2022 and 2024: Local Council of Women Halifax – George Wright House):

- 30 March 2016: four wreaths
- 4 April 2018: four wreaths
- 14 April 2021 (US): six wreaths
- 22 April 2022: four wreaths
- 11 April 2024: four wreaths

Designed with Safety in Mind

While *Titanic* did have several safety innovations – including its double-bottom, watertight compartments, sub-division and modern electronic watertight doors – that aided the escaping crew and passengers during the sinking, it was agreed at both the British and US inquiries that *all* ships should incorporate these kind of advanced safety features to avoid a repeat of the *Titanic* tragedy. This applied to already existing ships, ships that were in the process of being constructed and any new ships that were built from 1912 onwards.

The British inquiry recommended five key changes to be made (the following is taken directly from the final report):[25]

1. Newly appointed Bulkhead Committee should enquire and report, among other matters, on the desirability and practicability of providing ships with (*a.*) a double skin carried up above the waterline; or, as an alternative, with (*b.*) a longitudinal, vertical, watertight bulkhead on each side of the ship, extending as far forward and as far aft as convenient; or (*c.*) with a combination of (*a.*) and (*b.*). Any one of the three (*a.*), (*b.*) and (*c.*) to be in addition to watertight transverse bulkheads.

2. The Committee should also enquire and report as to the desirability and practicability of fitting ships with (*a.*) a deck or decks at a convenient distance or distances above the waterline which shall be watertight throughout a part or the whole of the ship's length; and should in this connection report upon (*b.*) the means by which the

necessary openings in such deck or decks should be made water-tight, whether by watertight doors or watertight trunks or by any other and what means.

3. The Committee should consider and report generally on the practicability of increasing the protection given by subdivision; the object being to secure that the ship shall remain afloat with the greatest practicable proportion of her length in free communication with the sea.

4. When the Committee has reported upon the matters before mentioned, the Board of Trade should take the report into their consideration and to the extent to which they approve of it should seek Statutory powers to enforce it in all newly built ships, but with a discretion to relax the requirements in special cases where it may seem right to them to do so.

5. The Board of Trade should be empowered by the Legislature to require the production of the designs and specifications of all ships in their early stages of construction and to direct such amendments of the same as may be thought necessary and practicable for the safety of life at sea in ships. (This should apply to all passenger carrying ships.)

The US inquiry also recommended changing ships' structural requirements. They suggested that ships carrying 100 passengers or more should:

> ... have a watertight skin inboard of the outside plating, extending not less than 10 percent of the load draft above the full-load waterline, either in the form of an inner bottom or of longitudinal watertight bulkheads, and this construction should extend from the forward collision bulkhead over not less than two-thirds of the length of the ship.[26]

Incorporating this double bottom into a ship's design would mean that if a ship collided with an object, be that another ship or an iceberg, the water would only fill a small part of the ship's interior. Granted, this would depend on the extent of the damage, but it would vastly improve a ship's chances of not sinking, or at least it prevent it from sinking long enough to rescue passengers and crew.

The US inquiry also agreed that the height of the bulkheads should be raised to prevent water spilling into other parts of the ship, as was the case with *Titanic*. Its bulkhead doors extended upwards to E Deck (10ft/3m above the waterline) but as the ship was pulled downwards, substantial amounts of water were able to spill into the other compartments, which dragged the ship down and down until it split in the middle. Higher bulkheads would prevent this. The US inquiry also concluded that the bulkheads be:

> … so spaced that any two adjacent compartments of the ship may be flooded without destroying the floatability or stability of the ship. Watertight transverse bulkheads should extend from side to side of the ship, attaching to the outside shell. The transverse bulkheads forward and abaft the machinery spaces should be continued watertight vertically to the uppermost continuous structural deck. The uppermost continuous structural deck should be fitted watertight.[27]

Water pressure was also taken into consideration. The US inquiry recommended that all watertight bulkheads should be able to withstand water pressure 'equal to 5 feet more than the full height of the bulkhead'[28] and that during testing phase, the designers should use actual water pressure to ensure this worked in practice, not just in theory.

The increased number of lifeboats on board ships, the creation of the Radio Act of 1912 and the International Ice Patrol, and the changes in ships' designs to make them safer were the main takeaways from the British and US inquiries, but both also made more general recommendations that were taken into consideration.[29]

The British inquiry recommended that:

- A police system should be devised on all ships to ensure control of the crew and passengers during an emergency situation, such as a collision or inevitable sinking.
- All steamship companies should incorporate into their legislation specific instructions regarding what to do when ice was sighted in a ship's path, or close enough to a ship to be of significant risk. The inquiry recommended that the captain should steer clear of the

danger and use moderate speed at night, to ensure no repeat of the *Titanic* tragedy occurred.

- All lookouts should undergo sight tests at regular intervals (while the lookouts on *Titanic* were not to blame at all for the disaster, for they were merely assisting the officers on watch, this suggestion is fair and understandable).

- In light of the issues caused by nearby *Californian* not coming to *Titanic's* aid during the sinking, all ship captains should be made aware that not aiding a ship in distress when it is possible to do so is a misdemeanour under the Maritime Conventions Act of 1911 (again, like the lookouts, the crew of *Californian* are not to blame, but they could played a much more substantial role in the tragedy that could have saved more lives).

- Common laws regarding ice management, the number of lifeboats, the installation of radio telegraphy equipment, ship construction and design, and the use of searchlights, should be agreed upon. During the International Sea Convention, which used the findings of the *Titanic* inquiries to inform its decisions, it was also agreed that common laws regarding the use of coloured rockets as distress signals be established thoroughly. *Titanic* used white rockets as she was sinking.[30] While the crew of *Californian* did see the white rockets, the intervals with which they were launched was ambiguous to the *Californian* crew, which was part of their reasoning for not going to its aid. They were unaware of the dire circumstances of the situation.

The US inquiry made similar recommendations, including emphasising the importance of searchlights to aid in detecting ice and firing rockets for distress purposes only, but its main concern was inspection. The inquiry stated that no ship would be licensed to carry passengers from US ports unless it conformed to the legislation set forth by their laws, and that inspection certificates of foreign ships should be common practice to maximise the safety of those on board.

Renewed Interest in *Titanic*: Cinematic Adaptations, Salvage Proposals and the Discovery of the Wreck (1912–85)

The *Titanic* tragedy captured people's attention immediately following the sinking. Songs and poems were composed, art was created and numerous books were published in quick succession to capitalise on the public's interest in the disaster. Its appeal, Jack Winocour notes, lay in the combination of 'the inevitability of a Greek tragedy with the ominous warning of the medieval morality play'.[1] Filmmakers understood the power of the story and began making films right away. An American silent film was made, *Saved from the Titanic*,[2] starring Dorothy Gibson, an actress and one of the survivors, less than a month after the sinking (the film was sadly lost in 1914 in a studio fire). For her costume, she wore the same clothes she had worn on the night of the sinking. The film was heavily criticised by journalists and audiences for capitalising on the disaster so soon, but it didn't stop two more films from being made that year. The Germans made *In Nacht und Eis* (*Night and Ice*),[3] a thirty-five-minute short film with innovative uses of tinted film to enhance the spectator's experience of the disaster (the stokers' scenes were tinted red, the night scenes tinted blue), and the French made *La Hantise* (*The Obsession*),[4] a twenty-four-minute short film focusing on a palm reader warning the wife of a passenger not to let him board the ship. A Danish film, *Atlantis*,[5] was released a year later. Though it was based on a novel, the similarities to *Titanic's* sinking were evident and the film was criticised for lacking taste.

Among the artistic and cultural responses to the tragedy, there were also talks almost immediately to salvage the wreck. According to John P. Eaton and Charles A. Haas, authors of *Titanic: Destination Disaster: The Legends and the Reality*, a consortium was formed by the surviving family members of the wealthier victims of the *Titanic*, including the Astors, the Wideners and the Guggenheims, to raise the ship.[6] They contracted Merritt-Chapman & Scott, a New York-based marine salvage and construction company, for the job. Merritt-Chapman & Scott was highly respected among the marine salvage community and was considered the ultimate authority on salvaging. In fact, it was this company that was contracted to salvage the wreck of SS *Florida* mentioned in Chapter 1; while it concluded that salvage was not possible, it is clear from the reception its decision received from the New York newspapers at the time that its expert opinion was decidedly valued. Much to the disappointment of the hastily formed consortium, Merritt-Chapman & Scott decided that salvaging *Titanic* was not feasible due to the pressure from the immense depths divers would have to go to reach its final resting place. A lack of advanced submarine technology at the time was also a contributing factor.

In March of 1914, innovative architect Charles Smith, who pioneered architectural designs that enhanced cleanliness and ventilation in American schools, proposed an idea. A custom unmanned submarine could be designed to feature electromagnets that, once the sub reached the hull of the ship, would attach themselves to the ship and release a buoy to indicate the location of the wreck. Once they were sure of its location, more magnets would be attached and the ship could be raised with winches attached to several strong barges. Some *Titanic* scholars consider this idea to be one of the most viable options for raising the ship and respect Smith for his idea, but it's highly doubtful this would have worked in practice because, at the time, the condition of the ship — which was split in two with an enormous debris field in the middle — was unknown and funding would have been incredibly difficult to secure.

People were captivated by the tragedy, but interest quickly fell away once an even bigger tragedy struck the world: the First World War (1914–18). Following that, the decadence of the Roaring Twenties encouraged those who had been traumatised and impacted by said war to look forward, not backward, and interest in *Titanic* faded to almost nothing, except among the survivors and the most avid of historians and *Titanic* buffs. The Great Depression of the 1930s destroyed the economy of the industrialised Western world and plunged people into abject poverty: no one cares about a lost ship at the bottom of the ocean when they can't feed their own family.

An idea for a lavish film about the disaster was considered in 1936 by Hollywood film producer David O. Selznick, whose company Selznick International Pictures produced Golden Age of Hollywood classics including *Gone with the Wind* (1939), *A Star is Born* (1937) and *Spellbound* (1945). Selznick wanted his version of *Titanic* to be directed by Alfred Hitchcock to mark his Hollywood debut, but the film never materialised. Selznick was threatened with various lawsuits and efforts from shipping companies to stop the production. It's likely that shipping companies didn't want the negative press: depicting a massive disaster at sea to millions of people would not be good for business. The British Chamber of Shipping wrote to the White Star Line board in 1938 demanding that they stop production. The reasons for abandoning the project remain unclear, but no culturally significant film about *Titanic* emerged until the middle of the Second World War (1939–45). This time, it did not come from Hollywood.

The first re-emergence of public interest in *Titanic* came about when a banned German propaganda film from the Second World War entitled simply *Titanic* was discovered.[7] Spearheaded by Joseph Goebbels, the Nazi party's chief propagandist, the film depicts the factual elements of the story – the ship's officers and famous passengers, hitting the iceberg and the subsequent sinking of the ship – but it leans heavily into a narrative that suited the Nazis' ideology; namely, that the sinking of *Titanic* was the result of British hubris, greed and pride. One of the biggest takeaways from the sinking was the idea of upstanding 'Britishness', a dignified way of dying, of 'going down like gentlemen'. Although this famous line was supposedly said by an American, the millionaire industrialist Benjamin Guggenheim who perished during the sinking, it quickly became part of *Titanic*'s lore. This idea of the bravery of the British was further supported by survivors who claimed that Captain Smith shouted, 'Be British, boys, be British!' to his crew as the ship went down.

Goebbels turned this notion on its head by portraying the British on board *Titanic* as villains and the German characters as heroes, including a fictional first officer called Petersen. The White Star Line executives were crooked and greedy – Bruce Ismay in particular – caring more about the speed and luxury of the ship than the safety of its passengers, and the officers were incompetent. The British passengers were portrayed as entitled, materialistic and cowardly, creating a stampede for the lifeboats as soon as it became clear that the ship was beyond saving. We know this to be untrue and, in fact, a behavioural economist at Queensland University of Technology, David Savage, actually found that British passengers on board *Titanic* were 7 per cent more likely to die simply because of British sensibilities; British passengers queued for the lifeboats rather than rushing towards them, as other nationalities did.[8]

The film cost the Third Reich a fortune to make ($180 million in today's money) and it had numerous production difficulties, including its original director going on a tirade about the failures of the Nazi regime and being fired and arrested for his outburst. (He was found hanged in cell by his own suspenders in a supposed suicide. Rumours circulated within the German film community that his suicide was staged, and that he had actually been strangled by Gestapo agents who then strung up his corpse, all under direct orders from Goebbels). The film was finished in November 1943, but it was not screened in any theatre in Germany or seen by German audiences. Some sources claim that high-ranking Nazi officials believed the film's dark content would be too distressing for German civilians who were already at the mercy of the horrors brought on by Allied bombing, while others claim that Goebbels was dissatisfied with the final result. According to journalist George Bass, Goebbels also 'feared that a film about a doomed vessel captained by incompetents might send the wrong message about the German war effort, which by 1943 was struggling' and that he 'objected to Petersen's recklessness, which flew in the face of the Nazis' *Führerprinzip*, a requirement to obey orders'.[9] There was a myth that the film was banned by Goebbels and was not shown in German theatres until after the war, when it was dubbed into Russian and shown in parts of the Soviet-controlled Eastern Bloc during the Cold War to support the Soviets' anti-capitalist ideology. However, research conducted by Robert E. Peck found that while the film was temporarily shelved during the war, it was not banned until after the war, at the request of the British, between 1950 and 1955.[10]

The 1950s saw two more cinematic portrayals of the *Titanic* disaster. The first was a melodrama made in 1953 staring Clifton Webb and Barbara Stanwyck.[11] Distributed by 20th Century Fox and directed by Jean Negulesco, its plot follows the stories of several fictional passengers on board *Titanic*. The screenwriters – Charles Brackett, Richard L. Breen, and Walter Reisch – were called into the office of Darryl F. Zanuck, the head of 20th Century Fox, who said that he had Clifton Webb under contract and that he wanted him to be given a chance to show his artistic range as a character actor. 'I now want to do something big, and in colour,' he told them.[12] Reisch pitched the idea of a *Titanic* story to Zanuck, with the intention of having Webb star as one of the ill-fated multimillionaires on board. According to *Interviews with Screenwriters of the 1940s and 1950s*, a fascinating collection edited by Pat McGilligan, Reisch wanted the film to be informed by real-life accounts from survivors, which he would get from old newspapers in New York and London. '60% truth, completely documentary,' he claimed. Many lines of dialogue, he said, were 'drawn almost exactly from life' and he reflected on the glee from the applauding audience who recognised the famous line 'no cause for alarm' from the newspaper accounts.[13]

Despite using real historical sources, however, the film is rife with inaccuracies. Some were included intentionally for the sake of an engaging story – though the actual story had enough of that already – while the decisions behind others are harder to gauge. Many people were irritated with the inaccuracies. Here is a snapshot of the details that were changed, or were just straight-up wrong:

- *Titanic* was not sold out as stated; it was underbooked in reality and passengers from other White Star Line ships were moved to *Titanic* to fill out the passenger list.
- The iceberg was correctly shown to hit *Titanic*'s starboard side, but the underwater shot shows the iceberg on the port side.

- Bruce Ismay was excluded from the film altogether, despite his presence being a crucial part of the story.
- *Titanic*'s officers did not wear Royal Navy uniforms on board; they had a White Star Line regulated uniform that they were required to wear.
- Isidor and Ida Straus boarded at Southampton, not Cherbourg as they were shown to do in the film.
- The ship's watertight doors closed horizontally in the film, but the real doors closed vertically (except deck E and F).
- The film added siren sounds to the sinking – the real ship did not have sirens.
- The ship's band did play *Nearer My God to Thee* as the ship went down, but there is no record of passengers standing on deck to sing its chorus, as portrayed in the film.
- The lookouts' names were changed – the real lookouts were named Frederick Fleet and Reginald Lee but, in the film, they were changed to Symons and Devlin.
- *Titanic*'s funnels collapsed during the sinking – this is not shown in the film.
- The film showed all lifeboats being launched successfully – one of the collapsible boats, Collapsible Lifeboat B, in reality, was not launched correctly and floated away upside down. A handful of survivors were able to climb on top of the upside-down boat, including Second Officer Lightoller and Charles Joughin.
- The ship did not sink as fast as shown in the film – we know that it hit the iceberg at 11.40 p.m. and sank beneath the water at 2.20 a.m.
- The ship in the film sank in one piece – we can forgive the film-makers for this one, as the state of the ship was unconfirmed until its discovery three decades later (eyewitnesses did attest that the ship split in two, but it could not be proven).

Despite these inaccuracies, the film was widely praised, winning the Academy Award for Best Original Screenplay and being nominated for Best Art Direction. Its success showed that there was a renewing interest in the story of *Titanic*, making it the ideal time for historian Walter Lord to publish what is still considered one of the definitive texts about the tragedy, *A Night to Remember*, in 1955.[14] Stephen Biel, author of *Down with the Old Canoe: A Cultural History of the Titanic Disaster*, wrote, 'Nobody deserves more credit for this rediscovery than Walter Lord', whose non-fiction account gave the disaster 'its fullest retelling since 1912 and made it speak to modern audiences and a new set of post-war concerns'.[15]

Lord had been fascinated by *Titanic* since his boyhood, in no small part thanks to his experience of travelling on *Olympic* when he was just 9 years old. According to Biel, Lord would prowl around the ship trying to imagine 'such a huge thing' going down.[16] By age 10 or 11, Lord was obsessively drawing pictures of *Titanic* and had started collecting memorabilia. *Titanic* refused to release its hold on him, and he felt compelled in his adulthood to become what Julian Fellowes in his foreword of *A Night to Remember*'s centenary edition calls the 'Chief Chronicler of the *Titanic*'.[17] Lord interviewed sixty-three survivors, noting down their specific memories from that night, and complied them into a factual, highly visual and personal narrative. Highlighting individual stories in disasters such as *Titanic* was becoming a popular characteristic of television reporting, which was booming in the 1950s, so Lord's narrative style was perfect for modern audiences. *The New York Times* said of Lord's approach: 'How people acted is the core of Mr. Lord's account, and explains its fascination, a pull as powerful in its ways as the last downward plunge of the ship itself.'[18]

Although there were already fifty books in the Library of Congress alone, none of them, according to Brian Lavery, 'matched the immediacy and impact of Lord's work'.[19] The book was short and easy to read. Lord spoke of its style as breezy and its form as fresh. Told from multiple perspectives – from White Star Line officers to the multimillionaires in first class, to the ordinary folk of third class – it offered a dramatic, heart-breaking almost minute-by-minute overview of the sinking in a way that had never been accomplished before. And, most importantly, Brian Lavery reflected, it 'put the ageing story of the *Titanic* back in the forefront of the public consciousness'.[20] A successful marketing campaign by publisher Henry Holt saw the book sell over 60,000 copies in less than three months. By March 1956, it had sold 100,000 copies. This was thanks to an NBC Live television play of the same name, narrated by Claude Rains, which attracted 28 million viewers.

Lord published his work at precisely the right time. Without it, Lavery reflected, 'it is quite likely that the *Titanic* would be almost forgotten now, or known only to specialists, if Walter Lord had not researched and published his most famous book at just the right moment'.[21]

After acquiring copies of *A Night to Remember*, Belfast-born producer William MacQuitty and director Roy Ward Baker decided to obtain the film rights. MacQuitty was drawn to the story not only because of his Belfast background, but also because of his vivid memories of witnessing *Titanic*'s launch at Harland & Wolff in 1911. In order to stay as true to the facts as possible, Lord was made a consultant throughout the production, and, alongside using action and dialogue lifted directly from the book, the production team reached out to several survivors, who were consulted as technical advisors throughout the making of the film. These included passengers Lawrence Beesley and Edith Russell, and White Star Line officer Joseph Boxhall. Second Officer Lightoller's widow Sylvia was also consulted, and even met with actor Kenneth More, who portrayed her husband in *A Night to Remember*.[22] Sylvia was particularly appreciative of the film, telling *The Guardian* that 'the film is really the truth and has not been embroidered'.[23] The visual aesthetic of the film was also as accurate as possible – it used real blueprints from *Titanic* to create thirty sets.

The film does make several changes to the events for the sake of the screenplay, including limiting the on-screen time of American passengers or portraying them as British, removing certain passengers altogether, such as J.J. Astor and the Duff-Gordons, the dramatisation of certain storylines or individual's actions, particularly Lightoller's as he is, arguably, the main character in this ensemble cast, and the ship not splitting in two (this one is fair, as the split was not confirmed until the wreck was discovered thirty years later). It also has some inaccuracies, though not as many as the 1953 production. Some examples include:

- The opening shows *Titanic* being christened but White Star Line did not approve of this practice, so the real ship was never christened.
- The painting in the first-class smoking room is one of New York Harbor rather than Plymouth Sound, but this was believed to be accurate at the time; Lord had reported as such in his book, but acknowledged the mistake in a documentary about the making of the film in 1993.

- Lifeboat 1 was depicted as being one of the last to leave the ship, whereas in reality it was one of the first.
- *Titanic*'s B Deck was not an open promenade.
- *Titanic*'s Junior Wireless Operator Harold Bride is shown attending a service on *Carpathia* after the survivors were rescued, but he did not attend as he was in the ship's hospital, unconscious, at the time.

Regardless, *A Night to Remember* is considered by historians and *Titanic* enthusiasts to be the most historically accurate cinematic depiction of the tragedy.[24] While only moderately successful commercially, it received critical acclaim, much more so than *Titanic* of 1953. Critic Bosley Crowther at *The New York Times* praised it for being a 'brilliant and moving account' of the tragedy, and for its 'tense, exciting, and supremely awesome drama'.[25]

This renewed public interest in *Titanic* sparked more salvage proposals. While there had been a previous attempt to salvage the wreck in 1953 by Risdon Beazley Ltd, a salvage company based in Southampton, it was unsuccessful and went widely unnoticed by other salvagers and the wider public. It was not until the 1960s that a very famous proposal was announced. The Titanic Salvage Company was formed to manage a proposal by Douglas Woolley. A hosiery worker who spent his days dying nylon stockings, Woolley proposed that *Titanic* could be located using a bathyscaphe, a self-propelled deep-sea submersible that could dive more than 10,000m and be raised using inflated nylon balloons attached to the ship's hull. It's important to note here that Woolley had absolutely no knowledge of oceanography, nor a formal education in science, and zero experience with deep-sea salvage expeditions. All he had was, as Lord puts it, was 'an obsession with the *Titanic*'.[26]

The reasoning behind the nylon balloons was the material's strength and durability, as well as its ability to adapt to external environments, which Woolley had a lot of experience with. His goal was to transform the raised wreck into a tourist attraction in Liverpool, with a chapel inside so visitors could pay their respects to all the souls who were lost. According to John Eaton and Charles Haas, authors of the 1987 book *Titanic: Destination Disaster – The Legends and the Reality*, this idea was considered a legitimate possibility and financial backing was offered by

Titanic–Tresor, a group of invested businessmen (some sources say it was three men, others as many as ten but we have no concrete evidence of how many were involved) based in West Berlin.[27] A boat was even promised to get Woolley out to the last known location of the wreck. A pair of Hungarian inventors also showed interest in the project, proposing that they could raise the wreck using plastic bags filled with hydrogen created by the electrolysis of the seawater.

The proposal was abandoned, however, when calculations revealed that it would take up to ten years to inflate the balloons with enough gas to overcome the intense water pressure at the bottom of the ocean – they would have required 85,000yds worth![3] And, as it turned out, the boat promised to Woolley was completely useless – it was a rust bucket hidden away in Newlyn, Cornwall, so old that the fishermen of the area had no faith in its ability to even make it out of the harbour, never mind get all the way to the North Atlantic.

But Woolley's interest in *Titanic* did not die with his proposal. In fact, he doubled down, claiming in 1981 that he actually owned the wreck itself, and he continues to make this claim (one of the last interviews with Woolley was in 2016 and, at the time, he would have been in his early eighties, so it is unclear if he is still with us). He does, however, have a LinkedIn profile, where he lists himself as the owner of *Titanic*'s salvage rights (and those of RMS *Queen Elizabeth*, which sank in 1972 in Hong Kong) and outlines his goals for the world to see:

Once the *Titanic* has been raised and towed under the water to a Loch in Scotland, where both parts will be joined to the best of our ability and cleaned. It will then be raised and sprayed with silicon to prevent further rust forming. The *Titanic* will then be towed to a dry dock in Liverpool UK, and it will be there that the *Titanic* and the *QE1* will be made safe enough for the public to view and then be made into a museum, and this will be the world's best tourist attraction. There will also be a chapel on board the *Titanic*, for any members of the public to pay their respects to the lives lost back in 1912. What we want companies to realise is that, whoever helps and backs the project, not only will the company receive a percentage of all profits gained by this, but will also have their mark in the history books.[28]

He tried various financial plans to fund the salvage of the ship, including crowdfunding and a supposed television production company that wanted to make a documentary about it, but he has never accumulated enough financial backing to support it. Most *Titanic* historians reject Woolley's claim to the wreck. One of the most prolific *Titanic* historians, Brian Ticehurst, described him as 'a lovely man but he is a dreamer who loves the publicity these stories bring him' and was dismissive of his ownership claim, commenting, 'Does he own the *Titanic*? Possibly, but no one has ever bothered to dispute his claim anywhere because it is just not worth disputing. He is a dreamer who is best left alone to dream.'[29] Ownership of the wreck remains a controversial issue as there is no single clear answer, and even interpretations of maritime law regarding issues such as this vary greatly depending upon the person you ask. At any rate, Woolley is certainly not the owner of the wreck and his dream of raising it will go unrealised.[30]

There were various salvage proposals in the 1970s, too, just a decade before the wreck was discovered, but they were even more ludicrous and impractical than Woolley's. In his follow-up work, *The Night Lives On*,[31] Walter Lord details a mad proposal for 180,000 tonnes of molten wax to be pumped into the wreck to lift it to the surface of the ocean. Vaseline was also suggested. Presumably the rationale behind this proposal was that wax is less dense than water – it floats and is very buoyant – so by pumping it into the wreck, the wax would rise and lift the ship with it. Unsurprisingly, this was deemed impractical and unlikely to work.

Another idea deemed impractical, and eventually discovered to be impossible, was filling the wreck with ping-pong balls, using the same rationale as the wax proposal. This would not work as the ping-pong balls would be crushed by the pressure of the water long before they reached the wreck. Mathematically, a standard ping-pong ball will only make it about 30m into the water before it collapses in on itself. So that proposal was out. But what about glass spheres? They could withstand the pressure – surely that would work? Possibly, but the cost to create the number of glass spheres required would be huge – a whopping $238 million!

What else? Oh, another iceberg. Arthur Hickey, a haulage contractor from Walsall in the West Midlands, who was unemployed at the time, proposed that the wreck could be encased inside an iceberg. As Lord describes, 'Like an ordinary cube in a drink, [the ice] would rise to the surface, bringing the *Titanic* with it.'[32] It would then, he proclaimed, be towed to Newfoundland, where it would be docked and allowed to melt, revealing the wreck for all to see. Obviously, this was impractical. The amount of liquid nitrogen required to do this equalled half a million tons and no financial backer or reputable scientist or explorer was willing to pump that much liquid nitrogen into the North Atlantic's seabed. And besides the huge financial commitment, there was no guarantee it would work, so the proposal disappeared.

The idea of salvaging the wreck of *Titanic* was as much an inspiration to writers and filmmakers as the sinking itself was. In 1976, author Clive Cussler based an entire novel on the concept, though his fictionalised account of raising the wreck was as ludicrous as the previous proposals. His novel, *Raise the Titanic!*,[33] is an American thriller that follows his protagonist Dick Pitt as he repairs holes in the ship's hull and pumps it full of compressed air, causing it to return to the surface in the same manner as a submarine. The purpose of this was to recover valuable, and fictional, exotic minerals that were on board when *Titanic* sank. The novel was written before the wreck was discovered, so Cussler's fictional version of the ship was still in one piece. Even if the wreck had been found in one piece – we know it split in two – it is highly unlikely this scenario would be possible. It's a visually stunning idea, but it would never work in real life.

It was not until 1977 that the eventual co-discoverer of the wreck, Robert Ballard, would make his first attempt at finding the lost ship. Working for the Woods Hole Oceanographic Institution at the time, Ballard had early negotiations with potential financial backers but quickly cut ties with them when he discovered they wanted to make, in severely poor taste, souvenir paperweights with material from the wreck. Ballard was sympathetic about the experiences of *Titanic*'s lost passengers from the outset, and he was determined only to be supported by a team with the same ethos and moral standing as he. Ballard decided to form his own company, Seasonics International Ltd, with financial backers who shared his vision. In October 1977, Ballard launched the Seaprobe, a deep-sea salvage vessel from the Alcoa Corporation. This vessel was a drillship, a vessel that has been modified to drill oil and gas wells, with sonar equipment and cameras, which were secured to the end of the drilling pipe. Ballard knew the last known location of the *Titanic* and he set off, but the expedition sadly ended in failure. The drilling pipe collapsed in the middle of the night, sending $600,000 worth of electronic equipment to the bottom of the North Atlantic.

While Ballard recuperated and re-strategised, The Walt Disney Company partnered with National Geographic to launch their own expedition to find the wreck. Their plan was to use *Aluminaut*, an aluminium submersible – the *Titanic* was within the submersible's depth limit, so it seemed like the perfect vessel. This plan was short-lived, however, due to financial reasons. Whatever those specific reasons were remains unclear. Another media-savvy figure jumped on the chance to find the wreck: Sir James Goldsmith, a British billionaire. He wanted to find the wreck to promote his new magazine *NOW!* The expedition was planned for 1980 but was quickly cancelled, again due to financial difficulties. Goldsmith was not the last adventurer to have his plans for glory thwarted by financial constraints. Fred Koehler, an electronics repairman from Florida, launched a plan to dive to the depths of the North Atlantic, which began with selling his electronics shop to finance the construction of the two-man deep-sea submersible Seacopter. His plans were just as nobly driven as Goldsmith's: he had heard tell of a rumour that the *Titanic* had a collection of diamonds deep within the ship's purser's safe. He was also unable to secure financial backing, and, quite frankly, that was a good thing.

The closest anyone came to discovering the wreck before Robert Ballard and Jean-Louis Michel was Jack Grimm, who conducted three expeditions between 1980 and 1983. Grimm was a colourful character. He grew up in Wagoner, Oklahoma, and was said by his family to be a seeker of treasure and adventure from a young age. So much so that he blew up a creek bed near his home, aged just 11, with dynamite he had bought from the local hardware store to find buried treasure his grandfather had told him about. Despite being disappointed with his findings – bullets, arrowheads and a single frying pan – Grimm never lost his thirst for treasure hunting. By his early adulthood, after befriending the son of billionaire oil tycoon H.L. Hunt, he'd convinced himself that he would discover treasure and become as rich as anyone could. He sincerely believed in the American myth of the self-made man, going so far as to incorporate panning for gold into his Californian honeymoon. Grimm struck oil shortly after returning to Oklahoma, and while he struggled financially for some time after – he had two children and a wife to support by this point – he got lucky a second time when he struck more oil in West Texas, which generated him $1,000 a day. He was a millionaire by the time he was 31.

His money secured, Grimm turned his attention to his extracurricular endeavours, though he adamantly assured people that these were legitimate business deals, not hobbies. These included locating the remains of the biblical Noah's Ark in Turkey (although he did not find the ark, he did return home with a hand-carved oaken timber dug out of a frozen peak, which he carried for the rest of his days in his briefcase) and proving the existence of the Loch Ness Monster, Big Foot (offering a staggering $500,000 for a definitive photograph) and the Abominable Snowman. In an interview with the *Abilene Reporter* in Texas in 1975, Grimm said of his fascination: 'I am inclined to believe the creatures exist. We knew they existed millions of years ago, why not now?'[34] He never did find proof.

It came as no shock to those who knew him when Grimm set his sights on the legendary *Titanic*. In 1979, Grimm was approached by Florida filmmaker D. Michael Harris (not to be confused with his son, *Titanic* explorer G. Michael Harris), who, having previously made documentaries on his search for Spanish treasure and having also searched for Noah's Ark, wanted to find the lost wreck. Grimm got to work immediately. He raised millions of dollars through his business ventures and sponsorship from friends and sold the media rights to the William Morris Agency, a talent agency based in Hollywood, to promote the North Atlantic expeditions. He even went as far as to commission a book and arrange for Orson Welles to narrate a documentary titled *Search for the Titanic*, which D. Michael Harris would create. He also hired singer Kenny Starr to record 'Ballad of the Titanic', a country song about the lost ship. He recruited reputable scientists, including Dr Fred Spiess of the Scripps Institute of Oceanography and Dr William B. Ryan of Columbia University, and acquired a stalwart crew of professionals to operate the expensive deep-water sonar-detection equipment from Columbia University and the Lamont-Doherty Geological Observatory. He was also briefly joined by a special crew member – a monkey named

Titan. Grimm had trained Titan to locate the wreck site on a map and believed Titan's unique ability would be good for publicity, but after the scientists gave Grimm an ultimatum – it's us or the monkey – Grimm was forced to leave Titan behind, much to his annoyance.

Grimm's three expeditions to find the wreck of *Titanic* were failures. The first was thwarted by bad weather, which made his findings inconclusive. The second admittedly found an object that looked like a propellor, but scientists refused to endorse his find due to lack of concrete evidence, and the third, while it was found to have passed over the wreck site, failed to definitively locate it and the expedition had to be cut short due to more bad weather. Although Grimm failed to locate the wreck, his expeditions did elucidate valuable data about the ocean floor and proved that the position given by *Titanic's* crew in 1912 during the night of the sinking was not accurate.

It was with this newly found knowledge and a rigid determination that Robert Ballard and his team returned to the wreck site in 1985, after making substantial discoveries about the site during an unrelated expedition to map the wreck site of the sunken submarines USS *Thresher* and USS *Scorpion*. After a week of searching, in the early hours of the morning on Sunday 1 September 1985, Ballard and Michel's team on board the research vessel *Knorr* watched as one of *Titanic's* boilers slowly appeared on their screens, unseen by human eyes since it had sunk over seventy years before.

And the rest, as they say, is history.

Contemporary Controversy: *Titanic* as a Shipwreck Versus *Titanic* as a Graveyard

Robert Ballard and Jean-Louis Michel's discovery of the wreck ignited another rise of *Titanic* enthusiasts, which only intensified, from professionals and the general public alike, following the release of James Cameron's 1997 adaptation of the story. The discovery of the wreck was not the beginning of its story; it was an epilogue, one that ignited a whole new era of deep-sea exploration. Of the estimated 3 million vessels lying on the ocean floor,[1] *Titanic* is arguably not only the most famous, but the most sought-after. While many reputable scientists have proved that any attempt to raise the ship would be detrimental to its integrity (though some maintain that raising the ship would actually save it, but that's a whole other argument) due to the damage inflicted upon it by deep sea microorganisms and rusticles (*halomonas titanicae*) – icicle-shaped rust left behind by iron devouring microbes – people still want to visit the wreck. They're on what Walter Lord refers to in *The Night Lives On* as a 'nostalgia binge', with *Titanic* standing 'for a world of tranquillity and civility which we have since lost'.[2] They want to see the wreck, and all it represents, with their own eyes. But should they be able to?

Ballard doesn't think so. He understands the allure of the ship, but he is adamant in his belief in the site as a gravesite, a memorial to those who were lost. In fact, during his 1985 expeditions to the wreck, he and his crew left a commemorative plaque on board as a homage to the victims who died on the night of the sinking. The ship should be studied and documented, yes, but disturbed as little as possible out of respect. James Cameron seems to mostly agree with Ballard's perspective. Curiosity alone, Cameron has said, is not enough to justify disturbing the wreck. Having made thirty-three dives himself, almost half of which were made for the purposes of research for his film, Cameron has stated that any curiosity surrounding diving to *Titanic* 'has to be science-based and solution-seeking curiosity; it has to be directed, and there is this challenge of doing it responsibly'.[3] He also emphasised that the ocean is a 'very, very unforgiving environment' that must be handled accordingly when mounting any kind of underwater expedition.[4]

This final chapter will explore the issues surrounding *Titanic* as a wreck versus a graveyard by putting it into context with maritime archaeology and the ethics surrounding the presence of human remains, comparative examples of other wrecks with souls lost as sea, and the 2023 *Titan* submarine tragedy, which resulted in the deaths of five people, including a 19-year-old.

This final chapter does not seek to provide in-depth explorations of incredibly complicated legislative, psychological, philosophical, moral or ethical issues regarding the treatment of human remains. I am not an expert on these topics, and I do not pretend to be, so I cannot give you expert analysis on these issues. Nor does this chapter provide definitive answers because, frankly, definitive answers are impossible in a situation like this. And in the context of *Titanic*, maritime archaeologist James Delgado put it best when he said, 'There are no simple answers to the questions posed by this wreck'.[5]

Rather, this chapter is a prompt. An encouragement to think about *Titanic* and its dead, and all the complications that accompany it in a way that is specific to you. Talk to your friends about it, talk to your family. Talk to your fellow history enthusiasts, your lawyer acquaintances. Talk to anyone who will listen. Because talking about, and becoming comfortable with, mortality in any capacity is important.

Perhaps *Titanic* can be your way of starting that conversation with your loved ones and, more importantly, with yourself.

Maritime Archaeology

For as long as humanity has braved the open ocean, there have been shipwrecks. People have been interested in the watery remains of sea vessels for thousands of years, but it is only in the last seventy years that underwater archaeology, specifically maritime archaeology, which deals predominantly with the study of shipwrecks, has been able to develop into a full-blown scientific discipline with the advancement of underwater technology. It is a 'young research field', Ballard states in his paper *Archaeological Oceanography*, 'with its roots deeply embedded in the technology of SCUBA (self-contained underwater breathing apparatus) diving that emerged in the early 1950s'.[6] Wrecks unseen for centuries can now be experienced, studied, archived and, arguably, exploited.

Maritime archaeology shares its roots with land archaeology in terms of its approach and goals, but it has a unique set of ethical considerations. For a long time, shipwrecks weren't looked upon as sites deserving of respect in the same way as, say, a battlefield or an ancient tomb. Some shipwrecks also hold the unique position of being in international waters, which has its own set of legislation regarding ownership of wrecks and regulation of salvagers or treasure hunters. Rather than being sites where knowledge could be gained, usually about the dead who died during whatever event caused the ship to sink in the first place, shipwrecks have been, and continue to be, seen as commercial items.[7]

This makes wrecks unique in archaeological terms because, as explained by Greene et al, archaeological research 'stands fundamentally apart from the exploitation of sites where the impetus is profit-driven'.[8] Archaeologists have worked diligently for decades, even centuries, to separate themselves from profit-driven treasure hunters and, for the most part, it has worked. But shipwrecks still have that romantic allure. Some shipwrecks also have the added bonus, to the treasure hunters, of lying in international waters so they have no single owner with whom they must contend. Some shipwrecks, to put it bluntly, are fair game. In his chapter 'The Ethics of Shipwreck Archaeology' in *Ethical Issues in Archaeology*, George K. Bass acknowledges that while he doesn't believe there should be a distinction between land-based archaeology and water-based archaeology, the 'undeniable romantic attraction of shipwrecks continues to separate underwater from terrestrial archaeology in most minds'.[9] He notes that 'print and television media, even those that campaign against the looting of archaeological sites on land, tend to sympathize with treasure hunting as long as it is under water'.[10] In simple terms, the consensus is that shipwrecks don't warrant the same respect as terrestrial archaeological sites and that they should be fair game for the public.

Wrecks are also distinctive archaeological sites because they only exist as a result of a catastrophe or accident (purposely scuttled vessels excluded). These catastrophes or accidents usually involve unexpected and often frightening death, giving these sites what Joseph Flatman calls a 'stench of the morgue' about them.[11] And due to the specificity of the environment they're in – the ocean – not all bodies of those who perished remain in a tangible sense (i.e., bones), but there is a sense of absent presence.[12] This is the notion that while the physical bodies do not exist anymore, the site in which they once were remains heavily associated with, and influenced by, their previously tangible presence. In the case of *Titanic*, the best examples are the leather shoes and coats of victims on the sea floor. Their flesh and bones may be gone, but these items of clothing indicate that the victims came to their final resting place here, and you can't ignore that. A graveyard on land is different as you don't see the remains of the deceased, in most cases, and burials at graveyards have a sense of purpose, an intent. Those bodies are meant to be buried there. The bodies of those who died during the sinking of *Titanic* are, in the most basic sense, not supposed to be at the bottom of the ocean. Their final resting place is not one that many, if any, of them would have chosen given the chance.

Many of the arguments regarding disturbing human remains for the sake of archaeology are in relation to graves on land – for example, the tombs of ancient Egyptian pharaohs – but it is difficult to compare that to disturbing the remains of those who perished on *Titanic*. One of the biggest arguments in favour of disturbing human remains is that we can learn from them, and this is very much the case with older shipwrecks, but does this apply to *Titanic*? *Titanic*, historically speaking, happened very recently. We have records on who died; we have primary and secondary accounts of their lives. We do not need to disturb their remains to learn about them.

It's an incredibly complicated issue because how we perceive and treat the dead can come from a variety of factors, two of the biggest being religious and cultural. There is also an idea that shipwrecked bodies do not warrant the same respect as bodies buried on land because the knowledge and value of what we can gain from the wreck itself is more important. Christopher Bryant, for example, argues that 'the historic, social, scientific, and monetary value of historic shipwrecks ... dictates that they should not be treated as underwater cemeteries protected from salvage or recovery'.[13] J.A.R. Nafziger takes this notion even further, arguing that since 'wrecked vessels do not belong in situ to the sea bottom but rather to their home ports and intended destinations' the site of a wreck becomes 'fortuitous and as a consequence they do not need to be preserved nor their remains respected'.[14] I disagree, and so do most modern maritime archaeologists. In the words of Geoffrey Scarre, 'To treat human remains without any regard to who they were, shows disrespect to those living persons and to humanity itself'.[15]

Other Ships with Human Remains

For a comparative study, and to prompt some questions and considerations, let's look at other ships with human remains and how they're treated: *Mary Rose*, USS *Arizona* and SS *Kamloops*. While there are an estimated 3 million shipwrecks on the sea floor, the number of physical human remains is significantly lower. This is for numerous reasons explored in chapter two, but some wrecks do have obvious human remains and they are treated differently depending on their context.

Mary Rose was Henry VIII's flagship and supposedly the monarch's favourite. It was built between 1509 and 1511, and rebuilt in 1527 and 1535 or 1536. Sources vary but we can be fairly certain that it served as a warship for over thirty years before sinking in July 1545 during the Battle of the Solent between Henry VIII and Francis I of France. It sank between Hampshire and the Isle of Wight, killing an estimated 700 of its crew, including its captain Sir George Carew. The reasons for the sinking remain unclear, but we know that it was carrying almost twice as many crew members as it was supposed to, which no doubt influenced its ability to right itself once it listed to one side, causing seawater to pour in through gunports and eventually capsizing it. After the Battle of Solent, the English tried to salvage the ship, but they were limited in what they could do, only raising it as high as its masts, and eventually abandoned the vessel. It remained untouched until the 1830s, when two divers briefly discovered it, but it went largely unnoticed until Alexander McKee, founder of Project Solent Ships, and his team discovered and successfully identified three of the ship's port frames in 1971. The ship was raised in 1982 and now stands, restored and on display, at the Mary Rose Museum in Portsmouth.

The ship lay in mudflats for over 400 years. These mudflats prevented oxygen erosion and preserved not only the 19,000 artefacts that were recovered from the wreck but almost 200 bones of the crew. These bones were not left on the seafloor either; they were brought back to land to be studied. DNA expert Dr Gary Scarlett of University of Portsmouth has successfully reassembled the bones to reveal the almost full skeletons of ninety-two crew members and is working with maritime archaeologist Alex Hildred to learn about the crew by scientifically analysing the bones. The approach allows them to recreate the faces of the crew and to identify various physical attributes, such as age, height, and any wounds or diseases they had. The research is driven by a desire to learn about and therefore remember the men of *Mary Rose*.

What makes *Mary Rose* different from *Titanic*? Is it that it's an older ship, so it feels further removed from our memory, and living descendants, and can offer us insights into a historical period we have few firsthand accounts or records of? As Sellevold argues, 'the further back in time, the less is the chance that the remains are identifiable as direct ancestors, and the less is the ethical concern'.[16] Is it that it was a warship, with crew who knew death at sea was a real and likely possibility, and a possible fate that was at the forefront of a navy man's mind? *Mary Rose* lacks the tragedy of *Titanic*'s story. It lacks the emotive resonance. The ship itself, which has had over 10 million visitors since being restored and preserved, is not seen as the tomb of the hundreds of crew members who died during its sinking. The area of the sinking between Hampshire and the Isle of Wight is not seen as a gravesite. Perhaps because it was a battlefield and there is a sense of psychological separation? Why is salvaging *Mary Rose* and disturbing the bones of the dead acceptable and celebrated, but not with *Titanic*?

Perhaps time is the most vital factor here. The idea of removing and analysing the bones of the dead is acceptable, even encouraged, in the context of older warships like *Mary Rose*, but could you imagine disturbing the bones of, say, the crew trapped within USS *Arizona*?

USS *Arizona* was an American battleship that sank after being attacked by Japanese forces at Pearl Harbor in Oahau Island, Hawaii during the Second World War. At the time of the attack, it was moored in 'Battleship Row' and, unlike *Mary Rose*, it was not prepared for war. The ship was hit by a projectile, causing flammable materials, including fuel and munitions, to ignite. The explosions were so powerful they reportedly lifted USS *Arizona* out of the water. It was attacked by more bombs as it sank. Between 334 and 355 (sources vary and are unclear) survived and 1,177 members of its crew were killed. More than 900 of those lost remain trapped within the wreck. USS *Arizona* did not sink in deep waters – it lies about 12m down – so it's easily visible and easily accessible. Surviving crew members and other navy men tried almost immediately to retrieve the bodies inside but the ship was deemed a loss and left in the water, only being returned to for salvaging parts to help the war effort.

By the 1950s, the wreck became an unofficial memorial where ceremonies were held to remember the dead, but it wasn't until 1958 that legislation was passed to grant it official memorial status and enable the construction of a memorial site. No federal budget was created for it, however, so the project relied on donations, which included a benefit concert staged by Elvis Presley in 1961. The money was raised, and the memorial was completed in 1962. It also operates as a visitor centre, providing contextual historical facts and thought-provoking stories from survivors for visitors to reflect on. Designed by Alfred Preis, who escaped from Austria to Honolulu to avoid Nazi prosecution during the war, the memorial sits over the wreckage to allow visitors to see the ship underneath them. According to Preis, the squashed milk carton look was intentional:

Wherein the structure sags in the center but stands strong and vigorous at the ends, expresses initial defeat and ultimate victory ... The overall effect is one of serenity. Overtones of sadness have been omitted, to permit the individual to contemplate his own personal responses … his innermost feelings.[17]

The bodies of the 900 men who died during the sinking remain entombed within the wreck, and, as far as I have been able to ascertain, no attempt, official or unofficial, has been made to remove their remains since the initial retrieval efforts immediately after the sinking. The idea of disturbing the wreck to remove the bodies feels disrespectful and morally wrong to many. Removing the bones from *Mary Rose* allows us to learn about the crew from a time when written records were not as freely available as they are now. That does not apply to USS *Arizona*. We can say with a fair amount of certainty who lies beneath the water, and we have more than enough written and oral records of who they were and what life was like during the Second World War that disturbing the bones for analytical reasons feels unnecessary. The bodies of these men also have a specific kind of respect and reverence, as they were not only navy men who were serving their country at the time, knowing full well the risks of what they were doing, but because their story does have a similar sense of evocative tragedy to it. USS *Arizona* is respected as the final resting place of these men, so their remains are not disturbed.

So, is the tragic and emotional aspect of a sinking, alongside what the ship represents on a wider cultural level, one of the most important things to consider when discussing disturbing a shipwreck, which, in essence, is someone's final resting place? Or is it whether living descendants remain? You can argue yes or no, and both could be correct. It's an incredibly contextual and nuanced thing to contemplate.

What about more ordinary shipwrecks? Ones that weren't warships or mighty explorers with that in-built sense of romanticism and adventure. What about the ones who were used daily as fishing vessels or cargo ships, with ordinary working people who died on the job? Do the bodies of their dead get the same respect and reverence of more famous shipwrecks like USS *Arizona*, which is such a crucial part of the United States's history and therefore identity? Arguably, no. These ships often aren't granted memorial status and are therefore open not only to scientific investigation but to recreational divers and thrill-seeking treasure hunters.

A great example is SS *Kamloops*. This was a lake freighter built in 1924 to aid in transporting imported goods from England to Canada, which was still a part of the British Empire in the 1920s. It sank in the freezing waters of Lake Superior – famously known as the lake that 'never gives up her dead' from the Gordon Lightfoot song immortalising another freighter ship that it claimed, the SS *Edmund Fitzgerald* – in 1927, the cause of the sinking still a mystery. It was a tragic loss for the families of the crew members, all of whom perished, and an economic loss for the Canada Steamship Lines, but it is a much smaller wreck historically, emotionally and culturally than *Mary Rose*, USS *Arizona* or *Titanic*. While it is not preserved as a memorial, it is protected by the National Parks Service as a cultural treasure, so only the most skilled and experienced divers are granted permission to go down there (though being skilled and experienced still doesn't make it ethical to do so).

What makes this wreck fascinating, and especially poignant for this specific discussion, is that while it is a matter of serious debate when it comes to the tangible, physical remains of those who died during the *Titanic* sinking being present within the wreck, we know for a fact that at least one body remains preserved within the wreck of SS *Kamloops*. His true identity is unknown, but since the 1970s, divers have captured photographs of a corpse that has become known as both Grandpa and Old Whitey. The lone corpse gained his nickname from the adipocere that has preserved him, as discussed in chapter three, which has turned his remains what appears to be a ghostly white. Few divers venture down to the wreck of SS *Kamloops* due to the extremely low temperature and depth, but the divers who have been there began to circulate stories of the corpse watching them 'quietly and calmly' from the crew bunks, of him going about his business on the ship, 'oblivious to the fact that it was sitting at the bottom of Lake Superior', or even that he would 'follow them as they made their way through the ship'.[18] Obviously, this is nonsense. The remains of the crew member may be preserved but there is nothing conscious left within that corpse. But it is interesting that many people's instinctive reaction to seeing a corpse within the wreck is to assume that it is haunted. Do they respect the wreck because they perceive it to be occupied by a spirit? Or is the psychological association between what the corpse is – an empty vessel – and what a corpse was – a living, breathing person – enough to justify respecting the wreck nonetheless? Perhaps a corpse like Old Whitey is more respected and disturbing his remains feels more ethically complicated because he still looks like a person. He's not bones, his remains aren't the empty shoes and coat he wore when he died; his body remains pretty much intact.

Nuanced context is key to how we treat shipwrecks with human remains, so there should not be a blanket approach to how we deal with individual wrecks. This isn't a case of whether something is clearly right or clearly wrong: it requires more thought and consideration than that.

Protecting the Wreck:
The Titanic Act and the Titanic Agreement

A huge driver in wanting to protect the wreck of *Titanic* is because of the absent presence of human remains associated with it. Almost immediately after the wreck was discovered, legal efforts to protect it began. Robert Ballard had not claimed salvage rights and there was no singular person or company who claimed to be the definitive owner of the wreck (unless you count Douglas Woolley, which I don't), so the 99th US Congress took matters into its own hands. It passed the first legislation enacted to protect the wreck: the RMS Titanic Maritime Memorial Act of 1986. The Congress had four findings:

1. The R.M.S. *Titanic*, the ocean liner which sank on her maiden voyage after striking an iceberg on 14 April 1912, should be designated as an international maritime memorial to the men, women, and children who perished aboard her;
2. The recent discovery of the R.M.S. *Titanic*, lying more than 12,000 feet beneath the ocean surface, demonstrates the practical applications of ocean science and engineering;
3. The R.M.S. *Titanic*, well preserved in the cold, oxygen-poor waters of the deep North Atlantic Ocean, is of major national and international cultural and historical significance, and merits appropriate international protection; and
4. The R.M.S. *Titanic* represents a special opportunity for deep ocean scientific research and exploration.[19]

Therefore, the purpose of the Act was to designate the wreck an international memorial to the victims, to ensure the regulation of exploration, research, and salvage of the wreckage and its contents with the goal of developing and implementing international guidelines, and to protect its value as a scientific, cultural and historical site of significance. The Act acknowledged that researching the wreck should continue because of these aspects, but it also acknowledged that the wreck was not owned by the United States, nor did it have any sovereign, exclusive rights or jurisdiction over it.

The act was well-meaning but also vague and open to interpretation, which meant it could be taken advantage of. In 1995, therefore, the US's National Oceanic and Atmospheric Administration (NOAA) and Department of State began negotiations with the UK, France and Canada towards an international agreement. This was signed by the UK in 2003 and the US in 2004 after research by NOAA and Robert Ballard highlighted the deterioration of the wreck since its discovery specifically related to increased human activity. It was not until 2019, after the US finally ratified it, that it came into effect – the Agreement Concerning the Shipwrecked Vessel RMS *Titanic*.[20]

A substantial portion of the agreement is about salvaging rights and the treatment of the wreck itself, but it also outlines how to approach human remains. It notes that the wreck serves as 'a memorial to those men, women and children who perished and whose remains should be given appropriate respect' and that 'further dives, if not properly regulated, risk disturbing the remains of those for whom RMS *Titanic* is their final resting place'.[21]

During this period between the first Memorial Act and the subsequent agreement, the wreck also became protected by UNESCO under the 2001 Convention on the Protection of the Underwater Cultural Heritage – which protects archaeological, historical and cultural objects such as shipwrecks that have been underwater for over 100 years – on 15 April 2012. This convention reflects what Greene et al. refer to as an 'international response to the looting and destruction of shipwrecks and other submerged sites'.[22] It ensures objects of significance are preserved in situ, that commercial exploitation is prohibited where possible, and that those who agree to comply with the legal framework cooperate to enhance education on the importance of cultural heritage and the object itself. Guidelines created by NOAA, in line with the 1986 act, were also created in 2001 to protect the wreck from further damage. No one owns the wreck, as it sank in international waters, so preserving it as a memorial is the best way to protect it.

So, the *Titanic* is legally protected and internationally recognised as a memorial. While most memorials are purpose-built, some objects and areas, such as the *Titanic* wreck, become memorials over time. According to Collins Dictionary, the definition of the countable noun version of the word 'memorial' means 'a structure built in order to remind people of a famous person or event', but it can also mean something that 'will continue to exist and remind people of them'.[23] In a similar vein, Merriam-Webster defines it as 'something that keeps remembrance alive'.[24] It is one reason James Delgado did not visit the wreck for a long time:

> Despite years of shipwreck exploration as a maritime archaeologist and a decade as director of a maritime museum, *Titanic* was never high on my list of lost ships to visit. I'd never considered it an archaeological site, but rather an underwater museum and memorial.[25]

This demonstrates that there is seemingly a moral obligation from those involved to protect the site and respect its sacredness.

But does its memorialisation make *Titanic* a graveyard, as many consider it? Technically, one could argue, no. According to Collins Dictionary, a graveyard is 'an area of land, sometimes near a church, where dead people are buried'.[26] Merriam-Webster keeps its definition even simpler: 'a place where dead people are buried.'[27] These definitions imply a sense of purpose and intent, so you could argue that while *Titanic* technically isn't a graveyard in the strictest definition of the word,[28] it is still the final resting place of some 1,500 people, and they deserve to have that respected. The words 'memorial' and 'graveyard', I believe, are often used interchangeably in the context of *Titanic*.

With this kind of understanding and appreciation of the wreck, there is often a desire to pay your respects to those who were lost and to learn about it. Some consider this desire to visit sites of death 'dark tourism'. Dark tourism, at its most basic definition, means 'tourism involving travel to places historically associated with death and tragedy'.[29] The term was first coined in the late 1990s and is usually used in relation to sites such as Pompeii, Auschwitz, Chernobyl, the Roman Colosseum, Alcatraz or Hiroshima. It can also extend to sites of cultural historical importance, like the murder sites of Jack the Ripper or the homes of serial killers, or assassination sites like those of JFK or John Lennon. The definition is vague and open to interpretation, so it can apply to a lot of sites depending on how one sees them. For example, a museum such as the Mütter Museum at The College of Physicians of Philadelphia may be seen as dark to some and not to others. But generally, dark tourism sites are sites connected to death. Unlike other tourist sites, where the main concern is usually being respectful and appreciative of a culture, history and way of life that is not your own, dark tourism comes with its own set of ethical and moral considerations. It opens up various debates into tourist etiquette, moral disengagement to justify transgressive behaviour and what Nitasha Sharma calls, 'the commercialisation of the macabre'.[30] *Titanic* is considered to be one such site. Arguments have been made in favour of opening the wreck site to tourists, based on the idea that visiting it isn't inherently unethical. A fantastic research paper by Albero Frigero demonstrates this well.[31] He argues, using various philosophical perspectives on ethics and morality:

> From the visitor's perspective, the act of accessing the site might ... be viewed as an enlightening and respectful commemoration of the tragedy rather than a mere recreational activity. From the perspective of the commercial provider, although the offered service is undeniably associated with the intent of monetary profit, it is also reasonably provided for educational and research aims. Arguably, such a good will in the intentions of the involved agents should allow a responsible and nonintrusive access to the *Titanic* wreck.[32]

He also acknowledges that the dark tourism sites previously mentioned are visited by hundreds of thousands of people per year, which 'might lead us to conclude that the site of the *Titanic* should also be made accessible as free, equal and rational individuals would commonly consent to that'.[33]

A huge part of *Titanic*'s appeal for many, including myself, is its connection to death, and many argue that seeing the wreck in person is a right everyone should have, regardless of how 'dark' it seems. I can appreciate that to an extent, but why do you have to risk your life to see it with your own eyes? Companies who are willing to take tourists to a, quite frankly, dangerous wreck site care more about the money you pay for your ticket than what you personally get out of seeing the wreck. The sites previously listed are places of immense death, tragedy and suffering, but you don't risk becoming part of that same site whenever you visit them.

This, thankfully, rarely happens, as these sites are controlled, monitored and respected to ensure the safety of those who visit. But, sometimes, tragedies do happen.

The *Titan* Submersible Implosion of 2023

On 18 June 2023, the world once again turned its attention to *Titanic*. But it was not the wreck itself that was of interest. This time, it was a smaller vessel that captured our attention: OceanGate Inc.'s *Titan* submersible. The 22ft vessel carried OceanGate's CEO and aerospace engineer Stockton Rush, who was also acting as the pilot; Paul-Henri Nargeolet, a *Titanic* expert who worked closely with RMS Titanic Inc. as its Director of Underwater Research; billionaire Hamish Harding, an active member of The Explorer's Club; Shahzada Dawood, a business-man and philanthropist; and his son Suleman, aged just 19. These men paid $250,000 per ticket for the privilege of seeing the wreck with their own eyes.

The sub began its some 4,000m (12,500ft) descent that morning, with the goal of reaching the wreck within about two hours. However, an hour and forty-five minutes into the journey, all communication with the sub was lost and it did not return to the surface as scheduled, prompt-ing a large-scale search from the US Coastguard and *Polar Prince*, *Titan*'s support vessel, with other commercial vessels and planes being called in for additional support. There was no sign of the sub but reports of banging sounds at thirty-minute intervals on 20 June sparked hope that the sub, and its passengers, were safe and would be found before their oxygen supply ran out – a mere 96 hours' worth that was likely deplet-ing faster and faster as the sub's inhabitants grew more panicked and frightened. By 21 June, more vessels were brought in to aid the search and the perimeter of the surface search was expanded to 10,000 miles, about 'two times the size of Connecticut'.[34]

Hope remained, but it was clear to some that this hope was misplaced. Retired navy submarine captain David Marquet explained the likely conditions on board the sub:

They're freezing cold. The water entirely surrounding the ship is freezing or slightly below. When they exhale, their breath condenses. There's frost on the inside of the parts of the submarine. They're all huddled together trying to conserve their body heat. They're running low on oxygen and they're exhaling carbon dioxide.[35]

There was still no sign of the vessel. 10 a.m. GMT on 22 June marked when the oxygen supply would run out and the rescue mission would become a retrieval mission. Later that day, a debris field with five major pieces of the sub was discovered some 500m off *Titanic*'s bow by a remotely operated vehicle. Officials from the US Coastguard told the world at a press conference that night that the *Titan* was gone, the five passengers on board killed instantly in a 'catastrophic implosion', with the debris field suggesting a 'catastrophic loss of the pressure chamber'.[36] Their deaths would have been quick and painless, according to Tom Dettweiler. A friend of Paul-Henri Nargeolet, Dettweiler surmised from a similar incident involving an Israeli submarine implosion in 1968 that 'For the crew, it was just like a light switch was switched off. They didn't even realise what was happening. They didn't suffer.'[37]

Five men died.

But their deaths were not a surprise to those who knew about the *Titan* submersible. One of the most vocal and well-known critics was James Cameron. He voiced his opinions to several journalists, but perhaps his most poignant observations came from the comments he made during an event organised by the Royal Canadian Geographical Society to open their exhibition 'PRESSURE – James Cameron into the Abyss'. During the talk, Cameron was asked several times about *Titan*. His anger and sorrow clear in his response, he said:

[OceanGate] forgot humility as well. You know, how can you dive *Titanic* without remembering the fundamental lesson of the history of *Titanic*, which is human arrogance and hubris, pride goeth before fall. So now there's two wrecks sitting side by side – I believe there's still some of the wreckage down there from the sub – and both are there for exactly the same reason, the human propensity to believe your own narrative and your own invincibility, and not be humble before the environment. If you're going into space, you have to be humble before what space is and how daunting that is. If you're going into the deep ocean, you have to be humble before the force of water, the pressure, the innate challenges of that world, and not be arrogant.[38]

His colleague and friend Dr Joe MacInnis echoed the frustrations, stating that the tragedy was 'a failure of technology but also a failure of psychology, a failure of leadership, a failure of the leadership of OceanGate to have empathy for the team, the task, the technology, the ocean'.[39]

Writers and investigative journalists Susan Casey and Ben Taub undertook in-depth investigations into what led to the tragedy, both of which are detailed in the end notes.[40, 41] The evidence they present could lead one to conclude that it was a combination of ego and ignorance, despite safety warnings and assistance offered by those within the industry. Nargeolet saw his presence as necessary: 'I can help them from doing something stupid or people getting hurt.'[42] Those who visited the wreck on *Titan* were required to sign waivers, which mentioned the risk of death several times, but rather than acting as a deterrent, this had the outcome Rush desired: it promoted his view that this was how pioneering exploration happened. What's the point in innovative practices without taking risks and pushing boundaries, even if that boundary is the one between life and death?

It was a risk that didn't pay off: 18 June 2023 became the first date on which a deep-sea submersible manned by an internal crew imploded. And hopefully it will be the last.

What interested me were the reactions of the general public to the *Titan* coverage. There were the typical gallows humour responses that were to be expected, as well as messages of hope and prayer, but throughout the news coverage of the tragedy I monitored several US and UK news outlets' YouTube comment sections and found similarities across various platforms. Several keywords and phrases appeared and reappeared. For example:

- **GB News:** mass grave, not a tourist attraction, cursed, ghoulish, graveyard, disrespectful, risk their lives, trouble, unsafe, grave-robbers, ghosts, left in peace[43]
- **CBS Boston:** ill-omened, leave the wreckage alone, cursed, stay away, graveyard, angry ghost, stop disturbing it, sacred place, a warning, final resting place, graves being treated like a tourist attraction to the mega-rich, haunted, deathtrap, karma, spirits[44]
- **BBC News:** grave-robbing tourists, irresponsible, death toll, avoidable, tragic, unsafe, selfish, isn't worth the risk, ignorant, let the dead rest, stop disturbing it, cursed[45]
- **ABC News:** *Titanic* has claimed 5 more, please leave *Titanic* alone, deaths were 100% avoidable, the *Titanic* is asking us to let her Rest In Peace, frightening, senseless, never play with watery graves[46]

It would be unethical, and quite frankly untrue, for me to claim that these keywords and phrases are representative of the general public's opinion of the *Titan* tragedy and, by extension, the *Titanic* wreck itself, as I have picked only a small sample to demonstrate, and all from a Western perspective.[47] It is interesting, however, that they appeared across various news outlets. Many people do appear to share the belief that the wreck should be left alone because it is a graveyard, a sacred place, the final resting place of some 1,500 souls. And this is presumably without having the specific knowledge of the legal, scientific, cultural and archaeological issues surrounding the wreck to influence their perception (though this is a general statement and not necessarily representative of what the general public actually knows).

The wreck is not haunted in the sense that there are literal ghosts trapped within the steel walls of the ship, but the tangible presence of those who died does haunt it. You cannot pretend their presence is not there, whether you visit the wreck for scientific research or not. Rush's positive contributions should be acknowledged: he did not use public taxes to fund his expeditions; he made the risks of visiting the wreck clear to his 'crew'; he helped satisfy demands for public visitation; and he was, in part at least, driven by the desire to enhance knowledge of the wreck via photographs and video footage provided by OceanGate, free for public view. However, whether you believe in an eternal soul and an afterlife or not, the dead deserve respect and disturbing the wreck without due cause is, I believe, unethical.

I believe Rush wanted to be remembered as an innovator, but it is far more likely that he'll be remembered for this. And, to echo James Cameron, the irony of people dying at the hands of a combination of hubris and the natural world is frustratingly apt in this case. While the factors that contributed to their end don't match up entirely, a convincing argument could be made that the victims of *Titanic* and the victims of *Titan* died for the same reasons, 111 years apart.

Investigations into the *Titan* implosion are still ongoing.

Conclusion

The ethics surrounding visiting the wreck of the *Titanic* are not only relevant to the dead, whose absent presence remains an integral part of the ship, but to people alive now. The people on board *Titan* visited a graveyard, and it became their own. I understand and appreciate the desire for thrill-seeking and adventure, but it also feels like a disrespectful and harmful way for the ultra-rich to get a thrill out of putting their lives, and the lives of others, at risk.

Opinions on what to do with the *Titanic* wreck vary, both among the general public and those who study the wreck historically, culturally and scientifically. It differs for those of us who believe artefacts should remain in situ and those who see the value in bringing them to the surface. It differs for those of us who think it should be left on the seabed and those who think it should be raised, either partially or completely.

There are many who believe visiting the wreck is a right everyone should have. It is a belief Paul-Henri Nargeolet staunchly held, and I respect him for that. James Delgado has also said he believes people should be able to visit the wreck if it's safe to do so. Part of me, the honest part, would love to see it, in the same way I love seeing graveyards. However, there is a fundamental difference between seeing a graveyard where burial was intended and something that became a gravesite through tragedy. Especially when some people visiting the wreck often go just to say they've seen it, not to pay their sincere respects.

For what it's worth, here's my opinion. In the case of *Titanic*, I believe visiting the wreck for leisure and unnecessarily disturbing the remains of its dead is unethical. Not because I don't think remains should be studied, not because I believe their spirits are still down there, but because the price you could pay for disturbing those remains could be with your own life. Visiting the wreck of *Titanic* is not the same as visiting Pompeii, Auschwitz, Parisian catacombs or Czech ossuaries.

The difference is that you don't risk your life to visit them.

Scientists, oceanographers, maritime historians and people with professional diving experience who visit the wreck in subs that have been checked, tested, and checked and tested again, again and *again*, fine. But I also think those trips should be limited. We have proof that even those visiting the wreck with pure intentions have accidently damaged it. Landing on the wreck damages it and we can see photographic proof of the damage. To account for the change in weight when bringing artefacts or parts of the ship to the surface, submarines must drop something else, be it chains or weight bags, some of them right beside the remains of the victims. And submarines have actually destroyed parts of the ship. For example, in an interview with Robert Ballard conducted by the US Naval Institute in 1996, he revealed that the crow's nest had been destroyed by an expedition taken by RMS Titanic Inc. in their quest to raise part of the ship's hull. Arguments were made that it was the result of severe decay, but Ballard firmly states that in the photographs from their expedition, you can clearly see the crow's nest intact in one and destroyed in another.[48] We have no definitive proof that this expedition was responsible for its destruction, but that's a pretty big coincidence. The same people who claim to desire to protect the wreck by bringing bits and pieces of it to the surface are the same people – accidently or not – damaging it. While I appreciate that currents and chemical erosion – the natural passage of time – have a continuing impact on the state of the wreck, I do believe that some submersibles have damaged it in ways that could have been avoided and have unintentionally accelerated its deterioration.

I also, however, believe people have and should have autonomy over their decisions. I do not have the right or desire to police what people decide to do with their time or their money. I also understand that disturbing a graveyard is not seen as unethical by everyone. It is not a universal perspective or belief. And it is, arguably, not even one that can be applied to *Titanic*.

All I can do is share my opinion, which I believe stands with various other scientists and historians who want to protect *Titanic* and the memory of those who died. I also acknowledge that *Titanic* is intrinsically tied to my identity, as someone from Northern Ireland – I feel very protective of this specific wreck, so there is a real sense of personal connection and responsibility for me when talking about it.

I stand with a suggestion Ballard made in 2012, and one he remains passionate about today: digitally preserve the *Titanic* and turn it into an underwater museum. We have the technology to facilitate this now. This approach would ensure it does not deteriorate any faster than nature intends, that the integrity of and respect for the artefacts and the items of clothing associated with the remains of the victims are undisturbed, and that tourists can visit the wreck without risking their lives. Leave the wreck, the artefacts and the remains in situ.[49]

I appreciate that my opinion on what to do with the *Titanic* wreck doesn't make complete sense, as I can understand the approach taken by those who have preserved *Mary Rose*. I'm not trying to say that it makes sense. *Titanic* is a contradictory and evocative topic, summed up in James Delgado's comment in the introduction to this chapter: there are no easy answers when it comes to *Titanic*.

What I can say for certain is this. I hope that this book has shown you a part of *Titanic*'s story that you haven't seen before, or perhaps haven't wanted to see before. I am, by no means, the first person to highlight this part of the tale. I am grateful to *Titanic* historians and enthusiasts who see this part of its story as being equally important as the well-known parts. I hope this book has taught you things you didn't know and has made you consider death in a new way. I hope it prompts you to discover more about *Titanic* and Halifax, and to explore your own relationship with death.

Most of all, I hope you remember the souls who died that night. This is for them.

Titanic's Lost and Recovered Souls

There are numerous sources one can go to for a comprehensive list of every single person who was lost during the sinking of *Titanic*. The best one I have come across in the course of my research is in Appendix A–Appendix F of *Report into the Loss of the SS Titanic*, compiled by Lester J. Mitcham. For the purposes of this book, I have compiled, as far as I was reasonably able, a list of the bodies recovered and their corresponding number. I have made a conscious decision not to include their class or crew status, but I have included those who remain unidentified. Sources vary from 316 to 337 bodies.

Van Billiard, Walter John #1
Marriott, John William #2
Henriksson, Jenny Lovisa #3
Goodwin, Sidney Leslie #4
Unidentified #5
Unidentified #6
Robins, Charity #7
Heininen, Wendla Maria #8
Dāhir, Abī Shadīd #9
Butt, Robert Henry #10
Shea, John Joseph #11
Rice, Margaret #12

Unidentifed #13
Williams, Leslie #14
Navratil, Michel #15
Rosenshine, George #16
Chapman, John Henry #17
Carbines, William #18
Greenberg, Samuel #19
Unidentified #20
Unidentified #21
Artagaveytia, Ramon #22
Turner, Leopold Olerenshaw #23

Unidentified #24
Hayter, Athur #25
Barnes, Frederick Charles #26
Monrós, Joan Javier #27
Unidentified #28
Unidentified #29
Unidentified #30
Evans, William Thomas #31
Sæther, Simon Sivertsen #32
Unidentified #33
Ashe, Henry Wellesley #34
Harbeck, William H. #35
Unidentified #36
Johnson, Malkolm Joackim #37
Holverson, Alexander Oskar #38
Unidentified #39
Unidentified #40
Stone, Edmund #41
Unidentified #42
Allāh, Niqūlā Khalīl Naṣr #43
Unidentified #44
Keeping, Edwin Herbert #45
Sutton, Frederick #46
Gilinski, Eliezer #47
Unidentified #48
Gill, Joseph Stanley #49
Tomlin, Ernest Portage #50
Draženović, Jozef #51
Mack, Mary #52
McNamee, Eileen #53
Unidentified #54
Lobb, Cordelia K. #55
Unidentified #56
Lloyd, Humphrey #57
Katavelos, Vasilios G. #58
Vear, William #59

Unidentified #60
Mangan, Mary #61
Douglas, Walter Donald #62
Unidentified #63
Rice, John Reginald #64
Unidentified #65
Hinckley, George Herbert #66
Sage, Anthony William #67
Farrell, James #68
Hansen, Henry Damsgaard #69
Kelly, James #70
Dunford, William #71
Ådahl, Mauritz #72
Jupe, Boykett Herbert #73
Unidentified #74
Hale, Reginald #75
Unidentified #76
Butt, William John #77
Unidentified #78
Ali, William #79
Jones, Charles Cresson #80
Stokes, Philip Joseph #81
Petty, Edwin Henry #82
Dashwood, George William #83
Unidentified #84
Hinton, Stephen William #85
Rudd, Henry #86
Unidentified #87
Unidentified #88
Olsvigen, Thor Anderson #89
Lawrence, Arthur #90
Smillie, John Downing #91
Unidentified #92
Roberts, Hugh H. #93
Unidentified #94
Unidentified #95
Straus, Isidor #96

Butler, Reginald Fenton #97
Gustafsson, Anders Vilhelm #98
Unidentified #99
Ricks, Cyril Gordon #100
Nicholls, Joseph Charles #101
Unidentified #102
Adams, John #103
Pedrini, Alessandro #104
Unidentified #105
Unidentified #106
Boothby, Walter Thomas #107
Leyson, Robert William Norman #108
Rowe, Alfred G. #109
Harrison, William Henry #110
Chisnell, George Alexander #111
Unidentified #112
Unidentified #113
Unidentified #114
Rigozzi, Abele #115
Butterworth, Jack #116
Unidentified #117
Unidentified #118
Robins, Alexander A. #119
Humblen, Adolf Mathias Nicolai Olsen #120
Louch, Charles #121
Newell, Arthur Webster #122
Tamlyn, Frederick #123
Astor, John Jacob #124
Unidentified #125
Long, Milton Clyde #126
Roberton, George Edward #127
Unidentified #128
Unidentified #129
Chapman, Charles Henry #130
Wirz, Albert #131

Unidentified #132
Dulles, William Crothers #133
Unidentified #134
Allison, Hudson Joshua Creighton #135
Unidentified #136
Unidentified #137
Fellowes, Alfred James #138
Unidentified #139
Waelens, Achille #140
Maytum, Alfred #141
Asplund, Carl Oscar Vilhelm Gustafsson #142
Johanson, Jakob Alfred #143
Wormald, Henry Frederick Charles #144
Allen, Henry #145
Anderson, Walter Yuill #146
Graham, George Edward #147
Birnbaum, Jakob #148
Hodges, Henry Price #149
Talbot, George Frederick Charles #150
Robinson, James William #151
Hill, James Colston #152
Lockyer, Edward Thomas #153
Unidentified #154
Gill, John #155
Johansson, Erik #156
McElroy, Hugh Walter #157
Watson, William #158
Barker, Ernest Thomas #159
Unidentified #160
Bailey, George #161
Unidentified #162
Woodford, Frederick Ernest #163

Unidentified #164

Kvillner, Johan Henrik Johannesson #165

Partner, Austin #166

Woody, Oscar Scott #167

Hewitt, Thomas #168

White, Richard Frasar #169

Unidentified #170

Connors, Patrick #171

Cavendish, Tyrell William #172

Olsen, Henry Margido #173

Bateman, Robert James #174

McCarthy, Timothy J. #175

Theobald, Thomas Leonard #176

Mayo, William Peter #177

Sedunary, Samuel Francis #178

Unidentified #179

Unidentified #180

Nofal, Mansouer #181

Unidentified #182

McQuillan, William #183

Saunders, Walter Ernest #184

Unidentified #185

Price, Ernest Cyril #186

Everett, Thomas James #187

Hanna, Mansour #188

Oviés Y Rodríguez, Servando José Florentino #189

Abbott, Rossmore Edward #190

Davies, Robert J. #191

Matherson, David #192

Hume, John Law #193

Unidentified #194

Shillabeer, Charles Frederick #195

Lymperopoulus, Panagiotis K. #196

Danbom, Ernst Gilbert #197

Unidentified #198

Unidentified #199

Davis, John #200

Meo-Martino, Alfonzo #201

Clarke, John Frederick Preston #202

Unidentified #203

Ingram, George #204

Ackerman, Joseph Francis #205

Pålsson, Alma Cornelia #206

Porter, Walter Chamberlain #207

Brandeis, Emil Franklin #208

McCrae, Arthur Gordon #209

Unidentified #210

Lefebvre, Paul Georges #211

Deslandes, Percival Stainer #212

Unidentified #213

Unidentified #214

Bernardi, Battista #215

Unidentified #216

Samuel, Owen Wilmore #217

Cave, Herbert #218

Unidentified #219

Unidentified #220

Allaria, Battista Antonio #221

Goree, Frank #222

Unidentified #223

Hartley, Wallace Henry #224

March, John Starr #225

Teuton, Thomas Moore #226

Dawson, Joseph #227

Unidentified #228

Unidentified #229

Minahan, William Edward #230

Roberts, Frank John #231

Righini, Sante #232
Unidentified #233
Østby, Engelhart Cornelius #234
Baxter, Thomas Ferguson #235
Fox, Stanley Harrington #236
Unidentified #237
King, Alfred John Moffat #238
Freeman, Ernest Edward Samuel #239
Unidentified #240
Unidentified #241
Hosgood, Richard William #242
Stone, Edward Thomas #243
Debreucq, Maurice Emile Victor #244
Van Der Hoef, Wyckoff #245
Wareham, Robert Arthur #246
White, Arthur #247
Unidentified #248
Millet, Francis Davis #249
Hutchison, James #250
Carney, William John #251
Dean, George Fox Hopkins #252
Couch, Frank #253
Unidentified #254
Van Billiard, Austin Blyler #255
Hickman, Lewis #256
Unidentified #257
Kent, Edward Austin #258
Allum, Owen George #259
Andersen, Albert Karvin #260
Storey, Thomas #261
Franklin, Alan Vincent #262

Nicholson, Arthur Ernest #263
Unidentified #264
Unidentified #265
Piazza, Pompeo Gaspro #266
Brown, John #267
Marsh, Frederick Charles #268
Crosby, Edward Gifford #269
Deeble, Alfred Arnold #270
Milling, Jacob Christian #271
White, Edward Joseph #272
Holloway, Sidney #273
Bogie, Norman Leslie #274
Gee, Arthur #275
Gradidge, Ernest Edward #276
Jaillet, Henri Marie #277
Unidentified #278
Unidentified #279
Reeves, Frederick Simms #280
Unidentified #281
Rogers, Edward James William #282
Kantor, Sinai #283
Sawyer, Frederick Charles #284
Johansson, Gustaf Joel #285
Faunthorpe, Harry Bartram #286
Norman, Robert Douglas #287
Unidentified #288
Unidentified #289
Bristow, Robert Charles #290
Unidentified #291
McCaffry, Thomas Francis #292
Weisz, Léopold #293
Swane, George #294
Del Carlo, Sebastiano #295
Unidentified #296

Giles, Ralph #297
Linhart, Wenzel #298
Buckley, Catherine #299
Cox, William Denton #300
Poggi, Emilio #301
Morgan, Thomas A. #302
Unidentified #303
Zakarian, Mampré #304
Givard, Hans Kristensen #305
Hendekovi, Ignjac #306
Hays, Charles Melville #307
Unidentified #308
Moen, Sigurd Hansen #309
Unidentified #310
Donati, Italo Francesco #311
Sa'b, Jirjis Yūsuf #312
Gatti, Luigi #313
Wiklund, Jakob Alfred #314
Wittman, Henry #315
Stanbrook, Augustus George #316
Elliot, Everett Edward #317

Unidentified #318
Howell, Arthur Albert #319
Cartwright, James Edward #320
King, Ernest Waldron #321
Fynney, Joseph J. #322
Mullin, Thomas #323
The last body the Minia *recovered was logged at #323 but the first body recovered by the* Montmagny *was logged as #326, so two records are missing.*
Unidentified #326
Reynolds, Harold #327
Jabbur , Hileni #328
Smith, Charles Edwin #329
McGrady, James #330
Beattie, Thomson #331
Keefe, Arthur #332
Unidentified #333
Cheverton, William Frederick #334
Kerley, William Thomas #335

Notes

Introduction

1 Willis, Sam, *Shipwreck: A History of Disasters at Sea* (London: Quercus, 2013).
2 *Ibid*.
3 Doughty, Caitlin, 'What Happened to Titanic's Dead?', YouTube, uploaded by Caitlin Doughty (formerly Ask a Mortician), 26 May 2016. Caitlin's video, at the time of writing, has had 4.4 million views, so it's clear that people are curious about this side of the *Titanic*'s story.

Chapter 1

1 *Encyclopedia Titanica*, 'The Shipbuilder' Special Edition, June 1911, www.encyclopedia-titanica.org/the-shipbuilder-olympic-and-titanic-special-contents.html.
2 Supposedly an employee of White Star Line said this during *Titanic*'s launch, 31 May 1911.
3 *Encyclopedia Titanica*, 'Thomson Beattie', www.encyclopedia-titanica.org/titanic-victim/thomson-beattie.html.
4 This quote has been attributed to Margaret Devaney but no source, as far as I could find, has been able to substantiate when and to whom she said this.
5 Gill, Anton, *Titanic: The Real Story of the Construction of the World's Most Famous Ship* (London: Channel 4 Books, 2012), p. 173.
6 This quote from *The Times* in May 1912 was referenced in Gittins, D., 'Too Few Boats, too Many Hindrances' in Halpern, S., Akers-Jordan, C., Behe, G., Beveridge, B., Chirnside, M., Fitch, T., Gittins, D., Hall, S., Mitcham, L. J., Weeks, C. and Wormstedt, B., *Report into the Loss of the SS Titanic: A Centennial Reappraisal* (Cheltenham: The History Press, 2016), p. 166.
7 Sir Alfred Chalmers's testimony at the British inquiry (day 23, question reference 22875), examined by Butler Aspinall.

8   Harold Sanderson's testimony at the British inquiry (day 18, question reference 19391), examined by Mr Scanlan.

9   Fitch, Tad, Layton, J. Kent and Wormstedt, Bill, *On a Sea of Glass: The Life & Loss of the RMS Titanic* (Stroud: Amberley Publishing, 2015), p. 40.

10 Harold Sanderson's testimony at the British inquiry (day 18, question reference 19398), examined by Mr Scanlan.

11 A quote from an article from the fifty-third session of the Institution of Naval Architects in March 1912, 'The Arrangement of Boat Installations on Modern Ships' by Axel Welin, read by Senator Smith at Joseph B. (Bruce) Ismay's testimony at the American inquiry (day 11).

12 Harold Sanderson's testimony at the British inquiry (day 18, question reference 19480), examined by Mr Scanlan. 6 June 1912.

13 Harold Sanderson's testimony at the British inquiry (day 18, question reference 19376), examined by Mr Scanlan. 6 June 1912.

14 Fitch et al., *On a Sea of Glass*, p. 41.

15 *Ibid.*

16 Grane, Thomas C. (Dir.), *Titanic: 20 Years Later with James Cameron*, National Geographic, 2017. Film.

17 Gittins, 'Too Few Boats ...' in Halpern et al., *Report into the Loss of the SS Titanic*, p. 164.

18 Fitch et al., *On a Sea of Glass*, p. 42.

19 Edward Wilding's testimony at the British inquiry (day 19, question reference 20491), examined by Mr Rowlatt.

20 Charles Lightoller's testimony at the British inquiry (day 12, question reference 14421), examined by the Solicitor-General.

21 *Philadelphia Inquirer*, 'Mrs E.W. Bucknell Says Carelessness Cost Many Lives: Survivor of the *Titanic* Condemns Lack of Boats and Failure to Have Drills', 20 April 1912.

22 Ruffman, Alan, *Titanic Remembered: The Unsinkable Ship and Halifax* (Halifax: Formac Publishing Company Limited, 2013), p. 70.

Chapter 2

1   *Tonopah Daily Bonanza*, 'Hundreds Drowned at Sea', 16 April 1912.

2   *Hawaiian Gazette*, '1200 Drown on Titanic', 16 April 1912.

3   World Health Organization, 'Drowning', www.who.int/news-room/fact-sheets/detail/drowning.

4   Paul Mauge's testimony at the British Wreck Commissioner's inquiry (day 19, question 20128), examined by the Attorney-General.

5   A valuable resource on the breaking of the ship is Bedford, J.G. and Hackett, C., *The Sinking of S.S. Titanic: Investigated by Modern Techniques* (London: Royal Institution of Naval Architects, 1996).

6   Beesley, Lawrence, *The Loss of the S.S. Titanic: Its Story and Its Lessons, by One of the Survivors* (Project Gutenberg, 2004; originally published in 1912).

7   Bruce Beveridge provided helpful comments on this during the feedback stage of the manuscript.

8   Newman, Friedrich, 'Titanic's Boilers: A New Theory', *Atlantic Daily Bulletin*, September 2014, pp. 13–15.

9   If you want to learn more about the incredible lives of *Titanic's* stokers, I highly recommend picking up de Kerbrech, Richard P., *Down Amongst the Black Gang: The World and Workplace of RMS Titanic's Stokers* (Cheltenham: The History Press, 2014).

10 *Encyclopedia Titanica*, 'John Arthur Priest: Titanic Survivor', www.encyclopedia-titanica.org/titanic-survivor/arthur-john-priest.html.

11 Ward, Christopher, *And the Band Played On: The Enthralling Account of What Happened After the Titanic Sank* (London: Hodder Paperbacks, 2012), p. 3.

12 Richards, Phil and Banigan, John. J., *How to Abandon Ship* (Ithaca, NY: Cornell Maritime Press, 1942), p.7.

13 *Ibid.*, p. 14.

14 *Ibid.*, p. 10.

15 This quote is from a letter sent by Laura Francatelli to someone named Marion, dated 18 April 1912, www.williammurdoch.net/mystery02_witness_08_francatelli.html.

16 'Appendix K: Shots in the Dark: Did an Officer Commit Suicide on the Titanic?' in *On A Sea of Glass* (pp. 305–21) covers this topic in depth and I would recommend reading it if you're interested in Murdoch's story.

17 This quote is from a letter sent by George Rheims to his wife, dated 19 April 1912. A photocopy of the letter is housed at Royal Museums Greenwich.

18 These quotes are from a letter sent by Eugene Daly to his sister, believed to have been written between 18 April and 21 April 1912. It was reprinted in almost its entirety in the *New York Herald*.

19 Halpern et al., *Report into the Loss of the SS Titanic*, p. 312.

20 This quote by Sjoblom is from articles in *The Tacoma Tribune*, dated 30 April 1912, and *The Seattle Daily Times*, dated 30 April 1912.

21 This quote by Whitley is from a *Washington Post* article dated 20 April 1912.

22 BBC News, 'Nephew Angered by Tarnishing of *Titanic* Hero', January 1998, news.bbc.co.uk/1/hi/uk/50203.stm#:~:text=Titanic%20First%20Officer%20William%20Murdoch,film%20will%20tarnish%20his%20reputation.

23 Störmer, Susanne, *Good-bye, Good Luck: The Biography of William McMaster Murdoch* (Stormer, Kosel, 1995).

24 McCluskie, Tom, Sharpe, Michael and Marriott, Leo, *Titanic & Her Sisters Olympic and Britannic* (London: Parkgate Books, 1998).

25 It's worth noting in this section that there is some conflicting evidence about deaths by gunshot more generally, not just, supposedly, among the officers. Steve A. Santini has quoted John Snow, the key undertaker in Halifax, as saying that he allegedly saw some bodies with bullet wounds, which supports claims of people being shot on board *Titanic*. For more information on guns on board the ship, I recommend *On a Sea of Glass*.

26 Lynch, Don, *Titanic: An Illustrated History* (New York: Chartwell Books, 1992).

27 Bier, Jess, 'Bodily Circulation and the Measure of a Life: Forensic Identification and Valuation After the Titanic Disaster', *Social Studies of Science*, vol. 48:5, 2018, pp. 635–62.

28 Lightoller, Charles Herbert, *Titanic and Other Ships* (Australia: Project Guttenberg, 2003; originally published in 1935, see gutenberg.net.au/ebooks03/0301011h.html).

29 Jack Dawson in Cameron, James (Dir.), *Titanic*, Paramount Pictures and 20th Century Fox, 1997. Film.

30 Orlowski, J.P., 'Drowning, Near Drowning and Ice-Water Submersions', *Paediatric Clinics of North America*, vol. 34:1, 1987, pp. 75–92.

31 Hiskey, Daven, 'Does Drinking Alcohol Really Keep You Warm When It's Cold Out?', *Mental Floss*, www.mentalfloss.com/article/32256/ does-drinking-alcohol-really-keep-you-warm-when-its-cold-out.

32 Barratt, Nick, *Lost Voices from the Titanic: The Definitive Oral History* (London: Arrow, 2009), p. 177.

33 *Ibid.*, pp. 199–200.

34 *Ibid.*

35 Barratt, *Lost Voices from the Titanic*, p. 177.

36 Gracie, Archibald, *The Truth about the Titanic* (New York: M. Kennerley, 1913), p. 89.

37 Everett, Marshall, *Wreck and Sinking of the Titanic* (Chicago: Homewood Press, 1912), p. 167

38 Bartlett, W.B., *Titanic: 9 Hours to Hell, the Survivors' Story* (Stroud: Amberley Publishing, 2011), p. 230.

39 *Ibid.*

Chapter 3

1 Captain Rostron's testimony for the US inquiry report.

2 Ballard, Robert, 'The Titanic Discovery: Professor Robert Ballard', YouTube, uploaded by UniversityOfRI, 20 April 2012.

3 Grane, Thomas C. (Dir.), *Titanic: 20 Years Later with James Cameron*, National Geographic, 2017. Film.

4 Ballard was quoted in an article for *The New York Times*, 'Experts Split on Possibility of Remains at Titanic Site', by William J. Broad, 14 April 2012.

5 Cameron was quoted in an article for *The New York Times*, 'Experts Split on Possibility of Remains at Titanic Site', by William J. Broad, 14 April 2012.

6 *Ibid.*

Chapter 4

1 *SS Atlantic*, 'SS Atlantic History', www.ssatlantic.com/ssatlantic/history.

2 For more information on this story, I recommend the www.ssatlantic.com website, where you can learn about the ship, Captain James Williams and the brave families who helped the survivors and victims, including Michael Clancy, his daughter, Sarah Jane O'Reilly, and Edmund and Dennis Ryan. There is also the work of historian and diver Bob Chalk, who has written two books about the ship and has been down to the wreck over 100 times.

3 *Oakland Tribune*, 'Titanic's Passengers Saved; Liner Sinking', 15 April 1912.

4 *Press and Sun-Bulletin*, 'Titanic Smashes Iceberg; 1,470 Saved', 15 April 1912.

5 *Star-Gazette*, 'White Star Liner Titanic Strikes an Iceberg. Passengers Are Safe and the Vessel is in Tow', 15 April 1912.

6 *The Evening World*, 'Liner Takes Off Passengers; Titanic Is Reported Sinking', 15 April 1912.

7 Ward, *And the Band Played On*, p. 15.

8 *Ibid.*, p. 41.

9 *Ibid.*, p. 30.

10 While 'coffin' and 'casket' are often used interchangeably, there is a difference between them. A coffin is broad at the shoulders and tapers down towards the feet to mimic the shape of the human body, whereas a casket is a simple rectangle and tends to be heavier. Various sources used throughout this book refer to both, but the photographs I have seen lead me to believe the victims were buried in coffins, not caskets.

11 Ruffman, *Titanic Remembered*, p. 28.

12 Van Beck, Todd, 'Call to Duty: The Funeral Director's Response to the Titanic Disaster – 1912' transcript for a presentation for the National Funeral Directors' Convention in Boston, Massachusetts, 1998.

13 *Encyclopedia Titanica*, 'An Echo of a Past Tragedy', Diary of Frederick A. Hamilton, cable engineer, *Mackay-Bennett*, 17 April 1912–1 May 1912, www.encyclopedia-titanica.org/diary-of-frederick-hamilton-cable-engineer-mackay-bennett.html.

14 *Ibid.*

15 Captain Larnder's log quoted in Ward, *And the Band Played On*, p. 29.

16 Johanna Stunke quoted in *Encyclopedia Titanica*, 'Floating Bodies in the Water', www.encyclopedia-titanica.org/floating-bodies-in-the-water.html.

17 *Encyclopedia Titanica*, 'An Echo of a Past Tragedy'.

18 *Ibid.*

19 Captain Larnder's log quoted in Ward, *And the Band Played On*, p. 31.

20 *Ibid.*, p. 33.

21 *Morning Chronicle*, 'Mackay-Bennett Returns to Port Freighted with Dead', 1 May 1912.

22 Captain Larnder quoted at a press conference in Halifax, 30 April 1912.

23 Maritime Museum of the Atlantic, 'Explosion in The Narrows: The 1917 Halifax Harbour Explosion', maritimemuseum.novascotia.ca/what-see-do/halifax-explosion.

24 'Fatality Reports' from the Nova Scotia Archives, archives.novascotia.ca/titanic/fatalities/?Search=.

25 *Britannica*, 'Embalming', www.britannica.com/topic/embalming.

26 Ward, *And the Band Played On*, p. 96.

27 *Ibid.*, p. 97.

28 Bier, 'Bodily Circulation and the Measure of a Life', p. 647.

29 *Encyclopedia Titanica*, 'The Life and Times of Hugh Walter McElroy', www.encyclopedia-titanica.org/the-life-and-times-of-hugh-walter-mcelroy-chief-purser-of-rms-titanic~part-18.html.

30 *San Francisco's The Call*, '64 Bodies of Titanic Victims Found', 22 April 1912.

31 *Encyclopedia Titanica*, 'An Echo of a Past Tragedy'.

32 Ruffman, *Titanic Remembered*, p. 30.

Chapter 5

1 Mosher's letter to his sister Agnes on 26 April 1912 was quoted in Ruffman, *Titanic Remembered*, p. 33.
2 Captain Larnder's log quoted in *Encyclopedia Titanica*, 'The Search at Sea for Titanic's Dead', www.encyclopedia-titanica.org/the-search-at-sea-for-titanic-dead-by-mackay-bennett.html.
3 *Encyclopedia Titanica*, 'An Echo of a Past Tragedy'.
4 Mosher's letter to his sister Agnes on 27 April 1912 was quoted in Ruffman, *Titanic Remembered*, p. 33.
5 Francis Rickards Dyke letter to his mother, April 1912. Dartmouth Heritage Museum, Dartmouth, Nova Scotia, uncatalogued and unindexed, 27 April, 2 pp., unpaged; transcript, *The Titanic Commutator*, Titanic Historical Society, vol. 7, No. 1, Spring, pp. 27–8.
6 *Encyclopedia Titanica*, 'An Echo of a Past Tragedy'.
7 Captain Larnder's log quoted in Ward, *And the Band Played On*, p. 39.
8 Francis Rickards Dyke letter to his mother, April 1912.
9 Mosher's letter to his sister Agnes on 27 April 1912 was quoted in Ruffman, *Titanic Remembered*, pp. 33–4.
10 Francis Rickards Dyke letter to his mother, April 1912.
11 *Dundee Evening Telegraph*, 'Captain P.C. Johnson Reports a Remarkable Discovery Made at the Scene of the Titanic Wreck', 14 June 1912.
12 *Encyclopedia Titanica*, 'Thomson Beattie'.

Chapter 6

1 Ward, *And the Band Played On*, p. 89.
2 Ruffman, *Titanic Remembered*, p. 45.
3 *Ibid.*, p. 30.
4 Ward, *And the Band Played On*, p. 91.
5 *The Washington Times*, 'Morgue Ship in Halifax; Captain Gives Dramatic Story of Finding Bodies', 30 April 1912.
6 Van Beck, Todd, 'Call to Duty: The Funeral Director's Response to the Titanic Disaster – 1912' transcript for a presentation for the National Funeral Directors' Convention in Boston, Massachusetts, 1998.
7 Ward, *And the Band Played On*, pp. 99–100.
8 *Ibid.*, p. 101.
9 Ruffman, *Titanic Remembered*, p. 45.
10 *The Washington Times*, 'Morgue Ship in Halifax; Captain Gives Dramatic Story of Finding Bodies', 30 April 1912.
11 *Ibid.*
12 Captain Larnder quoted in Ward, *And the Band Played On*, p. 93.
13 Mowbray, Jay, Henry, *Sinking of the Titanic: Thrilling Stories Told By Survivors* (Harrisburg: The Minter Company, 1912).
14 Ward, *And the Band Played On*, p. 106.

15 Snow quoted in *The Halifax Evening Mail* in Ward, *And the Band Played On*, p. 101.
16 Armstrong quoted in the *Morning Chronicle* in Ward, *And the Band Played On*, p. 102.
17 Ruffman, *Titanic Remembered*, p. 50.
18 *Ibid.*

Chapter 7

1 If you want to learn more about the real Ismay, I'd recommend reading Cliff Ismay's book *Understanding J. Bruce Ismay: The True Story of the Man They Called 'The Coward of Titanic'* (Cheltenham: The History Press, 2022).
2 This telegram was auctioned in April 2024 in Wiltshire as part of the Auction of *Titanic*, White Star and Transport Memorabilia. Its value was estimated at £2,000–£3,000.
3 Ruffman, *Titanic Remembered*, p. 47.
4 *Ibid.*, p. 48.
5 Some sources claim the victims were given crosses rather than slabs, but I am inclined to believe Ruffman's research rather than that of others, due to his access to the archives of the Maritime Museum of the Atlantic.
6 Ruffman, *Titanic Remembered*, p. 54.
7 *Ibid.*
8 For more information on this topic, Eugene Nesmeyanov recommends Goodwin, Carol, *Titanic's Unknown Child* (Newcastle: Newcastle Lane Publishers, 2016).
9 *Ibid.*, p. 48.
10 It should be noted that there are some contradictory issues with this. According to Alan Ruffman, the young Syrian girl's burial was overseen by Dean Crawford of All Saints Cathedral. Dee Ryan-Meister pointed out that the cathedral is Anglican, and so she would have thought that the burial of Hileni Jabbour (Zabour), listed as age 14–16 depending on the source, would have been officiated by a Catholic priest. As Alan Ruffman is no longer with us, this remains unclear for now.

Chapter 8

1 Comber, Northern Ireland. The Thomas Andrews Memorial Plaque was designed and sculpted by Rosamond Praeger.
2 Cobh, Ireland.
3 Liverpool, England. Historic England, 'Memorial to Heroes of the Marine Engine Room', *National Heritage List for England*. Listed March 1975.
4 Southampton, England.
5 Southampton, England.
6 Sir Archibald was quoted in an article for the *Daily Echo*, 'Memorial for Brave Titanic Engineers to Be Restored', August 2010.
7 Lichfield, England.
8 While there was no mention of Harley's violin case in the body inventory conducted in Halifax – which seems odd, as a violin surviving the sinking would have made

an impression – Hartley's violin is, as of 2024, in the Titanic Belfast museum. It is water damaged and features an engraving that reads, 'For WALLACE on the occasion of our ENGAGEMENT from MARIA'. There is an ongoing debate among historians and auctioneers about the authenticity of this item, but it seems pretty authentic to me.

9   Lancashire, England.

10 Eastbourne, East Sussex, England.

11 *The Pall Mall Gazette*, 'How the Mail Steamer Went Down in Mid Atlantic by a Survivor', March 1886.

12 Stead, William, *From the Old World to the New: A Christmas Story of the Chicago Exhibition* (Norderstedt: Hansebooks, 2017; originally published in 1892).

13 *Titanic Memorials*, 'W T STEAD TABLET', www.titanic.memorial/post/memorial/william+t+stead+memorial+tablet+london/.

14 London, England.

15 London, England.

16 London, England.

17 London, England.

18 Scarborough, England.

19 Godalming, Surrey, England.

20 Broadway, Worcestershire, England.

21 Glasgow, Scotland.

22 Cherbourg, France.

23 New York City, USA.

24 New York City, USA.

25 Washington DC, USA.

26 President William Taft in a telegram from the White House in April 1912. Shapell, 'President Taft's Eulogy for his Aide, Archibald Butt, Who Went Down with the Titanic Just Days Before', www.shapell.org/manuscript/president-taft-mourns-life-lost-on-titanic/#transcripts.

27 New York City, USA.

28 Boston, USA.

29 Broken Hill, New South Wales, Australia.

30 Nesmeyanov, Eugene, *The Titanic Expeditions: Diving to the Queen of the Deep: 1985–2021* (Cheltenham: The History Press, 2022).

31 titanicmap.org.

Chapter 9

1   Hartman, Cody (Dir.), 'Unsinkable: The Titanic Untold', Brian Hartman and Jeff Stephan, 2024. A cinematic portrayal of the US inquiry was released in 2024 and I was invited by the Belfast Titanic Society to attend the first screening in Belfast. It was an incredibly moving experience.

2   The complete transcripts for both inquiries are available online at www.titanicinquiry.org and they are invaluable resources for any *Titanic* enthusiast, expert or novice.

3 Lightoller, *Titanic and Other Ships*.
4 Barczewski, Stephanie, *Titanic: A Night Remembered* (London: Continuum International Publishing Group, 2004).
5 United States Senate Inquiry Report, Speech of Senator Isidor Raynor in the Senate of the United States, 28 May 1912.
6 Barczewski, *Titanic*.
7 United States Senate Inquiry Report, Speech of Senator William Alden Smith, in the Senate of the United States, 28 May 1912.
8 Barczewski, *Titanic*.
9 Gittins, 'The International Convention on the Safety of Life at Sea (SOLAS)' in Halpern et al., *Report into the Loss of the SS Titanic*, p. 240.
10 This letter from Harold Bride was reprinted in full and is available to read at www.titanicofficers.com/article_16.html.
11 This story is also wildly disputed, but for the sake of this chapter, the accuracies of the story aren't strictly relevant, since we're discussing the general legislation that was put in place after the disaster.
12 United States Senate Inquiry, Final Report, Reporting Disaster, 'Wireless'.
13 *Ibid.*
14 British Wreck Commissioner's Inquiry Report, 'Account of Ship's Journey Across the Atlantic / Messages Received / Disaster, Action That Should Have Been Taken'.
15 *Ibid.*
16 British Wreck Commissioner's Inquiry Report, 'Recommendations'.
17 It is important to note here that this seems to be Lord Mersey's personal opinion, rather than one shared by the entire collective.
18 Eugene Nesmeyanov notes that contemporary research shows that *Titanic* was indeed driven to arrive in New York on Tuesday night instead of Wednesday morning. And that they clearly were making a speedy crossing with a view of breaking *Olympic*'s maiden arrival time.
19 British Wreck Commissioner's Inquiry Report, 'Account of Ship's Journey Across the Atlantic / Messages Received / Disaster, Action That Should Have Been Taken'.
20 Charles Lightoller's testimony at the British inquiry (day 11, question references 13566, 13570 and 13657), examined by the Solicitor-General.
21 United States Senate Inquiry, Final Report, 'Voyage'.
22 International Conference on Safety of Life at Sea (London, Cd (Great Britain. Parliament), 7246), p. 5.
23 *Ibid.*
24 International Conference on Safety of Life at Sea. Messages from the President of the United States transmitting an authenticated copy of the international convention relating to safety of life at sea, the detailed regulations thereunder, a final protocol and the *voeux* expressed by the conference, all signed in London, 20 January 1914; and a report from the United States commissioners together with the report of Andrew Furuseth, submitted to the president after his resignation as commissioner. Memorial of International Seamen's Union of America (Govt. print. off., 1914), p. 82. Available via www.HathiTrust.org.
25 British Wreck Commissioner's Inquiry Report, 'Recommendations'.

26 United States Senate Inquiry Report, 'Recommendations'.

27 *Ibid.*

28 *Ibid.*

29 In Chapter 12, 'The Aftermath of the Disaster', Mark Chirnside discusses the changes made specifically to *Olympic* and *Britannic* in 'Effect of the Disaster on Modifications Made to Olympic and Britannic' in Halpern et al., *Report into the Loss of the SS Titanic*, pp. 236–40. It's a fascinating piece and I'd recommend reading it if you want to learn more.

30 Thank you to Eugene Nesmeyanov for providing clarification on this. In the original draft of this book, I had discussed the use of red and white rockets, but Eugene noted that 'according to the Rules of the Road at Sea in force at the time, rockets or shells of ANY colour thrown at short intervals were used as distress signals'. It was more than likely it was the intervals that were used which caused confusion rather than specific colours.

Chapter 10

1 Winocour, Jack, *The Story of the 'Titanic' as Told by Its Survivors* (Mineola: Dover Publications, 2003), p. viii.

2 Arnaud, Étienne (Dir.), *Saved from the Titanic*, Eclair Film Company, 1912. Film.

3 Misu, Mime (Dir.), *In Nacht und Eis*, Continental-Kunstfilm, 1912. Film. For more information on this, refer to Eugene Nesmeyanov's excellent chapter '*Titanic* in Literature and Cinema since 1912' in *The Titanic Expeditions: Diving to the Queen of the Deep: 1985–2021*.

4 Feuillade, Louis (Dir.), *La Hantise*, Gaumont, 1912. Film.

5 Blom, August, (Dir.), *Atlantis*, Nordisk Film Kompagni, 1913. Film.

6 Eaton, John P. and Haas, Charles A., *'Titanic': Destination Disaster – The Legends and the Reality* (Somerset: Patrick Stephens Ltd, 1996).

7 Selpin, Herbert (Dir.), *Titanic*, Deutsche Filmvertriebs, 1943. Film.

8 *Independent*, 'More Britons than Americans Died on Titanic "Because They Queued"', www.independent.co.uk/news/world/australasia/more-britons-than-americans-died-on-titanic-because-they-queued-1452299.html.

9 *Washington Post*, 'Ship in German "Titanic" Film Sank, Killing Far More than the Real One', www.washingtonpost.com/history/2022/12/18/germany-titanic-film-disaster.

10 Bergfelder, Tim and Street, Sarah, *The Titanic in Myth and Memory: Representations in Visual and Literary Culture* (London: Bloomsbury Publishing, 2004), p. 21.

11 Negulesco, Jean (Dir.), *Titanic*, 20th Century Fox, 1953. Film.

12 McGilligan, Patrick, *Backstory 2: Interviews with Screenwriters of the 1940s and 1950s* (Berkeley: University of California Press, 1991), pp. 237–8.

13 *Ibid.*

14 Lord, Walter, *A Night to Remember* (New York: Henry Holt and Company, 1955).

15 Biel, Stephen, *Down with the Old Canoe: A Cultural History of the Titanic Disaster* (New York: W.W. Norton & Co., 1960), p. 141.

16 *Ibid.*, p. 142.

17 Julian Fellowes's foreword in Lord, Walter, Lavery, Brian and Fellowes, Julian, *A Night to Remember: The Classic Bestselling Account of the Sinking of the Titanic* (London: Penguin, 2012), p. 1.

18 *The New York Times*, 'The Nightmare of April 14, 1912; The Titanic Nightmare A NIGHT TO REMEMBER. By Walter Lord. Illustrated. 209 pp. New York: Henry Holt & Co. $3.50', November 1955.

19 Brian Lavery's introduction in Lord et al., *A Night to Remember*, p. 12.

20 *Ibid.*, p. 3.

21 *Ibid.*

22 Baker, Roy Ward (Dir.), *A Night to Remember*, The Rank Organisation, 1958. Film.

23 *Encyclopaedia Titanica*, 'Widow of Titanic Officer Visits Chorley', www.encyclopedia-titanica.org/widow-titanic-officer-visits-chorley.html.

24 It should be noted that James Cameron's 1997 film also has minor inaccuracies to aid the storytelling – the Renault town car being transported in an open (not crated) condition, third-class passengers being locked below deck by the crew (though this remains a contentious issue), the rudder being too small, and the hull rising as high as 45 degrees, etc.

25 *The New York Times*, 'Screen: Sinking of *Titanic*; A Night to Remember Opens at Criterion', December 1958.

26 Lord, Walter, *The Night Lives On* (New York: William Morrow and Company, 1986), p. 228.

27 Eaton, John P. and Haas, Charles A., *Titanic: Triumph and Tragedy* (Wellingborough: Patrick Stephens, 1994), p. 302.

28 Douglas Woolley, Owner, Seawise Titanic Salvage Co., LinkedIn. www.linkedin.com/in/douglas-woolley-65a88921/?original_referer=https%3A%2F%2Fuk%2Elinkedin%2Ecom%2F&originalSubdomain=uk.

29 *Daily Echo*, 'Douglas Woolley Claims He Owns the Wreck of the RMS Titanic', November 2009.

30 Dan Stone covers Douglas Woolley's story extensively in his book *Unsinkable: Obsession, the Deep Sea, and the Shipwreck of the Titanic* (London: Penguin, 2022).

31 Lord, *The Night Lives On*, p. 231.

32 *Ibid.*, p. 230.

33 Cussler, Clive, *Raise the Titanic!* (New York: Viking Press, 1976).

34 *Mental Floss*, 'Grimm Prospects: Jack Grimm, the Eccentric Billionaire Hell-Bent On Finding the "Titanic", Bigfoot, and Noah's Ark', April 2022.

Chapter 11

1 UNESDOC Digital Library, 'The UNESCO Convention on the Protection of the Underwater Cultural Heritage', p. 4, unesdoc.unesco.org/ark:/48223/pf0000152883.

2 Lord, *The Night Lives On*, p. 18.

3 *Global News*, 'Titanic Sub Disaster: James Cameron Says Lack of "Discipline" Led to Implosion', 18 July 2023.

4 *Ibid.*

5 Delgado, James P., 'Diving on the Titanic', *Archaeology Magazine*, vol. 54:1.

6   Ballard, Robert, 'Archaeological Oceanography', *Oceanography*, vol. 20:4, pp. 62–7, p. 62.

7   Baehr, Leslie G., *Troubled Waters: The Battle Over Shipwrecks, Treasure and History at the Bottom of the Sea* (Cambridge, Massachusetts: Massachusetts Institute of Technology), p. 21.

8   Greene, Elizabeth S., Leidwanger, Justin., Leventhal, Richard M. and Daniels, Brian I., 'Mare Nostrum? Ethics and Archaeology in Mediterranean Waters', *American Journal of Archaeology*, vol. 115:2, pp. 311–19, p. 313.

9   Bass, G.F. 'The Ethics of Shipwreck Archaeology' in Zimmerman, Larry J., Vitelli, Karen D. and Hollowell-Zimmer, Julie, *Ethical Issues in Archaeology* (Walnut Creek: AltaMira Press, 2003), pp. 57–69, p. 60.

10 *Ibid.*

11 Flatman, J., 'The Origins and Ethics of Maritime Archaeology – Part I', *Public Archaeology*, vol. 6:2, pp. 77–97, p. 79.

12 For a more detailed exploration of the subject, I recommend the work of Elena Perez-Alvaro, particularly her paper 'Shipwrecks and Graves: Their Treatment as Tangible Heritage'. She discusses the complexities of human remains management using the legally recognised concept of Cultural Heritage, and how they're valued based on culture, temporal influences, science and funerary considerations. She is very much the expert, not I.

13 Bryant, Christopher R., 'The Archaeological Duty of Care: The Legal, Professional, and Cultural Struggle Over Salvaging Historic Shipwrecks', *Albany Law Review*, vol. 65:1, pp. 97–145.

14 Nafziger, J.A.R., 'The Titanic Revisited', *Journal of Maritime Law and Commerce*, vol. 30:2, pp. 311–29.

15 Scarre, G., 'Archaeology and Respect for the Dead', *Journal of Applied Philosophy*, vol. 20:3, pp. 237–49, p. 243.

16 Sellevold, Berit, 'Ancient Skeletons and Ethical Dilemmas' in Fossheim, H., *More than Just Bones: Ethics and Research on Human Remains* (Olso: The Norwegian National Research Ethics Committee), pp. 139–63, p. 144.

17 Langmead, Donald, *Icons of American Architecture from the Alamo to the World Trade Center* (Westport: Greenwood Press, 2009), pp. 447–70.

18 *Week in Weird*, 'Meet Old Whitey, the Preserved Corpse of the SS Kamloops, Lake Superior's Most Haunted Shipwreck', Greg Newkirk on 27 November 2016, www.reddit.com/r/submechanophobia/comments/gls2ij/ here_is_a_closer_image_of_old_whitey_in_the_ss/.

19 RMS Titanic Maritime Memorial Act of 1986, www.un.org/depts/los/ LEGISLATIONANDTREATIES/PDFFILES/USA_1986_Act.pdf.

20 Agreement Concerning Shipwrecked Vessel RMS Titanic (2019), assets.publishing. service.gov.uk/media/5dfa072de5274a08dd355be0/TS_8.2019_Agreement_ concerning_Shipwrecked_Vessel_RMS_Titanic.pdf.

21 *Ibid.*

22 Greene et al., 'Mare Nostrum?', in *American Journal of Archaeology*, p. 311.

23 Collins Dictionary, definition of 'memorial', www.collinsdictionary.com/ dictionary/english/memorial.

24 Merriam-Webster, definition of 'memorial', www.merriam-webster.com/ dictionary/memorial.

25 Delgado, James P., 'Diving on the Titanic', *Archaeology Magazine*, vol. 54:1.

26 Collins Dictionary, definition of 'graveyard', www.collinsdictionary.com/ dictionary/english/graveyard.

27 Merriam-Webster, definition of 'cemetery/graveyard', www.merriam-webster. com/dictionary/cemetery#:~:text=%3A%20a%20place%20where%20dead%20 people,Etymology.

28 During the drafting stages of this book, Eugene Nesmeyanov informed me that 'strictly and technically, the bow section of *Titanic* can be labelled a graveyard since the remains of a treasure-hunter, Mel Fisher (namely, his ashes in a plastic vial), were placed on the bridge under the telemotor. The vial is still there.' So, while *Titanic* may not be a graveyard in the way we typically think of it (in the context of the victims who died in 1912), it *is* the final resting place of Mel Fisher.

29 Foley, Malcolm and Lennon, John J., 'JFK and Dark Tourism: A Fascination with Assassination', *International Journal of Heritage Studies*, vol. 2:4, pp. 198–211.

30 Sharma, Nitasha, 'Dark Tourism and Moral Disengagment in Liminal Spaces', *Tourism Geographies*, vol. 22:2, pp. 273–97, p. 276.

31 Frigero, Alberto, 'Opening the Public Accessibility to the Wreckage of the RMS *Titanic*: Some Ethical Reflections', *Journal of Heritage Management*, vol. 7:1, pp. 118–22.

32 *Ibid.*, p. 119.

33 *Ibid.*, p. 120.

34 *The Standard*, '"More Noises" Heard Underwater in Search for Missing Titanic Sub – But "Not Clear" What They Are', 22 June 2023.

35 CNN, 'June 21, 2023 – Missing Titanic Sub Search News', 21 June 2023.

36 *The Guardian*, 'Titanic Sub Crew Believed to Have Died Instantly in "Catastrophic Implosion"', 23 June 2023.

37 CNN, 'The Unsettling Days After the Titanic Submersible's Demise', 24 June 2023.

38 CTV News, 'James Cameron on Deep Sea Exploration, Artificial Intelligence', 18 July 2023.

39 *Ibid.*

40 *Vanity Fair*, 'The Titan Submersible Disaster Was Years in the Making, New Details Reveal', 17 August 2023.

41 *The New Yorker*, 'The Titan Sub was "an Accident Waiting to Happen"', 1 July 2023.

42 *Vanity Fair*, 'The Titan Submersible Disaster Was Years in the Making, New Details Reveal', 17 August 2023.

43 GB News, 'Missing Titanic Sub Running Out of Time: "Crucially, Only Two Days of Oxygen Left": Paul Hawkins', YouTube, uploaded 20 June 2023.

44 CBS Boston, 'Missing Submarine Heading to Titanic Wreckage Had 5-Person Crew, Lost Contact Sunday Morning', YouTube, uploaded 19 June 2023.

45 BBC News, 'Titan Sub Passengers Died After Catastrophic Implosion Says US Coast Guard – BBC News', YouTube, uploaded 22 June 2023.

46 ABC News, 'ABC News Special Report: Titanic Submersible Passengers "Have Sadly Been Lost", OceanGate Confirms', YouTube, uploaded 22 June 2023.

47 Input from Eugene Nesmeyanov revealed that the general public of Russia reportedly had an even worse response, full of gloating, insults, swear words, accusations of ignorance, greed and faulty design from Anatoly Sagalevich.

48 Schultz, Fred L., 'It's a Carnival: An Interview with Robert Ballard', *Naval History*, vol. 10:5.

49 There is a section within 'The Agreement Concerning the Shipwrecked Vessel RMS *Titanic*' that allows artefacts to be brought to the surface in some cases, particularly when something threatens them while at depth. While this is technically allowed through agreed legislation, I personally disagree with it.

Bibliography

Books

Barczewski, Stephanie, *Titanic: A Night Remembered* (London: Continuum International Publishing Group, 2004).

Barratt, Nick, *Lost Voices from the Titanic: The Definitive Oral History* (London: Arrow, 2009).

Bartlett, W.B., *Titanic: 9 Hours to Hell, the Survivors' Story* (Stroud: Amberley Publishing, 2011).

Bedford, J.G. and Hackett, C., *The Sinking of S.S. Titanic: Investigated by Modern Techniques* (London: Royal Institution of Naval Architects, 1996).

Beesley, Lawrence, *The Loss of the S.S. Titanic: Its Story and Its Lessons, by One of the Survivors* (Project Gutenberg, 2004; (originally published in 1912, see www.gutenberg.org/files/6675/6675-h/6675-h.htm).

Bergfelder, Tim and Street, Sarah, *The Titanic in Myth and Memory: Representations in Visual and Literary Culture* (London: Bloomsbury Publishing, 2004).

Biel, Stephen, *Down with the Old Canoe: A Cultural History of the Titanic Disaster* (New York: W.W. Norton & Co., 1960).

De Kerbrech, Richard P., *Down Amongst the Black Gang: The World and Workplace of RMS Titanic's Stokers* (Cheltenham: The History Press, 2014).

Doughty, Caitlin, *From Here to Eternity* (New York: W.W. Norton & Company, 2017).

Eaton, John P. and Haas, Charles A., *Titanic: Triumph and Tragedy* (Wellingborough: Patrick Stephens, 1994).

Eaton, John P. and Haas, Charles A., *'Titanic': Destination Disaster – The Legends and the Reality* (Somerset: Patrick Stephens Ltd, 1996).

Everett, Marshall, *Wreck and Sinking of the Titanic* (Chicago: Homewood Press, 1912).

Fitch, Tad, Layton, J. Kent and Wormstedt, Bill, *On a Sea of Glass: The Life & Loss of the RMS Titanic* (Stroud: Amberley Publishing, 2015).

Fossheim, Hallvard, *More than Just Bones: Ethics and Research on Human Remains* (Olso: The Norwegian National, 2012).

Gennard, Dorothy, *Forensic Entomology: An Introduction* (Oxford: John Wiley & Sons, 2012).

Giesbrecht, Gordon and Wilkerson, James A., *Hypothermia, Frostbite and Other Cold Injuries: Prevention, Survival, Rescue and Treatment* (Washington: Mountaineers Books, 2006).

Gill, Anton, *Titanic: The Real Story of the Construction of the World's Most Famous Ship* (London: Channel 4 Books, 2012).

Gittins, D., 'Too Few Boats, Too Many Hindrances' in Halpern, S., Akers-Jordan, C., Behe, G., Beveridge, B., Chirnside, M., Fitch, T., Gittins, D., Hall, S., Mitcham, L.J., Weeks, C. and Wormstedt, B., *Report into the Loss of the SS Titanic: A Centennial Reappraisal* (Cheltenham: The History Press, 2016).

Gracie, Archibald, *The Truth about the Titanic* (New York: M. Kennerley, 1913).

Gunn, Alan, *Essential Forensic Biology* (3rd edition) (Hoboken, New Jersey: Wiley, 2019).

Hart, Eva, *A Girl Aboard the Titanic* (Stroud: Amberley Publishing, 2012).

Hayman, Jarvis and Oxenham, Marc, *Human Body Decomposition* (Cambridge, Massachusetts: Academic Press, 2016).

Ismay, Clifford, *Understanding J. Bruce Ismay: The True Story of the Man They Called 'The Coward of Titanic'* (Cheltenham: The History Press, 2022).

Jaekl, Phil, *Out Cold: A Chilling Descent into the Macabre, Controversial, Lifesaving History of Hypothermia* (New York City: Public Affairs, 2021).

Lightoller, Charles, *Titanic and Other Ships* (Australia: Project Gutenberg, 2004; originally published in 1935, see gutenberg.net.au/ebooks03/0301011h.html).

Lord, Walter, *A Night to Remember* (New York: Henry Holt and Company, 1955).

Lord, Walter, Lavery, Brian and Fellowes, Julian, *A Night to Remember: The Classic Bestselling Account of the Sinking of the Titanic* (London: Penguin, 2012).

Lord, Walter, *The Night Lives On* (New York: William Morrow and Company, 1986).

Lynch, Don, *Titanic: An Illustrated History* (New York: Chartwell Books, 1992).

McCluskie, Tom, Sharpe, Michael and Marriott, Leo, *Titanic & Her Sisters Olympic and Britannic* (London: Parkgate Books 1998).

McGilligan, Patrick, *Backstory 2: Interviews with Screenwriters of the 1940s and 1950s* (Berkeley: University of California Press, 1991).

Mowbray, Jay Henry, *Sinking of the Titanic: Thrilling Stories Told by Survivors* (Harrisburg: The Minter Company, 1912).

Nesmeyanov, Eugene, *The Titanic Expeditions: Diving to the Queen of the Deep: 1985–2021* (Cheltenham: The History Press, 2022).

Richards, Phil and Banigan, John J., *How to Abandon Ship* (Ithaca, New York: Cornell Maritime Press).

Roach, Mary, *Stiff: The Curious Lives of Human Cadavers* (London: Penguin, 2004).

Ruffman, Alan, *Titanic Remembered: The Unsinkable Ship and Halifax* (Halifax: Formac Publishing Company Limited, 2013).

Sellevold, Berit, 'Ancient Skeletons and Ethical Dilemmas' in Fossheim, H., *More than Just Bones: Ethics and Research on Human Remains* (Oslo, Noruega: The Norwegian National Research Committee, 2019).

Sorg, Marcella H. and Haglund, William D., *Forensic Taphonomy: The Postmortem Fate of Human Remains* (Boca Raton, Florida: CRC Press, 1996).

Stead, William, *From the Old World to the New: A Christmas Story of the Chicago Exhibition* (Norderstedt: Hansebooks, 2017; originally published in 1892).

Stone, Dan, *Unsinkable: Obsession, the Deep Sea, and the Shipwreck of the Titanic* (London: Penguin, 2022).

Störmer, Susanne, *Good-bye, Good Luck: The Biography of William McMaster Murdoch* (Stormer, Kosel, 1995).

Troyer, John, *Technologies of the Human Corpse* (Cambridge, Massachusetts: The MIT Press, 2006).

Valentine, Carla, *Past Mortems: Life and Death Behind Mortuary Doors* (London: Speare Books, 2018).

Ward, Christopher, *And the Band Played On: The Enthralling Account of What Happened After the Titanic Sank* (London: Hodder Paperbacks, 2012).

Willis, Sam, *Shipwreck: A History of Disasters at Sea* (London: Quercus, 2013).

Winocour, Jack, *The Story of the 'Titanic' as Told by Its Survivors* (Mineola: Dover Publications, 2003).

Journals, Website Articles, Reports & Government Documentation

Aftermath: Specialists in Trauma Cleaning & Biohazard Removal, 'Human Body Decomposition in Water', www.aftermath.com/blog/human-body-decomposition-in-water.

'Agreement Concerning Shipwrecked Vessel RMS Titanic' (2019), assets.publishing. service.gov.uk/media/5dfa072de5274a08dd355be0/TS_8.2019_Agreement_ concerning_Shipwrecked_Vessel_RMS_Titanic.pdf.

Ashworth, Hannah, 'How Long Does It Take for a Body to Decompose at Sea?', BBC: Science Focus, 2023, www.sciencefocus.com/the-human-body/ how-long-does-it-take-for-a-body-to-decompose-at-sea.

Ayers, Laura E., 'Differential Decomposition in Terrestrial, Freshwater, and Saltwater Environments: A Pilot Study' (San Marcos, Texas: Texas State University, 2010).

Baehr, Leslie G., *Troubled Waters: The Battle Over Shipwrecks, Treasure and History at the Bottom of the Sea* (Cambridge, Massachusetts: Massachusetts Institute of Technology, 2013).

Ballard, Robert, 'Archaeological Oceanography', *Oceanography*, vol. 20:4, pp. 62–7.

Bass, G.F, 'The Ethics of Shipwreck Archaeology' in Zimmerman, Larry J., Vitelli, Karen D. and Hollowell-Zimmer, Julie, *Ethical Issues in Archaeology* (Walnut Creek: AltaMira Press, 2003), pp. 57–69.

BBC News, 'Nephew Angered by Tarnishing of Titanic Hero', January 1998, news. bbc.co.uk/1/hi/uk/50203.stm#:~:text=Titanic%20First%20Officer%20William%20 Murdoch,film%20will%20tarnish%20his%20reputation.

Bier, Jess, 'Bodily Circulation and the Measure of a Life: Forensic Identification and Valuation After the Titanic Disaster', *Social Studies of Science*, vol. 48:5, 2018, pp. 635–62.

Britannica, 'Embalming', www.britannica.com/topic/embalming.

British Wreck Commissioner's Inquiry Report, 'Account of Ship's Journey Across the Atlantic / Messages Received / Disaster, Action That Should Have Been Taken'.

British Wreck Commissioner's Inquiry Report, 'Recommendations'.

Bryant, Christopher R., 'The Archaeological Duty of Care: The Legal, Professional, and Cultural Struggle Over Salvaging Historic Shipwrecks', *Albany Law Review*, vol. 65:1, pp. 97–145.

Caruso, J.L., 'Decomposition Changes in Bodies Recovered from Water', *Acad Forensic Pathol*, vol. 6:1, 2016, pp. 19–27.

CNN, 'June 21, 2023 – Missing Titanic sub search news', 21 June 2023. edition.cnn. com/americas/live-news/titanic-missing-sub-oceangate-06-21-23/index.html.

CNN, 'The unsettling days after the Titanic submersible's demise', 24 June 2023. www.cnn.com/2023/06/24/us/missing-titanic-submersible-timeline/index.html.

Cussler, Clive, *Raise the Titanic!* (New York: Viking Press, 1976).

Daily Echo, 'Douglas Woolley Claims He Owns the Wreck of the RMS Titanic', November 2009. www.dailyecho.co.uk/news/4765970.douglas-woolley-claims-he-owns-the-wreck-of-the-rms-titanic.

Daily Echo, 'Memorial for Brave Titanic Engineers to Be Restored', August 2010. www.dailyecho.co.uk/heritage/8353018.memorial-for-brave-titanic-engineers-to-be-restored.

Delgado, James P., 'Diving on the Titanic', *Archaeology Magazine*, vol. 54:1, 2001

Dundee Evening Telegraph, 'Captain P. C. Johnson Reports a Remarkable Discovery Made at the Scene of the Titanic Wreck', 14 June 1912.

Dyke, Francis, letter to his mother, April 1912. Dartmouth Heritage Museum, Dartmouth, Nova Scotia, uncatalogued and unindexed, 27 April, 2 pp., unpaged; transcript, *The Titanic Commutator*, Titanic Historical Society, Vol. 7, No. 1, Spring, pp. 27–8.

Encyclopedia Titanica, 'An Echo of a Past Tragedy', Diary of Frederick A. Hamilton, cable engineer, *Mackay-Bennett*, 17 April 1912–1 May 1912. www.encyclopedia-titanica. org/diary-of-frederick-hamilton-cable-engineer-mackay-bennett.html.

Encyclopedia Titanica, 'Floating Bodies in the Water', www.encyclopedia-titanica.org/floating-bodies-in-the-water.html.

Encyclopedia Titanica, 'John Arthur Priest: Titanic Survivor', www.encyclopedia-titanica. org/titanic-survivor/arthur-john-priest.html.

Encyclopedia Titanica, 'The Search at Sea for Titanic's Dead', www.encyclopedia-titanica. org/the-search-at-sea-for-titanic-dead-by-mackay-bennett.html.

Encyclopedia Titanica, 'The Shipbuilder' Special Edition, June 1911, www.encyclopedia-titanica.org/the-shipbuilder-olympic-and-titanic-special-contents.html.

Encyclopedia Titanica, 'Thomson Beattie', www.encyclopedia-titanica.org/titanic-victim/thomson-beattie.html.

Encyclopedia Titanica, 'Widow of Titanic Officer Visits Chorley', www.encyclopedia-titanica.org/widow-titanic-officer-visits-chorley.html.

Flatman, J., 'The Origins and Ethics of Maritime Archaeology – Part I', *Public Archaeology*, vol. 6:2, pp. 77–97.

Foley, Malcolm and Lennon, John J., 'JFK and Dark Tourism: A Fascination with Assassination', *International Journal of Heritage Studies*, vol. 2:4, pp. 198–211.

Frigero, Alberto, 'Opening the Public Accessibility to the Wreckage of the RMS Titanic: Some Ethical Reflections', *Journal of Heritage Management*, vol. 7:1, pp. 118–22.

Global News, 'Titanic Sub Disaster: James Cameron Says Lack of "Discipline" Led to Implosion', 18 July 2023, globalnews.ca/video/9840356/titanic-sub-disaster-james-cameron-says-lack-of-discipline-led-to-implosion.

Greene, Elizabeth S., Leidwanger, Justin, Leventhal, Richard M. and Daniels, Brian I., 'Mare Nostrum? Ethics and Archaeology in Mediterranean Waters', *American Journal of Archaeology*, vol. 115:2, pp. 311–19.

Hawaiian Gazette, '1200 Drown on Titanic', 16 April 1912.

Hiskey, Daven, 'Does Drinking Alcohol Really Keep You Warm When It's Cold Out?', *Mental Floss*, www.mentalfloss.com/article/32256/does-drinking-alcohol-really-keep-you-warm-when-its-cold-out.

Historic England, 'Memorial to Heroes of the Marine Engine Room', *National Heritage List for England*. Listed March 1975.

International Conference on Safety of Life at Sea (London, Cd (Great Britain Parliament), 7246).

International Conference on Safety of Life at Sea. Messages from the President of the United States transmitting an authenticated copy of the international convention relating to safety of life at sea, the detailed regulations thereunder, a final protocol, and the *voeux* expressed by the conference, all signed in London, 20 January 1914; and a report from the United States commissioners together with the report of Andrew Furuseth, submitted to the president after his resignation as commissioner. Memorial of International Seamen's Union of America (Govt. print. off., 1914), p. 82. Available via www.HathiTrust.org.

Langmead, Donald, *Icons of American Architecture from the Alamo to the World Trade Center* (Westport: Greenwood Press, 2009), pp. 447–70.

Marks, Kathy, 'More Britons than Americans Died on Titanic "Because They Queued"', *Independent*, 2009, www.independent.co.uk/news/world/australasia/more-britons-than-americans-died-on-titanic-because-they-queued-1452299.html.

Mayo Clinic, 'Hypothermia', www.mayoclinic.org/diseases-conditions/hypothermia/symptoms-causes.

Nafziger, J.A.R., 'The Titanic Revisited', *Journal of Maritime Law and Commerce*, vol. 30:2, pp. 311–29.

Newman, Friedrich, 'Titanic's Boilers – A New Theory', *Atlantic Daily Bulletin* September 2014, pp. 13–15.

NHS, 'Hypothermia', www.nhs.uk/conditions/hypothermia.

Nova Scotia Archives, 'Fatality Reports', archives.novascotia.ca/titanic/fatalities/?Search=.

Oakland Tribune, 'Titanic's Passengers Saved; Liner Sinking', 15 April 1912.

Orlowski, J. P., 'Drowning, Near Drowning and Ice-Water Submersions', *Paediatric Clinics of North America*, vol. 34:1, 1987, pp. 75–92.

Philadelphia Inquirer, 'Mrs E.W. Bucknell Says Carelessness Cost Many Lives: Survivor of the *Titanic* Condemns Lack of Boats and Failure to Have Drills', 20 April 1912.

Press and Sun-Bulletin, 'Titanic Smashes Iceberg; 1,470 Saved', 15 April 1912.

Proc, Jerry, 'Wireless Aboard the Titanic', jproc.ca/radiostor/titanic.html.

RMS Titanic Maritime Memorial Act of 1986, www.un.org/depts/los/LEGISLATIONANDTREATIES/PDFFILES/USA_1986_Act.pdf.

Rossen, Jake, 'Grimm Prospects: Jack Grimm, the Eccentric Billionaire Hell-Bent On Finding the "Titanic", Bigfoot, and Noah's Ark', *Mental Floss*, April 2022, www.mentalfloss.com/posts/jack-grimm-explorer-titanic-bigfoot.

Royal Lifesaving Society UK, 'Cold Water Shock – the Facts', www.rlss.org.uk/cold-water-shock-the-facts.

Scarre, G., 'Archaeology and Respect for the Dead', *Journal of Applied Philosophy*, vol. 20:3, pp. 237–49.

Schultz, Fred L., '"It's a Carnival": An Interview with Robert Ballard', *Naval History*, vol. 10:5.

Shapell, 'President Taft's Eulogy for His Aide, Archibald Butt, Who Went Down with the Titanic Just Days Before', www.shapell.org/manuscript/president-taft-mourns-life-lost-on-titanic/#transcripts.

Sharma, Nitasha, 'Dark Tourism and Moral Disengagment in Liminal Spaces', *Tourism Geographies*, vol. 22:2, pp. 273–97.

Star-Gazette, 'White Star Liner Titanic Strikes an Iceberg. Passengers Are Safe and the Vessel is in Tow', 15 April 1912.

The Evening World, 'Liner Takes Off Passengers; Titanic Is Reported Sinking', 15 April 1912.

The Guardian, 'Titanic Sub Crew Believed to Have Died Instantly in "Catastrophic Implosion"', 23 June 2023.

The New York Times, 'Experts Split on Possibility of Remains at Titanic Site', 14 April 2012.

The New York Times, 'Screen: Sinking of Titanic; A Night to Remember Opens at Criterion', December 1958.

The New York Times, 'The Nightmare of April 14, 1912; The Titanic Nightmare A NIGHT TO REMEMBER. By Walter Lord. Illustrated. 209 pp. New York: Henry Holt & Co. $3.50', November 1955.

The New Yorker, 'The Titan Sub Was "an Accident Waiting to Happen"', 1 July 2023.

The Pall Mall Gazette, 'How the Mail Steamer Went Down in Mid Atlantic by a Survivor', March 1886.

The Standard, '"More Noises" Heard Underwater in Search for Missing *Titanic* Sub – but "Not Clear" What They Are', 22 June 2023.

The Washington Times, 'Morgue Ship in Halifax; Captain Gives Dramatic Story of Finding Bodies', 30 April 1912.

Titanic Memorials, 'W T STEAD TABLET', www.titanic.memorial/post/memorial/william+t+stead+memorial+tablet+london.

Titanic Wiki, 'List of Recovered Victims', titanic.fandom.com/wiki/List_of_recovered_victims/No%27s_1-50.

Tonopah Daily Bonanza, 'Hundreds Drowned at Sea', 16 April 1912.

UNESDOC Digital Library, 'The UNESCO Convention on the Protection of the Underwater Cultural Heritage', p. 4, unesdoc.unesco.org/ark:/48223/pf0000152883.

United States Senate Inquiry, Final Report, Reporting Disaster, 'Wireless'.

United States Senate Inquiry, Final Report, 'Voyage'.

United States Senate Inquiry Report, Speech of Senator Isidor Raynor in the Senate of the United States, 28 May 1912.

United States Senate Inquiry Report, Speech of Senator William Alden Smith, in the Senate of the United States, 28 May 1912.

Van Beck, Todd, 'Call to Duty: The Funeral Director's Response to the Titanic Disaster – 1912' transcript for a presentation for the National Funeral Directors' Convention in Boston, Massachusetts, 1998.

Vanity Fair, 'The Titan Submersible Disaster Was Years in the Making, New Details Reveal', 17 August 2023.

Washington Post, 'Ship in German "Titanic" Film Sank, Killing Far More than the Real One', www.washingtonpost.com/history/2022/12/18/germany-titanic-film-disaster.

Weather.gov, 'Cold Water Hazards and Safety', www.weather.gov/safety/coldwater.

Week In Weird, 'Meet Old Whitey, the Preserved Corpse of the SS Kamloops, Lake Superior's Most Haunted Shipwreck', Greg Newkirk, 27 November 2016, weekinweird.com/2016/11/27/old-whitey-preserved-corpse-kamloops.

William Murdoch, 'Miss Laura Mabel Francatelli, first class passenger', www.williammurdoch.net/mystery02_witness_08_francatelli.html.

World Health Organization, 'Drowning', www.who.int/news-room/fact-sheets/detail/drowning.

Other Sources

ABC News, 'ABC News Special Report: Titanic Submersible Passengers "Have Sadly Been Lost," OceanGate Confirms', YouTube, uploaded by ABC News, 22 June 2023.

Arnaud, Étienne (Dir.), *Saved From the Titanic*, Eclair Film Company, 1912. Film.

Baker, Roy Ward (Dir.), *A Night to Remember*, The Rank Organisation, 1958. Film.

Ballard, Robert, 'The Titanic Discovery: Professor Robert Ballard', YouTube, uploaded by UniversityOfRI, 20 April 2012.

BBC News, 'Titan Sub Passengers Died after Catastrophic Implosion Says US Coast Guard – BBC News', YouTube, uploaded by BBC News, 22 June 2023.

Blom, August (Dir.), *Atlantis*, Nordisk Film Kompagni, 1913. Film.

CBS Boston, 'Missing Submarine Heading to Titanic Wreckage Had 5-Person Crew, Lost Contact Sunday Morning', YouTube, uploaded by CBS Boston, 19 June 2023.

Collins Dictionary, definition of 'graveyard', www.collinsdictionary.com/dictionary/english/graveyard.

Collins Dictionary, definition of 'memorial', www.collinsdictionary.com/dictionary/english/memorial.

CTV News, 'James Cameron on Deep Sea Exploration, Dangers of AI and Titan Tragedy', YouTube, uploaded by CTV News, 18 July 2023.

Dawson, Jack in Cameron, James (Dir.), *Titanic*, Paramount Pictures and 20th Century Fox, 1997. Film.

Doughty, Caitlin, 'What Happened to Titanic's Dead?', YouTube, uploaded by Caitlin Doughty (formerly Ask a Mortician), 26 May 2016.

Douglas Woolley, Owner, Seawise Titanic Salvage Co, LinkedIn, www.linkedin.com/in/douglas-woolley-65a88921/?original_referer=https%3A%2F%2Fuk%2Elinkedin%2Ecom%2F&originalSubdomain=uk.

Feuillade, Louis (Dir.), *La Hantise*, Gaumont, 1912. Film.

GB News, 'Missing Titanic Sub Running Out of Time: "Crucially, Only Two Days of Oxygen Left": Paul Hawkins', YouTube, uploaded by GB News, 20 June 2023.

Grane, Thomas C. (Dir.), *Titanic: 20 Years Later with James Cameron*, National Geographic, 2017. Film.

Hartman, Cody (Dir.), *Unsinkable: The Titanic Untold*, Brian Hartman and Jeff Stephan, 2024. Film.

Merriam-Webster, definition of 'cemetery/graveyard', www.merriam-webster.com/dictionary/cemetery#:~:text=%3A%20a%20place%20where%20dead%20people,Etymology.

Merriam-Webster Dictionary, definition of 'memorial', www.merriam-webster.com/dictionary/memorial.

Misu, Mime (Dir.), *In Nacht und Eis*, Continental-Kunstfilm, 1912. Film.

Negulesco, Jean (Dir.), *Titanic*, 20th Century Fox, 1953. Film.

Selpin, Herbert (Dir.), *Titanic*, Deutsche Filmvertriebs, 1943. Film.

Zimmerman, Robert (Dir.), *City of the Dead: Halifax and the Titanic Disaster*, Morning's Mist Films, 2013. Film.

Acknowledgements

I never intended to write a book about *Titanic*. I have been a writer my entire life and I have been fascinated by the ship my entire life, but I never imagined the two combining.

This book would not exist without Mark Chirnside. I attended a talk he gave at the Public Record Office Northern Ireland (PRONI) in April 2022 called '*Titanic* at 110: Learning, Unlearning & Relearning History' and it reignited my love for the ship and its story. For that, Mark, I extend my deepest gratitude. I also owe a huge debt of thanks to Aidan McMichael of the Belfast Titanic Society. Aidan was so enthusiastic when I approached him to enquire about giving a talk on *Titanic*'s dead and Halifax's role in their recovery, identification and care. I was almost certain he would say no, but he did not. For that, I will be forever thankful.

When I realised that giving my talk wasn't enough and that I wanted to delve deeper into the story, Aidan passed on the contact details of Dee Ryan-Meister. Dee, without you, this book would not be what it is. Thank you for being patient with a *Titanic* newbie and sharing your valuable knowledge and resources with me. Your sincere kindness, wealth of knowledge and passion for Halifax's role in the tragedy is nothing short of spectacular. I can't wait to read your own book someday.

I owe an enormous thanks to The History Press and my commissioning editor Amy Rigg. Thank you for taking a chance on a first-time author and fledgling *Titanic* historian, Amy. Your faith in my abilities as a writer and researcher has helped me more than you know. I would also like to thank the seasoned *Titanic* historians who stepped up to help shape this book into what it is. Eugene Nesmeyanov and Bruce Beveridge, thank you. Your insights taught me so much and I will be forever grateful for the part you played in bringing *The Death Ship* together. And Steve Hall, thank you for your kind words and for writing a fantastic foreword.

I am grateful to the people in my personal life who have played crucial parts in making this book a reality. My family – Mum, Dad, Emily, Charlotte, Granny Pearl, Auntie Sharon, Megan, Olivia, Great-Auntie Mona and Great-Uncle David – have always encouraged my love of history and my passion for reading and writing. Your support means more to me than you'll ever know. Those who have passed on and whom we miss dearly – Nana and Uncle Wayne – would have been so proud of me. I wish I could share this with you both. Your love is with me, always.

My friends Bekka and Shannon are two of the most important people in my life. We have been through everything together and when I told them I was writing *The Death Ship*, they were unbelievably supportive. They have been my cheerleaders throughout this entire process and I don't think I will ever be able to express how much they mean to me. When I was offered a publishing contract, they turned up at my home with flowers, presents, balloons and a card. Bekka's daughter, Freya, picked out a notebook for her Auntie Tori that I will keep and treasure forever. When the cover for *The Death Ship* was revealed, I did not tell Shannon straight away because her hen party was coming up and I didn't want to take the focus off her. I showed her after the party and explained why I hadn't shown her immediately. In response, she said, 'You should have shown me and every single person at that table.' I hope *The Death Ship*'s readers experience this kind of friendship in their lives.

I have many supportive friends in my social circles too, to whom I am exceedingly grateful. Special thanks go out to my friends at BanterFlix, The Fright Club NI, and The Readers in the Rue Morgue Book and Film Club, particularly Joe (and your love for PG). Your support has meant the world to me.

Chris, my partner, has been my rock throughout this. I can't fully express how much your love and support has sustained me throughout the harder times writing this book. You constantly checked in on my progress, reassured me during the more difficult periods and cheered for me during the good periods. Thank you, my love.

Lastly, I want to thank my four-legged companion, Asher. My personal life changed drastically while writing *The Death Ship* and he has been there through every single step. He kept me company during the research phase, he provided me with comfort during the writing phase, and he was an adorable distraction throughout the editing phase. Our human friends and family are important, but our pets are too.

Index

Note: index terms are of key persons, places, vessels and submersibles